A Writer Teaches Writing

A Writer Teaches Writing: A Practical Method of Teaching Composition

Donald M. Murray

Houghton Mifflin Company / Boston / New York / Atlanta / Geneva, Illinois / Dallas / Palo Alto

Printed in the U.S.A.

This book is dedicated to Dick Goodman
who must accept full responsibility
for luring the author into the maze of
elementary and secondary education.

Contents

Preface *xi*

The Author *xv*

One
The Writer's Seven Skills

1 He Discovers a Subject *2*
2 He Senses an Audience *3*
3 He Searches for Specifics *5*
4 He Creates a Design *6*
5 He Writes *8*
6 He Develops a Critical Eye *10*
7 He Rewrites *11*

Two
The Writing Teacher's Seven Skills

8 He Listens *15*
9 He Coaches *18*
10 He Is a Diagnostician *19*
11 He Is Flexible *20*
12 He Writes with His Students *21*
13 He Hones Creativity with Discipline *22*
14 He Keeps His Distance *23*

Three
The Experience of Writing

15 The Student Discovers a Subject *27*
16 The Student Senses an Audience *42*
17 The Student Searches for Specifics *43*
18 The Student Creates a Design *51*
19 The Student Writes *70*
20 The Student Develops a Critical Eye *72*
21 The Student Rewrites *82*

Four
A Climate for Writing

22 Why Writing Isn't Taught Effectively *103*
23 The Classroom: A Writing Laboratory *109*
24 Why a Lesson Plan? *110*
25 A Smorgasbord of Lesson Plans *112*
26 Writing in the Regular English Course *125*

Five
The Techniques of Teaching Writing

27 How to Teach the Student to Teach Himself *129*
28 How to Create Assignments *133*
29 How to Not Correct Papers *135*
30 How to Edit Papers *139*
31 How to Run a Conference *150*
32 How to Motivate Students *151*

33 How to Reach the Unreachable *154*
34 How to Publish Papers *161*
35 How to Plan in Time of Panic *162*
36 How to Teach Writing *170*

Six
Resources for the Teacher of Writing
37 The Writer Writes *173*
38 The Teacher Teaches *215*
39 What the Masters Know *230*

The Writing Teacher's Library *247*

Index *255*

Preface

A Writer Teaches Writing gives English teachers an effective method of teaching composition based on the experience of professional writers. The book, tested by teachers in hundreds of classrooms, shows how the skills of the publishing writer can be learned by the student. The ability to write is not a gift, it is a skill. *A Writer Teaches Writing* shows the teacher how to help the student develop the ability to write—in school on an essay test, a term paper, an examination, a book report; beyond school in a business letter, a scholarly paper, an engineering report, a news release, a corporate memo, a poem—whatever is appropriate to the student's individual ability and need. This method does NOT train students to be professional writers but it does encourage students to teach themselves the lessons professional writers have taught themselves.

The author of the book is a writer who was brought into the classroom after the need for a new approach to the teaching of composition was given priority by the Executive Board of the New England School Development Council in 1965. The Council represents more than three hundred school systems in New England, and its board is made up of superintendents who head representative urban, suburban and rural school districts. The administrators agreed that they needed a new approach to the old problem of teaching writing to a large number of students.

NESDEC approached the author, who teaches a course in writing for English Education majors at the University of New Hampshire and is also a professional writer. He had isolated and defined the steps followed by most effective writers—businessmen and poets, scientists and journalists—and then made his students experience the process of writing as followed by most professionals. His students, in turn, had success in making their students learn by experiencing the process of writing as practiced by the publishing writer.

The author met with eighteen experienced secondary school teachers, all but one of whom had taught for more than ten years, and presented his approach to them. They considered, reacted, attacked, debated, and discussed his ideas. The author then went home and hammered out the draft of a book, presenting his methods in a manner which might be appropriate for the secondary school teacher.

The author met again with the teachers and they tore into a draft of his book line by line. This draft was also shown to professional writers, to other teachers, to teachers of teachers, and to English professors. The book was twice rewritten and a third draft completed. At the beginning of the school year in September 1966 the third draft of the book was read by more than a thousand English teachers, college students who planned to become English teachers, writers, college professors, and public school administrators. The approach, in one form or another, was tried in hundreds of classrooms. The author used parts of the book in his university courses, and also tested it in Hollis, New Hampshire, High School in a program supported by Sanders Associates of Nashua, New Hampshire. Each page of the book was criticized by many teachers and students.

During the winter of 1967–68 NESDEC and the *Reader's Digest* Educational Division sponsored a project through which the ideas in this book were tried in eight elementary schools which draw their children from a wide variety of social, racial and economic backgrounds. The project revealed that the basic concepts and methods in this book can be applied in the elementary school.

Now the book has been completely redesigned and greatly expanded. It is a book by a publishing writer who is a practicing teacher. It has evolved from the writing desk experience of the author, confirmed by the experience of many other writers, as well as from the classroom experience of the author, confirmed by the experience of hundreds of other teachers.

It is impossible to give credit to all who have participated in the development of this book, but some deserve special mention.

A Writer Teaches Writing would not have been written without Richard Goodman, Executive Secretary of the New England School Development Council. When Dick was a superintendent of schools he involved the author in a project in Hollis, New Hampshire, High School. Then, when he went to NESDEC, he developed Project WRITE. NESDEC has supported this book in every way, financially and spiritually. This support has made it possible for the author to work on the job at hand without distraction and with the expert counsel of many secondary school teachers.

The book is also an indirect product of the author's own teachers of writing—Mortimer B. Howell of Tilton, New Hampshire, the late Carroll Towle of the University of New Hampshire and Gerald Warner Brace of Boston University.

The book could not have been written without the help of the eighteen teachers who worked in NESDEC's Project WRITE. They are: William E. Dubee, Old Saybrook High School, Old Saybrook, Connecticut; Sally Byrne, Milford High School, Milford, New Hampshire; Owen L. Egan, Jr., Tiverton High School, Tiverton, Rhode Island; Joseph Gernsheimer, South Kingstown High School, South Kingstown, Rhode Island; John M. Gray, Jr., Walpole High School, Walpole, Massachusetts; John Harris, Conard High School, West Hartford, Connecticut; Ralph W. Hawkes, Portland High School, Portland, Maine; Juanita Jacobs, Brattleboro Union High School, Brattleboro, Vermont; Patricia Khoury, Belmont High School, Belmont, Massachusetts; Virginia Lewis, Framingham South High School, Framingham, Massachusetts; Miriam B. Moody, Sanford High School, Sanford, Maine; Terence Ortwein, Hanover High School, Hanover, New Hampshire; Richard H. Pervonga, Classical Senior High School, Springfield, Massachusetts; Paul Quimby, Kingswood Regional School, Wolfeboro, New Hampshire; Irene W. Sherwood, Duxbury High School, Duxbury, Massachusetts; Esther Urie, South Burlington High School, South Burlington, Vermont; Edward A. Watts, Beverly High School, Beverly, Massachusetts; George Griewank, Timberlane Regional High School, Plaistow, New Hampshire and the University of New Hampshire.

Other teachers who have read the book and made helpful comments include: John Ragle of Hartford High School, White River Junction, Vermont and Dartmouth College; Grace Whittaker of Lewis Junior High School, Roxbury, Massachusetts; Bruce Crowder of Barre, Massachusetts, High School; Marcia Stearns of Barrington, New Hampshire; Beverly Strout of Oyster River High School, Durham, New Hampshire. Mr. Bill Sims, now of Portsmouth, New Hampshire, High School, the teacher with whom I worked at Hollis, New Hampshire, High School, made many contributions to the book and to my education. Thomas Payzant, now of the New Orleans, Louisiana, school system, made helpful suggestions while he was at the Harvard Graduate School of Education. Students who have been particularly helpful include, Miss Susan Beckler, now an English teacher in Salem, New Hampshire, High School, Richard Burrows, now of Hanover, New Hampshire, High School, Miss Helen Powroznek, David Mayberry and Mark Ramsdell. The book has also been read by Charles L. Allen of the Baltimore, Maryland, school system and Alverda Gaspard of the New Orleans, Louisiana, school system, and by Mrs. Beverly Hotaling of Somersworth, New Hampshire, High School.

The elementary school teachers and their supervisors who worked on a special project with this approach to writing are: Mrs. Lynn Nalchajian and Mr. Ernest L. Hunter, Brook School, Weston, Massachusetts; Mrs. Margaret Clark and Mrs. Ethel Bears, Franklin School, Lexington, Massachusetts; Mrs. Priscilla Brown and Mr. Robert McCaffrey, Batchelder School, North Reading, Massachusetts; Mr. Neil Cronin and Miss Dorothy Calahan, John Marshall School, Boston, Massachusetts; Mrs. Mary Armstrong and Miss Charlotte Danoff, Holmes School, Malden, Massachusetts; Miss Brenda Simon and Mr. Enrico Caruso, Liberty School, Revere, Massachusetts; Mrs. Judith Stavis and Mr. Walter Doucette, Happy Hollow School, Wayland, Massachusetts; Miss Carol Mansfield and Miss Hava Kane, Bridlepath School, West Hartford, Connecticut. Mrs. Joan E. Zelonis of the Oyster River School in Durham, New Hampshire, has also made a number of helpful suggestions.

The book has been read by my colleagues in many departments of the University of New Hampshire, and a few of those to whom I am particularly indebted are: Dr. J. C. Richardson, Chairman of the English Department; Dr. Sylvester H. Bingham, former Chairman of the English Department; Dr. Lewis Goffe, Director of the English Education Program; Mr. Hidde van Duym; Robert Read, librarian; Dr. Charles Jellison, historian and biographer; Dr. Manley Irwin, writer on economics; Mr. James Sullivan, Director of Freshman English; Dr. Robert Hapgood; Dr. Jack Mulhern, physicist; Dr. Dwight Ladd; Dr. Hugh Potter; Mr. Edward Hanrahan; Dr. Philip Nicoloff; Mrs. Nancy Deane; Dr. Herman Gadon; Dr. Richard Balomenos, who has been very active in developing math programs for public schools. It has also been read by the teachers of writing at the University of New Hampshire, who are writers themselves—Tom Williams, John Yount, Mark Smith and Ted Weesner.

Many other professional writers and teachers have read the book and commented on it: Evan Hill, who is a Professor of Journalism at the University of Connecticut as well as a writer; Kenneth Andler, attorney and writer; Dr. Fredelle Maynard, a writer who also teaches a special writing course at Dover, New Hampshire, High School; Dr. Eugene Yarrington, a poet who teaches at Boston University; Ed Linn; Dr. George Snook, surgeon and writer; Daniel Ford; Lorus and Margery Milne, naturalists, teachers and writers; Joan Mills; Nancy Otis; Richard Watt; Walter Bonney; Max Gunther; Dr. David Emmerich of the State University of New York at Stony Brook, Long Island, N.Y.; William Brodrick, who was an English teacher before he became a newspaperman; Charles Coombs; newspapermen Harold E. Clancy, William T. Stewart, and Leonard Wheildon; and Senior Editor James Monahan of the *Reader's Digest* and Burton Albert, Jr., a former teacher who is with Reader's Digest Services, Inc., Educational Division. Mrs. Dwight Ladd picked many a nit. As usual, my wife's contribution has gone far beyond the chore of typing and re-typing and re-typing. . . .

There are many, many others, and I am grateful to them all. I am particularly indebted to my students who have taught me while I have attempted to teach them.

Donald M. Murray
University of New Hampshire

The Author

Donald M. Murray, a professor of English at the University of New Hampshire, teaches and supervises both undergraduate and graduate courses in writing and the teaching of writing. He has conducted a composition program in Hollis, New Hampshire, High School for two years, directed the New England School Development Council's Project WRITE, headed NESDEC's summer workshop for the teaching of writing at Bowdoin College, taught a NESDEC course in the teaching of writing for English teachers. He is teaching at a NDEA institute at the University of New Hampshire in the summer of 1968. As a teacher of writing he has also participated in the Fourteen Professor Project sponsored by the New England School Development Council and the New England Board of Higher Education for the National Institute for Disadvantaged Youth. He has directed a NESDEC program to determine the implications of his approach to composition for pupils in primary and elementary grades. Most important, he is a teacher of writing who spends hours in conference with students every week of the school year.

He is also a professional writer. He won the Pulitzer Prize for editorials he wrote for the *Boston Herald*. He has been a contributing editor of *Time* magazine, has sold several hundred magazine articles, and has been a regular contributor to the *Reader's Digest*. He is the author of five books, including two juvenile nonfiction books, and his latest novel, *The Man Who Had Everything*, was called "one of the most memorable books in years," by a critic on the *New York Herald Tribune Book Week Magazine*.

One The Writer's Seven Skills

How does the writer write?

We must be able to answer this question to teach writing effectively. But we cannot discover how the writer works merely by studying what he has left on the page. We must observe the act of writing itself to expose to our students the process of writing as it is performed by the successful writer.

The successful writer is the person who conveys information, ideas and experience across the barriers of time and distance. The writer may be a novelist, a salesman, a lawyer, a historian, a member of the League of Women Voters, an engineer, a journalist, a general, a philosopher, a politician, an advertising copywriter, a union official, a businessman, a scientist. Those categories simply identify the material he has to communicate, they do not indicate whether he is a writer or not. The man who creates an effective memo is as much a writer as the man who produces an effective sonnet. We should isolate and identify the fundamental skills of the writer, who is able to take an idea from his brain and transplant it into the minds of people beyond the range of his voice.

We teach the student to write because he has to be a writer, revealing his knowledge to his teachers before he is allowed to graduate. Once the student becomes a working member of our complex society he will probably write reports, letters, proposals, memoranda, in order to work with people beyond his office and his community.

The student can learn to write if he is encouraged to discover and to practice the publishing writer's basic skills. It is the job of the writing teacher to create a climate in which his students can experience the act of writing as it is performed by the professional writer.

Writing is exploration—discovery of meaning, discovery of form—and the writer works back and forth, concentrating on one of the writer's seven basic skills at a time, so that he can discover what he has to say and how to say it more efficiently. The act of writing is complicated, but in the tidal conflict between the artist's freedom and the craftsman's discipline there is a consistent pattern of work which can be identified and passed on to the student writer.

The student writer and his teacher, however, must first understand what every writer knows: there are no absolute laws of composition. Each principle of writing may be broken to solve a particular problem in a specific piece of work. The only test a writer applies to a page is the craftsman's question, "Does it work?" But in making language work—forcing it to carry its burden of meaning to the reader—most writers discover they have to practice, consciously or subconsciously, the following seven skills.

1 He Discovers a Subject

The writer knows what he has to say determines how he says it. He takes part in a constant search for subject, for he has discovered the strength of his writing will depend directly on the vigor of his thinking. Content and form, form and content—which comes first? The answer has to be content. Form is not an empty jug into which the writer pours meaning; form grows out of meaning, so much so that many writers come to believe that form, in a very real sense, is meaning.

Most of a writer's time is spent trying to perceive his subject. His business is perception—to see and to understand so that he can make the reader see. Elizabeth Bowen in "The Roving Eye," reprinted on page 28, has described the process by which the imaginative writer finds his subject. We should realize that non-"creative" writers are also "see-ers." What the lawyer tries to do when he sits down to write a brief is to bring the case into perspective, into focus. The person who is writing a police report, an account of a Ladies Aid meeting, a memorandum on a new sales process, is trying to see the subject so clearly that he can make the reader see it equally well.

How does the writer develop a sense of subject so that he can identify a good subject? This process of spotting, developing, shaping and completing a subject may be described as what happens when an idea is developed into a thought. The idea is quick, fragile, a passing thing. For example, an idea might be that our town needs a school for high school graduates who cannot afford to go away to college but who have not yet developed into college material. That is an idea. A thought is a well-considered proposal for the establishment of a two-year community college. This thought would have some firm indication of the need, of the way in which a college could be founded and supported. The difference between an idea and a thought might be described as the difference between a kiss and marriage.

The writer gets ideas by spending part of his time in a state of open susceptibility. One person has said that a writer is a man with his skin off. He is particularly aware, uniquely receptive to impressions and ideas. He reads, he listens, he looks, he tastes, he touches. He is in contact with life in an uncritical way, accepting life; he hears what his students really say; he watches how the town develops as the shopping center is built on the outside of town; he sees the silent, threatening signs of a developing street fight late on an August night.

The writer is sensitive, but not in any dainty, limp-wristed sort of way. If one is going to be sensitive, aware of life, caring, then one must be tough. The writer is sensitive the way high-speed film is sensitive. It is the best film and the toughest film which can record the horror and the beauty of life. The novelist, the company speechwriter, the newspaperman, the scholar—all writers—should first of all be able to see, to listen, to record and accept what is happening around them.

The writer is not looking for ideas so much as he is trying to handle the ones he has. He feels that the ocean of ideas will overwhelm him. In the same way, some aphasic children cannot be taken to a supermarket for the impressions made on their brains by the lights, the colors, the sounds, the cold of the air-conditioning, the clatter and the chatter, the shapes and forms, are all a jumble. The children panic because their damaged brains cannot sort out the difference between an unimportant and an important sound. The writer escapes a similar confusion and panic by seeing patterns in the jumble of impressions. He ties ideas together and sees relationships as he is on the way to developing a thought.

Mozart used the same notes as other composers, but he saw many more connections or relationships. This is how the writer builds. He sees a connection between a production statistic, a new development in transportation, the findings of a market report; and he weaves these all together into a thought: we should develop a new product. The man in the company, the community, or the government agency who is given the task of writing is usually the person who not only sees more, but sees patterns. The writer is the person who brings order to disorder. That is his most important job, to create order where disorder existed. The ghost-writer, for example, does not just rearrange the words of the person for whom he is writing; he puts together ideas for the person for whom he is writing; he creates a pattern, an order, a form.

As the writer searches for his subject he goes through a focusing process, developing a vague idea into a well-aimed thought. Lucile Vaughan Payne in her book *The Lively Art Of Writing,* talks very effectively about the informed opinion. This is what the writer has, a focused generalization. He has worked from specifics, from unrelated ideas to a synthesis, a generalization, but not toward, as the inexperienced writer seems to think, a vague generalization. The writer's generalizations are nailed down, they are well-made and documented; they have been built, thought through, constructed, composed. This is why we use the term "composition," an old-fashioned but a good word for writing. The subject is composed when the writer has achieved a sense of completeness in his thinking, when he has been able to put a frame around the picture, fitting everything inside that frame which belongs there and ruthlessly discarding that which does not belong there.

The writer finds his subject by being open to ideas, by making connections between ideas, by defining that connection in a focused generalization. He builds a thought on the page which is so well-constructed that the reader will accept it as his own.

2 He Senses an Audience

The professional writer may write for himself, but he does not write to himself. The writer does not exist without a reader. The purpose of writing is not to arrange ink on paper, to provide a mirror for the author's thoughts, but to carry ideas and information from the mind of one person into the mind of another.

To do this the writer speaks in terms the reader will understand. He does not talk down to the reader, nor up to the reader, but across to him. He must know what his reader knows, what his reader doesn't know, what his reader needs to know, and what his reader wants to know. He may know this subjectively, and many of the world's most popular writers have never been aware of their audience; they have merely written in terms they themselves understand. They have been very much the common man. This does not mean that they do not know an audience, it means that they know it subconsciously; and if we are to discover what the writer does, we must develop this conscious sense of audience if we do not have an unconscious sense of audience. The writer may be his own audience, but only after he has found by publication of some form or another that there are many other people who believe, think, and feel as he does.

There is another way of describing this process: the writer is on a search for himself. If he finds himself he will find an audience, because all of us have the same common core. And when he digs deeply into himself and is able to define himself, he will find others who will read with a shock of recognition what he has written. But this requires a depth of honesty few students are able to achieve. They are not old enough to have found themselves; they are trying on roles; they are trying to discover themselves by being other people for a moment, for an hour, for an evening. The adolescent lives in the world of imitation, that is the way he learns. He will imitate other writers, other men's experiences, and will write to titillate or please an audience—sometimes his classmates, too often his teacher.

Writing merely written for an audience will have the appearance of cheap plastic. The good writer does not change his truths for the audience he wishes to achieve, he does not toady to that audience, but he does develop his truth and then put it in terms which the reader will understand.

The professional writer and the professional teacher speak to a special audience. The teacher does not teach the first grade the same way he teaches the twelfth grade, or an eleventh-grade college group the same way he teaches an eleventh-grade general class. He knows his audience. The writer too must know his audience. He may be writing a memo for the president of the firm, his audience is one; he may be writing a report for the board of directors, his audience is twelve; he may be writing a statement for the stockholders, his audience is twenty-five hundred; he may be writing a statement for the general public, his audience is almost unlimited; he may be writing a statement which is aimed at his corporation's workers, and again his audience is limited. Whether he is speaking to workers or customers or stockholders, he must speak in terms which each audience can understand. His tone must be appropriate. As soon as he knows his subject he must discover his audience.

The inexperienced writer repeats the refrain, "But I know what I mean." The professional writer knows that that is no test at all. Many of us paint beautiful pictures in our head, but no one else sees them; we compose imaginary symphonies in our daydreams, but no one else hears them. When we write we are not speaking to ourselves, we are speaking to others. The tests are simple—and terrifying. Does the reader know what I mean? Does the reader understand me? Have I spoken clearly to the reader? We have poor readers, but it is not the job of the writer to bemoan the poor reader. It is the job of the writer to speak to the poor reader, to speak in terms which he understands and which make the issues absolutely clear. It is easy to confound and confuse. That is why the writer is in such demand: he is the one who clarifies.

The professional writer does not know what facts to seek to document his truth, which quotations or statistics will appeal to his readers until he knows his audience. He will discover the form of what he has to write, its length, its shape, its tone, when he knows to whom he is speaking. We do not speak the same way in church as we do in the beer hall; we do not talk to old friends, parents, colleagues, superiors and inferiors with the same words or in the same voice. We shape what we have to say so that we will be understood. If we are honest we do not change what we have to say, but we speak appropriately. The writer cannot write in an effective tone unless he knows his audience. He must discover his audience before he begins to write so that he can design his writing in such a way that it will effectively carry his thoughts into the reader's head.

3 He Searches for Specifics

The contractor does not build a house by wandering through a lumberyard picking out lumber, nails, bricks and glass at random. Neither does the writer wander through the area of his subject picking up quotations, statistics, statements and facts without reason or purpose. The writer makes a calculated search for his raw materials. This search is based on the knowledge of his subject and of his audience.

What are the raw materials of the published writer? Robert Frost is reported to have snarled, "intellectuals deal in abstractions. It's much safer that way." The writer searches for specifics. A specific is many things: it is the statistic, the quotation, the anecdote, the parable, the authoritative conclusion, which will document what the writer has to say. The writer, as much as possible, wants to show instead of tell. He wants the reader to see the subject so that the reader will accept the conclusion for himself. He wants to convince the reader.

The reader knows that the authenticity of what he has to say comes from the specifics he uses. He will be believed by the reader if he uses concrete details which have the ring of truth. Read something that you like, a piece of writing that you have saved or that you return to, and you'll probably find that it is more than a generalization, that it is specifically written, that it has the ring of authority because of the specifics in it.

Where does the writer find his specifics? First of all, he uses recorded sources. He goes to the library and reads books, pamphlets, monographs, articles and news clippings about his subject. He may work through laboratory reports, scientific articles, recorded computer calculations, or he may work among old letters and diaries. His sources are also tape-recordings, video tapes, movies, news pictures, oil paintings; they are whatever sources are appropriate to his subject.

He uses live sources as well. He talks to the people who are experts in their field. They may be scientists, investigators, laboratory technicians, or they may be salesmen or policemen or soldiers or voters. He talks, and listens, to the individuals who can reveal the subject to him in greater clarity. When he is doing a profile or a biography, for example, he searches for the revealing details. How did his subject act with his family, with his subordinates? What were his hobbies, what did he wear, what was his home like, what were his work habits? The biographer looks for the revealing actions, which will expose his subject to his audience. This is what the novelist does and it is also what a man does when he writes a report for an advertising agency on a potential market or a report for the Secretary of State. How does the buyer or the voter reveal himself? What does he say about his prejudices and his wants? When we are told that the helicopter pilot in Vietnam stuffs his nostrils full of Vicks to avoid the smell of death, then something about a battlefield is revealed directly to us. The writer wants the specific details which relate the subject to the reader.

The writer also uses himself as a source. He is a writer—and a voter, a buyer, a parent. He sees what others do not see in the world around him. One city editor said that a good reporter is forever astonished at the obvious. A good writer sees the subject, has a feeling about it, and is aware of the significant details. He fills his notebook with materials gathered from written sources, from talking to people and from seeing the subject himself.

"You must write from abundance," Professor Carroll Towle used to repeat to me. He was right. The Managing Editor of *Time,* Otto Fuerbringer, used to say you could tell a good story, or a good issue, by the amount of good material thrown away. As a free lance writer, I used to keep a fifty-gallon wastebasket by my desk, and I filled it. This book is the distillate of boxes and files of materials. It was written from sixteen two-inch-thick notebooks, almost 300 pages drawn from perhaps 4,800 pages. This is the way the professional writer works. He writes from abundance.

The amateur thinks that the writer has an idea, perhaps a vague thought, and a few facts. He doesn't. He has shelves of reports, miles of tape-recorded interviews, notebooks of quotations and facts and ideas and possible constructions. It takes thirty gallons of sap to make a gallon of maple syrup; it takes hundreds of pages of notes to make one *Reader's Digest* article.

The good writer is wasteful. He saws and shapes and cuts away, discarding wood ends, shavings, sawdust, bent nails—whatever doesn't fit and doesn't work. The writer cannot build a good, strong, sturdy piece of writing unless he has gathered an abundance of fine raw materials.

4 He Creates a Design

"Prose is architecture, not interior decoration," stated Ernest Hemingway.[1] The amateur thinks the decorative touches come first in writing. That is no more true than the idea that one hangs a picture before he builds a house. Victor S. Navasky, in an interview with John Kenneth Galbraith, described his comments on the writing of *The New Industrial State* as follows: "his system is four drafts, and then on the fifth, he puts in 'that note of spontaneity everybody likes.' "[2]

The published writer creates a design before he writes. The design may be informal or formal. It may be in the writer's mind or on his page. That is not important. What is important is that the structure is there. Faulkner outlined one novel on the walls of his workroom. Many writers make charts. Richard Watt, a businessman and historian, outlines his books on great, eighteen-column sheets of accounting paper. He keeps making his outlines more detailed, more formal, filling in the holes, and his outlines eventually turn into first drafts. He designs his books.

The art of writing is no more spontaneous than the art of marriage. There are moments of spontaneity, seconds of inspiration or insight, minutes of delight, but most of the time it is hard work. The writer must plan and calculate, scheme and decide. He makes a thousand executive decisions every time he outlines a chapter. The lawyer chooses a defense from all the laws and past cases and judicial opinions with which his experience has

[1] *Death in the Afternoon.*

[2] *The New York Times,* June 25, 1967.

made him familiar. The writer briefs his article or speech or essay or report in the same way.

The writer usually finds it helps to chart what he has to write, to be able to see the structure on the page. He may create a formal "Harvard" outline in which each point is in a complete sentence. It is more likely, however, that he doesn't follow the rules of Roman numerals and Arabic numbers, of capital letters and small letters, but draws what he has to say in a circle or a square, develops it in a chart form, or scribbles it very informally, putting ideas down in random patterns and then drawing lines between ideas. The important thing is that he sees the design. He is not trying to win a contest by the clarity of his design. No one has to see or understand his design but himself. But he must have, in his mind's eye or on paper, an idea of where he is to begin and where he is to end.

The amateur driver may just go out for a drive, having no idea where he is headed or where he will end up. It is fun, and amateur writing is fun. But the professional writer has a clear idea of where he is going. He doesn't start out with a gallon of gas to drive from Los Angeles to Chicago. He doesn't leave Philadelphia to go to Chicago and wander through Miami on the way. The writer knows where he is going and how he wants to get there.

The writer understands that writing is a process, not a rigid procedure. He constantly rediscovers his subject. He gets to know his audience better and sees what they need to know. When he gathers facts, the facts will change, refine or perhaps even destroy his subject. When he creates a design of what he has to say, his outline may show him he needs to expand or limit the subject. He may discover he cannot speak to the people he wanted to speak to, and he must find a new audience. Sometimes he will give up what he has to say and start on a new subject. He must be open to these changes, for writing is a continuing state of discovery. He is doing something, building something, creating something, and it will change under his hands. That is part of the terror and the excitement of writing.

Most writers find out what the journalist knows: the lead is all-important. In journalism the lead may be as short as the first line of copy, or it may be as long as ten lines, but never more. You either capture the reader in the first hundred words or you don't. The introduction is just as important in a textbook, a sales letter, a proposal for federal funds, and in a political speech. The professional knows how to write a variety of leads, and he works hard at the lead. Quite often the lead takes approximately eighty-five per cent of the effort. It is not unusual for a magazine writer to write fifty or sixty leads for an article.

The amateur asks, "Why not just plunge in?" And it is true that a few writers just start off writing and worry about the first page later on. But most writers can't do this. There are too many things decided in the lead: the lead limits the subject; the lead makes it clear where the piece of writing is headed; the lead establishes the tone. There are words you can use and words you cannot use after you have written the lead. Before the lead is constructed anything is possible. After it is constructed, the length, the subject, the mood, the shape of the piece of writing is largely determined. It is the lead which gives the writer the control over his subject. The professional writer spends a great deal of time on leads. Most of this book was written by dictation after I had spent a considerable time scribbling down the leads for each chapter. Once the lead was clear, the points in the chapter laid out, then it was possible to "write" the chapter, hard and fast.

Once the writer has created the design he is able to ask the question, "Does it work?" When the writer asks that question he is examining the structure of what he has to say: Does the piece of writing go from beginning to end? Will it support the ideas which it is designed to convey?

This step, the fourth of seven, the central step, may be the most important one, for it is the job of the writer to bring order to disorder, to create a design of meaning which will bring form and content together in such a way that the writer will make the reader understand.

The writer generally practices these four skills before what the layman calls writing. But, of course, he has been writing, for most of the writer's effort must be spent in finding what he has to say, discovering to whom he will say it, completing the research which will give him the raw materials so he may say it effectively, and designing the form which is appropriate to his subject, his audience, and his documentation. The writer has learned the importance of pre-writing, of knowing what he is going to do before he does it, of solving as many problems as possible off the page. The writer does not try to write too soon; he does not go into battle until his troops are trained, in position, given ammunition, and provided with tactics to carry out that strategy. The writer does not write until he has a good idea of what he has to say and how he can say it.

5 He Writes

I am afraid of height. I do not like to stand near the edge of a cliff, climb a ladder, look down from a skyscraper, or drive across a high bridge, but I served in the paratroops during World War II. I was trained to overcome my fear, to jump despite it. Yet, as much terror as I felt stepping out of an airplane, I feel more terror facing the empty page.

"A writer is a person for whom writing is more difficult than it is for other people," is a definition attributed to Thomas Mann. The writer may have begun his career because he had a facility with words, or because he saw a structure in what had to be said more clearly than other people did. But as he goes on with his career, writing the stockholders' reports for the corporation, the annual reports for the school board, or his third novel, writing becomes more difficult for him.

The most elemental reason that writers do not write, that scholars perish rather than publish, is the fact that writing is a commitment. The writer is a doer, a person who expresses himself to other people. Before we write, our knowledge is our own, after we write we have revealed ourselves to other people.

The essay test, and eventually the thesis and the dissertation, is still the most demanding form of examination. The student is given the time to reveal what he knows about the subject on the page so that it can be examined by a knowledgeable reader. No wonder so many students find it hard to take an essay test, and so many teachers find it discouraging to read an essay test. Professor John Mulhern of the Physics Department at the University of New Hampshire has taught a physics course in which the student must write an essay on physics. He said the course covers much less material than courses with objective examinations but the students know the subject far better when they have had to discover, through trying to write, how little they know. They had to work to fill in the holes in their knowledge which their essays revealed.

The awful moment of writing: before you write the words are all clear in your mind, the arguments convincing, the paragraphs well-designed and the sentences graceful; then you are revealed to yourself on the page. The more experienced the writer, the more critical is his eye. His standards become higher, his technical choice is greater. The more he knows about writing the more effective a writer he is, but the harder it becomes for him to write. As we have seen, he discovers the importance of pre-writing, of defining and refining his subject and his audience, of searching for raw materials, of creating designs. He has good excuses not to write, and it becomes harder and harder to overcome the inertia. Most writers do this by artificially establishing a deadline when it is no longer possible to put off writing. Most writers create a ritual of work, the same place each day, the same hour each day, the same number of pencils sharpened, the same number of cups of coffee drunk.

The professional writer must be an effective critic of his own writing, but for the first draft he must suspend his ruthless eye. He must find some way to put aside his good, sharp, critical judgment and write a draft, as hard and fast as possible. Some writers find they must get each paragraph or each page right; others find they can create a very rough draft. But all writers know they must put the process of pre-writing behind them. They can no longer delay. They stand at the top of the slope and they must ski down. They have to find some way of pushing off and doing it, and they must go on to completion.

When the writer writes he discovers what he has to say. This is the moment of revelation, of excitement and discouragement. As he moves on down the page his ideas fill out, are developed. His subconscious mind dredges up the metaphors, the comparisons and the specific details which he needs to make each point. The writer finds that in writing the first draft, or what Peter Drucker calls the zero draft, he has to put his notes aside. He writes from abundance, and his subconscious mind edits out that which is unnecessary and brings up that which is necessary. He feels, as much as he sees, the shape of what he has to say. His characters or his theories develop; his arguments are completed and answered; his paragraphs are full.

The happy accidents of language occur while he writes. He plays with a word, and it leads to a phrase which in turn can lead to a revelation about the subject.

As he writes, the writer has a feeling of emptying. What he knows is being sucked out by some enormous vacuum cleaner and placed on the page so others can see it. He has the feeling of giving birth, a sense of pride and a sense of embarrassment that that red and squirming thing is his. At that moment of composition all that he knows, and doesn't know, is there on the page.

When he writes he discovers the holes in his argument, the logical steps which are passed over, the sentences which grow tangled upon themselves, the paragraphs which collapse, the words which are inadequate. But still he must push on through the first draft. He cannot allow himself to be discouraged at this stage, or to be too critical. The happy accidents will be matched by the misfortunes, but still he must complete this piece of writing. He must achieve his destination.

This is the turning point. Before he wrote he had in his mind what he wanted to say. Once he has written he has lost his innocence. His hopes have become an actuality; instead of dreams he has a reality.

When he completes his first draft the professional writer has a feeling of relief, but this does not mean he feels he has completed his job. Now he can go to work on it, now he has begun, now he can become a craftsman. Before the completion of this first draft all was intangible; there were fragments of notes, bits and pieces of what he had to say, a sketch, a design, a plan, an idea, a hint. Now he has a piece of writing. And now that he has completed this piece of writing he can begin to write.

6 He Develops a Critical Eye

The uncritical writer who completes a first draft becomes a most critical reader when the draft is done. This is the point at which the amateur thinks the job is finished, and the professional knows the job has just begun.

Now he is the ruthless reader. He rethinks the entire piece of writing: What has he said? Does it make sense? Does it stand up? Is it said in terms the reader understands? Is it clear? Does it move easily from the beginning to the end? Does it work? The writer must be his own devil's advocate, his own best enemy, challenging what he has said with a cold eye. He is a thinker before he is a writer, and he must think through his entire piece of writing, rediscovering his subject and his audience.

Once he has affirmed his subject and his audience he can research his raw materials. Has he used the most effective documentation? Does he need to go back and search out facts which are missing? Must he develop new statistics? Will he have to go back to the laboratory and run some more experiments? Will he have to go back and retranslate a basic document? Must he get new facts run through the computer? Does he have to interview more people? The question he asks himself is, Would he believe the subject? Would he be convinced by what he has said? If he is not, then he must develop materials which will convince him. He must get the best possible raw materials from which to build his arguments.

If necessary, he must redesign the entire piece of writing. He may outline what he has written to see whether its structure stands up, or he may see the need for a new outline. Sometimes a writer will make quick marks in the margin on a re-reading. This point must be cut (X), this one must be developed (//), or expanded (>). Another one must be included that is not there. Other ones must be eliminated completely. He is searching for a shape that will work, for a structure that will stand up to the most critical reader—himself. And he wants to solve the problems of the writing off the page before he does another draft.

The writer is now deeply within the process of writing. He is changing and shaping and developing what he has to say. He is a craftsman who has choices to make. This point can be moved down here, that one built up over there. The writer is always forming, always changing, until he has composed a piece of writing which is not too long, not too short, which has a tone which is neither too frivolous nor too severe, which has just enough documentation, which is limited to the subject it starts out to present—in other words, a piece of writing which works. It should be as firmly built as a house which can stand up to weather and to time.

7 He Rewrites

All effective writers know writing is rewriting. The inexperienced writer feels a revision is a failure. The amateur believes the writer is the person who can sit down and rip off an essay or a report. The professional writer knows better. Rewriting is what you do when you are a writer, for it is an essential part of the process of writing. It is the way in which you fit ideas into language.

The writer often revises by completing a new draft. If this is necessary he still pays little attention to details, pushing on until he has the shape of his subject completed. He goes through the same process with much the same attitude that he had when he completed his first draft. He wants, of course, to have the right word, the right sentence, the right paragraph. But he cannot stop, usually, until he has the whole piece fixed, until he knows what he wants to say and has it in focus, until he has seen and fitted in the documentation which is needed at each point. The process of writing and rewriting is very much like the process of developing a picture: slowly it evolves before your eyes. It is a physical process almost as much as a mental process. The writer may dictate, or use a fountain pen or pencil, a crayon or a felt-tipped pen. He may type, or occasionally work from printed proofs. Whatever his technique, the result is the same. He attempts to achieve a draft that works, a piece of writing that has the subject defined, developed, completed. The piece of writing seems to come alive, to have, indeed, a life of its own. It has a sense of its own wholeness. It has something to say and it says it in an appropriate tone. When the writer has that draft completed he can become an editor. He takes a craftsman's care with the manuscript, working it over line by line. At this moment no detail is too small to be examined carefully, no nit cannot be picked. He knows what he wants to say and the form in which to say it. Now there can be no fat, no wordiness, no inaccuracy.

The writer first looks to see if the order is right, if each paragraph leads into the next paragraph. In a piece of fiction each act should be motivated so that it is believable. In a piece of non-fiction each paragraph should answer the immediate questions in the reader's mind. It should give the reader the information he needs when he needs it, building point upon point until he has reached the end of the piece of writing with the information in hand to convince him of its conclusion. The editor will rearrange a sentence or a paragraph or a page to make sure that everything is in the right order.

Next, the editor looks to the paragraph. Most writers write in paragraphs, and in general a paragraph should have one idea. The paragraph may be a formal one with a topic sentence, the idea developed, and a concluding sentence, or it may be much more informal. But in every case the paragraph has a shape. It must have unity: it should all be about the same subject. It must have coherence: each point should lead to the next point. And it must have emphasis: the most important points should be in the most important places. The editor will rework the shape of the paragraph to make sure that it has unity, coherence and emphasis, to make certain it adequately develops the idea which has been assigned to it.

Next, the editor looks at the sentence. Every sentence should move the idea forward. The sentences are similar to freight cars in a train and each should carry forward a meaning. Sentences should be neither simple nor complex; they should just do their job. When a writer becomes tangled in a sentence his editor (himself) will go back and start again. The sentences should be clear, with just enough clauses to qualify and develop the subject, with the verbs in the places which will provide emphasis, with the nouns so that they can be understood, with the adjectives and adverbs used sparingly.

The editor's focus narrows. He looks at the phrases, the clichés and the jargon, which sneak into everyone's writing. Some clichés may be all right, some jargon may be effective when speaking to a specialized audience. But clichés and jargon are the blank checks which the lazy writer gives to the reader, hoping that he will fill them in himself. The good editor will slash away at each cliché and every example of jargon, which clutter a piece of writing. He will slash at the wordiness which hides rather than clarifies the meaning.

Finally the editor looks at the word. The editor seeks active verbs and concrete nouns. He wants neither too few words nor too many words, but exactly the right number, and he wants those words used with precision. For the writer is the person who sees language as a tool. Pen in hand, ready to stab, cut, change the word, the writer ultimately is the seeker of the word. He has an almost religious feeling about it.

We communicate to each other as effectively as we are able to use words. We understand when the right word is used; we misunderstand when the wrong word is used. We live in peace because of words, and go to war because of words. A few words wrong and the teacher may lose a child who might have become a leader. A few words right and we inspire another child. It comes back to the word, using the right word in the right way and in the right place. And how do you know what is the right word? The writer knows that it all goes back in a great circle to the beginning of the writing process. What you have to say decides the words you use to say it. Content comes before form, but the search for the right form illuminates content. You know what you have to say so you choose the word to say it and, in choosing the word, you discover what you have to say.

This is the great circle of craft in which the writer is involved. He is searching for words and for meaning. He works back and forth, seeking a subject, an audience, raw materials, a design; he writes, rethinks, researches, redesigns, rewrites, searching for his meaning and for a way to communicate his meaning to other people. The professional writer rewrites and rewrites and rewrites.

A Summary of What the Writer Does

The Writer Sees The writer sees what we do not see in what we all see. He finds the ordinary extraordinary and old truths new.

He has the gifts of reception and perception. He appears to receive more impressions than other men, but in their confusion he discovers patterns. He has ability to be specific, to see with precision and accuracy.

He disbelieves to believe, destroys to rebuild. The writer has to impose order on disorder.

The Writer Writes The writer has the courage or the compulsion to reveal himself. He commits himself.

The writer is obsessed with form, but not as an empty vessel into which he pours meaning. He knows he has to have something worth saying. What he wants to say determines which tools he will use. For him words are never isolated from meaning, grammar segregated from subject, rhetoric divorced from purpose.

The writer works through specifics to generalizations and back. Hemingway said writing is "architecture not interior decoration." The writer builds with specific details, writing by selection. He forms, fits, shapes, and wastes. He knows the value of what he completes might properly be judged by what he has ruthlessly tossed away.

He respects brevity, knowing its challenge, and attempts to cut away from complexity to clarity. His goal is simplicity—the flight of the seagull. He seeks the least complicated way of expressing the most complicated idea. The writer tries to see and then make the reader see. He does not want to tell but to show. He believes he is successful when he is invisible, when the reader discovers the subject for himself.

The Writer Rewrites Art is beyond craft, but art grows out of craft. Craft is the calculation which turns inspiration into creation.

The craftsman writes by rewriting, and he rewrites by re-seeing and re-thinking. He seeks the inspiration of the writing desk. He understands that writing is a way of perceiving, a method of discovery, and refinement and synthesis and clarification.

The writer dreams of art, but he works at craft.

To ~~the~~ a Sky-Lark.

Hail to thee blithe Spirit!
Bird thou never wert—
That from Heaven or near it,
Pourest thy full heart
In profuse strains of unpremeditated art.

insert

In the golden lightning
Of the sunken Sun—
O'er which clouds are brightening
~~They~~ ~~wings~~ Thou dost float & run;
Like an unbodied joy whose race is just begun

The pale purple even
Melts around thy flight,
Like a Star of Heaven
In the broad daylight
Thou art unseen,—but yet I hear thy ~~blithe~~ shrill delight

Two The Writing Teacher's Seven Skills

"Let [the teacher of rhetoric] therefore adopt a parental attitude to his pupils, and regard himself as the representative of those who have committed their children to his charge. Let him be free from vice himself and refuse to tolerate it in others. Let him be strict but not austere, genial but not too familiar; for austerity will make him unpopular, while familiarity breeds contempt. Let his discourse continually turn on what is good and honorable; the more he admonishes, the less he will have to punish. He must control his temper without however shutting his eyes to faults requiring correction: his instruction must be free from affectation, his industry great, his demands on his class continuous, but not extravagant. He must be ready to answer questions and to put them unasked to those who sit silent. In praising the recitations of his pupils he must neither be grudging nor over-generous: the former quality will give them a distaste for work, while the latter will produce a complacent self-satisfaction. In correcting faults he must avoid sarcasm and above all abuse: for teachers whose rebukes seem to imply positive dislike discourage industry. He should declaim daily himself and, what is more, without stint, that his class may take his utterances home with them. For however many models for imitation he may give them from authors they are reading, it will still be found that fuller nourishment is provided by the living voice, as we call it, more especially when it proceeds from the teacher himself, who, if his pupils are rightly instructed, should be the object of their affection and their respect."

Quintilian—*Institutio Oratoria*

8 He Listens

You're assigned to a group of persons and marched each day at the same hour to the same room. You sit at a desk which is assigned to you. You are given a pen and paper and commanded to write for forty-five minutes on a topic written in large letters on the front wall of the room. There is a large clock on the wall. While you write a guard paces the aisles between the desks. There is the sound of pens, the footsteps of the guard, and the clock. You write until a bell rings, and your paper is collected. Another day you are marched back to the room. You are given back your paper which is covered by red marks. You have failed. The guard tells you how badly you write. The next time you return to the room you are forced to write again. And again your paper is returned with red marks. Day after day, week after week, at the same hour there are other topics on the board, and you write, and the papers come back, and the guard gets mad because you failed again, as you did the year before, and the year before that, and as you will fail next year.

Percy Bysshe Shelley, **Ode to a Sky-Lark.** By permission of the Harvard College Library.

Is that the description of some monstrous Communist brainwashing technique? No, that is a description of English composition classes as experienced by too many students. The usual student feels he is writing trivia for an uninterested critic under impossible conditions, and many times he is right.

The teacher of writing, first of all, must be a person for whom the student wants to write. The teacher must have a receptive eye.

This does not mean that the writing teacher should be so understanding that he has no standards. Students will accept and even seek criticism if it is fair and if it is meaningful. They must be shown that the teacher is teaching them for a reason. When they cannot communicate to him or to their classmates, and they have something they want to communicate, then the teacher can give them the skill to communicate it.

The first job of the teacher, and not an easy one, is to be himself as much as possible. Students can spot a phony, and the teacher must have the courage to reveal himself honestly to his students. He must show something of his own interests and his own concerns and his own personality, so that the students can be themselves and can communicate to him on an individual basis. The class does not write for the teacher; each student writes for the teacher.

The content of a writing course belongs to the student, not to the teacher. The instructor of writing must recognize this fact. In a writing course the content comes from the student. The writing teacher cannot tell the student what to say, but he can tell the sudent how to find something that he wants to say, and then how to find a way to say it effectively. If the teacher wants the student to write with honesty and precision and grace, he must listen to the individual student to find out how he really sees the world and how capable he is of using language, so that the teacher may help the student find his own style as well as his own subject matter.

This does not mean that you accept the student's view of the world if it is irrational, illogical and expressed in an illiterate manner. It does mean that you listen to what he has to say—not what you wish he would say but what he has to say—and then show him where his logic or his language is faulty. Each student is at a different point. The writing class unlike the history class does not move on from the Revolutionary War to the War of 1812 to the Civil War; each student in the class is facing his own problems at his own pace. One student must work on spelling for it is impossible to read what he has said and there can be no communication until he can spell. Another student who spells beautifully says absolutely nothing; she must be brought to a point where she has something to say.

Teaching individual students is exciting—and tiring. Another teacher may have only five classes while you have one hundred thirty individuals, but you still should not try to fit the writing student into the mold of the class. I have found in my own teaching that there is remarkably little difference between the papers from some elementary and some graduate students. We all, as writers, face the same problems, and we must be brought to see our problems and to find our way of solving them. We should not accept the evaluation of other teachers—Johnny is an A student, Bill is a D student. We must listen to this student, to what he has to say. Rarely in our educational system do we allow the student to say anything. We tend to breed parrots, and it takes a while in the writing course for the student to believe that he is allowed—in fact encouraged—to speak honestly, candidly, directly. He must be taught to see his own importance, not self-importance, not pomposity, but to see that as an individual human being he can have his own view of the world and his own critical opinion of it.

Listening to the individual student usually means, in the beginning, that you listen to his autobiography. This is appropriate. The Chaucer scholar has made scholarship part of his autobiography. When he writes of Chaucer he writes subjectively, caring deeply and knowing deeply. The student knows little of the world except what he has experienced. He must begin by writing about his world, and then he must be led to more objective materials, to reading, to studying what other people have said about the same world he sees, so that he may see and understand his world better and sharpen his critical talents on the ideas of other people.

The teacher of writing must be able to get out from behind the desk, to face students individually, to be encouraging to one and discouraging to another, to lead one student, drive another, support a third. He must at all times be understanding. This certainly does not mean that he likes all students or that all students like him. The teacher who gets to know his students will find that some are slobs, some may even be evil. The teacher of writing is a member of the faculty; he is not a student, a friend, confidant or pal of the people he is teaching writing. There is a distance of age, experience and responsibility, but the distance must be established between the individual student and the individual teacher. The teacher of writing must know his students by name, know their own problems, and work with their problems. He must listen to what the student has to say, and if the student has nothing to say, it is the job of the writing teacher to show him that he does have something to say, for the writing teacher knows that what you have to say determines how you say it. Content precedes form and writing is not words and sentences, but ideas which are honed into thoughts.

Archibald MacLeish has pointed out in his article "The Teaching of Writing"[1] that "the whole situation in a writing course is a reversal of the usual academic pattern. Not only is there no subject, there is no content either. Or, more precisely, the content is the work produced by the students. And the relation of the teacher to his students is thus the opposite of the relationship one would expect to find. Ordinarily it is the teacher who knows, the student who learns. Here it is the student who knows, or should, and the teacher who learns, or tries to. The student writes. The teacher reads. And the object of the teacher's reading is to learn if he can see how closely the knowing of the words approximates the knowing of the writer . . . the only question the man who undertakes to teach can ask, is the question of the adequacy of the writing to its own intent."

In a time of mass society, mass communications and mass mind, the writing teacher must find ways to listen to the individual student. This can be done, and it is done by the best teachers of writing. Some are stern disciplinarians, others are quite permissive. Some are traditional, and some keep changing their approaches from year to year. But those teachers who teach writing effectively, in every case, have students who want to write for them: one single human being speaking to another single human being.

[1] *Harper's Magazine,* October 1959.

9 He Coaches

The English teacher who wants to be a good writing teacher should spend some time watching a good athletic coach in action. Out on the football field he will find that the coach has organized the afternoon's work so that the team is broken into small units, each player learning and practicing the skills he needs the most. And then he will find the coach walking from player to player, showing one how to get a quick start, another how to throw a block, a third how to cut to the left, a fourth how to catch the ball.

If he talks to the coach he will find him saying that the good coach does not over-coach, and he will learn that these people, who have dedicated their lives to teaching skills, work with individual students. They do not try to take an uncoordinated fourteen-year-old and ask him to be a great athlete, or to play to professional standards right away. Yet that is what we do when we ask our students to write as professional literary critics when they are in the tenth grade. The coach takes an individual student and tries to teach him one skill at a time. First the fundamentals: how to block, how to tackle; step by step these skills are broken down. And you will find that he is motivating his students in different ways. One boy has to be told to take it easy in practice, another one has to be driven to try. Some are lazy, some are ambitious, some are afraid. A coach develops a team out of individuals who have quite different talents and capabilities, and he accepts those. I played football in the days before contact lenses. I was big, clumsy, near-sighted, and I played in the line, where my beef outweighed my disadvantages as a half-blind, poorly coordinated teen-ager.

Not all our students will look at the world through the eyes of the literary scholar. We should be grateful for that. We should be quite willing, even honored, to be allowed to give the student the skills he needs. He may want to write business reports, news stories, legal briefs, laboratory reports. No matter, we should not be snobbish about the kind of writing or its purpose. The literary scholar may be writing for money, and we should remember to write for money may be more honest than to write for fame.

Some students have a certain facility with words. We should encourage that facility and coach them so that they can use it to the very best of their ability. Other students who are not articulate can be shown how to use language effectively. As coaches we may see an even greater challenge in these students, and the longer we teach the more we realize that the student with the smaller amount of talent and the greater amount of desire may go further in life. We should not judge our students on their genetic advantages.

As a coach the writing teacher should design, out of his own knowledge and experience, an ever-changing course for each student. The writing coach must lead each student along week by week, so that he is developing his own talents at his own pace, never relaxing, never going stale, but always practicing and stretching, so that he is doing a little more than he did the week before but never faced with impossible goals. The good coach does not try to make a long-distance runner out of a sprinter, a high-jumper out of a shotputter. He works with each student's potential, and he should get his satisfaction from developing that potential. The student who can become a fine secretary may be more satisfying to teach than the student who will become a very poor poet. The writing teacher should think of himself as a coach who encourages the student to develop his own skills.

10 He Is a Diagnostician

The English teacher too often plays the role of judge. The student, through his paper, comes before him guilty of multiple crimes and is given concurrent sentences. The student is more than a three-time loser; on one page alone he may be a twenty-time loser.

There is a great satisfaction in passing back a paper covered with red, and the pride of the English teacher is to mark up all his papers completely, no sentence fragment, no ambiguous pronoun reference, no misplaced comma, no spelling mistake is overlooked. The paper is covered with comments, with "awks," and sarcastic remarks about split infinitives and dangling prepositions. If the paper is graded the student needs only to look at the grade to know precisely where he stands, but he has no idea what to do about it. I have even visited schools where I have seen numerical grades, an 83 or 67. The teacher's comments are often more destructive than constructive. They overlap each other and appear contradictory and, in fact, they may be contradictory.

The writing teacher must not be a judge, but a physician. His job is not to punish, but to heal. Most students are bad writers, but the more serious the injuries, the more confusing the symptoms, the greater the need for effective diagnostic work. When an accident victim is carried into the hospital emergency ward, the doctor does not start treating the patient at the top and slowly work down without a sense of priority, spending a great deal of time on the black eye before he gets to the punctured lung. Yet that is exactly what the English teacher too often does. The doctor looks for the most vital problem; he wants to keep the patient alive, and he goes to work on the critical injury.

The same thing is true when you visit the family doctor. He doesn't treat the headache, the difficulty in breathing, the stomach cramp, the lack of sleep or loss of weight; he tries first to diagnose their cause. Is it an organic problem? Is it a tumor, a problem of circulation, or is it psychiatric?

The writing teacher must train himself to be an expert diagnostician. This is central to the job of teaching writing. He wants to spot the most critical problem in each student's writing to give that student a prescription which will be effective for him. If you look at a paper, as we will in a later chapter, which is covered with red, you will usually find that twelve or fifteen of the problems are really symptoms of one problem. A student, for example, who has not given order to his views, who is illogical in his structure, will run into all sorts of problems in syntax. Confused and complex syntax usually is an attempt to fit information in where it doesn't belong. If the student has this problem diagnosed and is taught how to think out what he wants to say before he says it, then his papers may clear up overnight, they may become clean and direct. The good diagnostician will know he did not have a problem in grammar, although he was writing ungrammatically; he had a problem in thinking, because he was not thinking logically.

The student should realize that he has many problems with writing, but most students know this. They simply do not know how to solve all these different and confusing problems. The good diagnostician will tell him one thing at a time, "This week we are going to solve this problem. We'll come back to the other ones, you cannot be an educated man if you cannot spell, but for the moment we are going to forget about the spelling and try to get the order of ideas right." Each student will be treated according to his own diagnosis. The doctor does not diagnose a neighborhood, even in the case of an epidemic. Penicillin may work for most people, but there are those who are allergic to penicillin. So even when there seems to be an epidemic in the classroom, the teacher must treat each student individually.

Once the teacher thinks of himself as a diagnostician he will be able to handle many more students much more effectively. He is not trying to identify and correct every fault on a paper; he is not trying to cover every point in a conference. He is trying to find one central problem on each paper and prescribe a treatment. When he sees that a number of students are having the same problem, then he will develop a class presentation which will show the students that problem clearly, individually, separating it from all other problems, and then he will show ways that problem may be treated.

Again, the teacher of writing is a teacher of a skill. He does not try to make his classes march to some abstract and theoretical goal. He tries to teach each student by diagnosing his most critical problems and prescribing an effective treatment. And the better his diagnostic eye, the more effective his teaching.

11 He Is Flexible

The writing teacher, because he is an English teacher, is usually considered to have a subject matter as do teachers of history and physics and mathematics and literature. He does not. He must learn from those who teach music and art and shop, for he does not have a vast amount of knowledge or information to communicate to the students. He does not have many concepts to develop. He has a few basic skills which he must communicate to the students repetitively, over and over and over and over again.

The great danger is that the repetition of the same rule—be specific, be specific, be specific, be specific—may become boring both for the student and for the teacher. The writing teacher must develop many ways of saying the same thing.

It is possible in a writing course to present almost all the content—for example, the writer's seven skills—in one class period, then spend the year helping each student practice them.

The writing teacher should have a library of books and a file of materials which can be introduced to the individual student when he needs it. The model which is appropriate for a girl may not be for a boy, and the book which speaks to the child from a middle-class family may not be the same book which is effective for the child from a working-class background. It is possible for the writing teacher in most schools to develop a library of paperback material and dittoed examples, so that the student can be shown the same thing in many ways.

One rule may be developed and demonstrated through the daily paper, or in materials from a science book or a history book. It may be shown by a piece of writing in progress, flashed on the board step by step by means of an overhead projector. The writing teacher should be able to demonstrate the same rule through critical analysis of fine pieces of writing and of pieces written by students in the class. He should be able to use classical and contemporary material. He should be able to lead a discussion which will help the students discover their own rules; he should also be able to present the rules with clarity and simplicity. He will never catch all the students with one device; he should have many lively devices which will appeal to a variety of classes, small groups or individual students.

It is helpful for the teacher to remember he is a physician. He will have many medications and treatments for the same ailment. His job is to diagnose the simple problems of the student and then to be flexible enough so that he can prescribe a treatment which will cure.

12 He Writes with His Students

Most students suffer a feeling of horrible inadequacy about their own writing. They do not understand that writing is a process. They believe it is a magic thing which their teacher can do and they cannot do. They are shown literature as something completed, written in stone, and they think each time they write, the first draft should be the final one.

The good student and the bad believe when they have completed a draft that it is the best they can do. It is on the page, it is finished. The writing teacher must take the student into the process of writing. One of my students said I do not teach writing, I simply expose it. He may be right, for I endeavor to show the students as I write with them that writing is not magic, but work, that the writer does not put on a velvet smoking jacket, pick up a quill pen and let God direct his hand across the page. Instead, the student discovers that the writer is engaged in a continual struggle to discover what he has to say and how to say it.

The student should be shown literature in the making. It should be made clear to him that the novel he is reading may be the fifth or sixth version of that novel. He should be *shown* that it is, and why; how it changed and improved. The student should see the first drafts of great writers so that he can understand how they made clumsy sentences graceful, incomplete ideas complete. Chapter Six includes testimony from writers so that you can document your case as a teacher with the words of the writers who have engaged in a lifelong process of writing.

The most convincing technique, however, is for you to write with the student. The writing teacher cannot afford to hide behind the myth of his own good writing. He should do assignments with the students and have his own papers dittoed and criticized by the class. He must accept their criticism if they are to accept his criticism, since the student must be convinced that criticism is not a sentence of ignorance, but an aid to effective writing. It may be a humbling experience for the teacher to reveal his writing difficulty to his students. I know. As a professional writer I have gone into the high school classroom and done assignments, and I did not perform as well as some students in the class. The students were disappointed, not elated, when they found this out. Another myth was destroyed. Their teachers also wrote, facing the same problems as their students. Sometimes they succeeded, sometimes they failed. This was discouraging to the students, but this is the way it is. Writing is a process, and the student must be brought into that process.

The student should not leave the writing course believing the legend that English teachers can write more easily than other people. No one sits down at the piano and plays a Beethoven sonata the first day. You cannot paint a great picture without training, or win the National Open without practicing your golf game. And yet many students believe that writing is a gift.

In doing some assignments with the students, step by step, the teacher reveals his own struggles to the student, and he is able to show the student what he was trying to do, how he was failing, and what steps he took to correct those failures. He should write on the board in front of the students, trying to develop a paragraph, editing and changing the words according to student suggestions. He can write down changes suggested by the class, and in this way the class may see the difference one word can make. This is the time to teach connotation and denotation. The teacher may use an overhead projector as he edits a paragraph of his own with the class to show that a word simply does not fit in the context of other words which surround it. Or he may trace the steps he has taken from first scratched ideas, to outline, to paragraph, to revision and revision and revision.

The student must also discover for himself in his own work, that writing is a skill, and the difficulty of the skill brings its own satisfactions. Once he understands that writing is a process he may want to engage in that process, finding his own ideas, defining and refining them, until other people can understand what he has to say. To convince the student of this process, the teacher must be willing to expose his own personal struggle with language. The teacher is not a lecturer or an evaluator alone, he is also a participant, and he must share with his students the personal process of writing.

13 He Hones Creativity with Discipline

Many English students receive the unfortunate impression that you have to make a clear choice between creativity and discipline. They have English teachers who thump into the room and demand discipline. They are precise, exacting, direct, rigid, disciplined. Then the next year they have a creative teacher, who dances into the room, telling the students to express themselves, everything goes, "We are to be creative."

Neither teacher understands the nature of art, for creativity and discipline cannot be divorced. As in marriage, there is constant tension, but it is a productive tension. In fact, it might be possible to define art as the momentary resolution of the conflict between creativity and discipline.

If discipline wins that conflict then you have, even at best, nothing but imitation, a rigid product of rule-following, a perfectly controlled and unimaginative product. If pure creativity wins then you have chaos, a nonselective, meaningless vomit on the page.

We must make our students understand that creativity comes not only out of an openness to life, a willingness to make courageous and imaginative connections, to turn life inside out and upside down, but ultimately out of the struggle to contain life, to give it form, shape, order, meaning. It is the problem of poetry to fit life into language, to be precise in the documentation of dreams, hopes, feelings, emotions. The writer dramatizes life's conflicts, isolating them, identifying them, and revealing them. The writer asks, "What if . . .," and then goes on to resolve what his eye and his mind can predict.

The writer delights in the possibilities of language. He uses form to discover relationships, reaching for a rhythm or a rhyme or even a scientific definition. We think in language and we think by language. In attempting phrases the writer discovers meaning. He toys with words, and out of the play comes his work.

The writer is also frustrated by the limitations of language, its inability to carry his meanings. So few words, so few words, and so many of those words have been rendered meaningless by the advertising writers and the popular singers and the radio announcers. He is angry with the persons who have cheapened language, devaluating the coin of his realm.

He rails against the limitations of the page, the article, the book, the report, and wants to stretch the form, to burst out of it. And yet he can't, for form is both his prison and his opportunity.

Seeing the vastness of life the novelist follows E. B. White's advice, "Don't write about Man, write about a man."[2] The novelist takes the generalization of love, for example, and gives it meaning in terms of one, or two, or three persons. The person who is creative is faced by the meaninglessness and shapelessness of the world about him. He respects form as a way of handling material, and discovers language and rhetoric are his tools.

The teacher of writing should not be afraid to discipline his students. Some, with great imagination or caring, will desperately need limitations and controls. No artist was ever ruined by a teacher who imposed too much discipline. The artist is tough and quite capable of rebelling, and the rebellion should be encouraged as long as the student has a reason for doing what he is doing. Any rule can be broken for a cause; anything can be done in writing if it works. The question is: Does the writer take an idea out of his head and put it into a reader's head?

The teacher of writing, teaching individuals, should at one time encourage discipline and at another time encourage creativity, trying to keep the two in a productive conflict, not in balance but in a healthy tension to make the student try to do just a little more than he can and to teach him just enough of form to pull him back to the point of effectiveness. Too much discipline and he is suffocated; too much creativity and he drifts away.

Nothing is absolute about the quantity of creativity and discipline. How much creativity shall we put in this lesson plan? How much discipline in tomorrow's exercise? One should never think this way. At every moment in the process of creating writing there is an inherent conflict which comes from the opposing tugs of discipline and creativity. Both lines must be kept taut, both pulls steady. Out of the search for form comes meaning, and out of meaning comes form. Out of the struggle for freedom comes the need for discipline, and out of discipline comes the hunger for freedom, never separate, never resolved. The student must be engaged in this perpetual form of artistic warfare.

14 He Keeps His Distance

The writing teacher works in the front lines of education, close to the student. He is in an exposed position. The student reveals himself to him, and he reveals himself to the student. There is no lectern or desk between them for the writing teacher soon finds that the student has to come around

[2] Quoted by Roderick Nordell in "The Writer as a Private Man," *The Christian Science Monitor,* October 31, 1962.

the desk to sit beside him to be able to see the teacher's pen on the paper during a conference. Side by side they attack the problems of the paper.

This is an exciting, rewarding, and very dangerous kind of teaching. When you have convinced your students that you are willing to listen to them, they will tell you about themselves but it may not be easy to hear what they have to say. Many students are disturbed and will solve their problems by writing them to you. That is all right, as long as they are brought to discipline what they have to say and as long as you do not imagine that you are a trained counselor or psychiatrist. The writing teacher cannot be a parent or an uncle, a psychiatric adviser or a social worker, he must keep his distance.

He must know his students by their first names, know where they come from and what their problems are, since the problems of language are usually a reflection of the writer. The students when they write will reveal the prejudices and limitations of their home life; they will expose themselves. But the teacher of writing must maintain his distance. He will not be an effective physician if he becomes involved with each student. The students will attempt to involve him, for the writing teacher may be the only adult with whom they have had a mature, intellectual relationship. Yet the teacher must remind them he is a teacher. He must have his times of privacy, he must establish lines beyond which the students cannot step.

He should have understanding, but if the students are to respect him he must have standards. The teacher must be tough enough to impose a rigorous discipline upon students he knows very well. His understanding must not erode into a bland acceptance. At times he will be patient, but most good teachers are known by their vigorous impatience. Some students must be driven as well as understood, and the teacher's appreciation of his students and what they say and how they say it is meaningless unless there are some students for whom he has little admiration. He should respect his students only if they earn it; he should praise them only if they are worthy of praise. He should criticize them if they need criticism. His relationship will change from class to class, from year to year, from individual to individual. He will always try to make the student better than he is, and this, he will find, is a frustrating and difficult job. He should be quite willing to let the student see his frustrations and irritation, but not his anger. He should not make the mistake he probably makes with his own children of becoming so involved with them, so angry at their failures, that he is no longer an effective teacher.

Keep your distance, don't overteach, don't take your students' problems home with you. Don't think you can solve their non-writing problems. Maintain your own identity and integrity. The mother who blubbers, "I just do everything for my children," is a bad mother; the teacher who makes himself a sacrifice upon the altar of education is a poor teacher.

The most valuable skill of the writing teacher is a sense of humor. He must not be carried away with his own importance. There are other teachers, other subjects, other students. He must remember that he cannot make his students more than they make themselves. He can bring them to a point where they can express themselves, and that can be a very painful success. The writing teacher without a sense of humor will be drained and destroyed. The writing teacher with a sense of humor will not try to do more than can be done. He will be a bit ruthless in giving his students the opportunity to learn, and the opportunity to reject the chance to sit at the feet of this particular master.

At the end of one semester a freshman wrote me a note, "All semester when you said that stuff I thought you had to be kidding. But I guess you meant it." The teacher who gets such a note has a clear choice: he can cry —or laugh.

17 to know that in a time when his ~~the King's~~
hard task is not sought for by sailors ~~with~~ such
avidity ~~alacrity~~ as should be; a time also when some ~~and some~~
shipmasters privily ~~secretly~~ resent the borrowing
~~of~~ from them ~~a~~ a tar or two for the service ~~sea~~;
~~short service~~; His Majesty, I say, will
be delighted to learn ~~know~~ that ~~so at least~~
~~of~~ one shipmaster at least cheerfully
surrenders to the King ~~Service~~ the ~~very~~
flower of his flock, a sailor ~~as~~ who with
equal ~~cheerfully ... assents~~ loyalty makes no dissent. — But
where's my beauty? Ah," looking
through the cabin's open door

Three The Experience of Writing

The student must learn through a private discovery of writing problems and their solution. He cannot only talk about written writing, listen to lectures on writing, or study the principles of writing, the student must also work with his own pen and his own mind, suffering the experience of writing until he is able, on his own, to identify the problems in a job of writing, choose an efficient solution and use it with a craftsman's skill. To learn to write the student must first be a writer.

15 The Student Discovers a Subject

"But I don't have anything to write about."

The student lament is real, for the student does not believe he has anything to say. He does not see stories around him. Yet the writer, except in rare, dark, barren moments, usually has too much to say. He has to choose one idea from hundreds. The problem is to teach the student to do what the writer knows.

A good subject has three elements. First, the author must have a point of view towards his subject. He cares about his subject and has an opinion of it. The writer's tone may be objective or subjective, but in each case he is inevitably, through the selection and ordering of his information, expressing a critical evaluation of his subject.

Next, we find information in the good subject. Even in fiction and poetry we are informed for we either enter into the poet's vision of the world, or we put on the skin of a character in a novel. In both cases we are informed as much as we are by facts and truths in a book of non-fiction. The subject we usually like most is the one which informs us most efficiently and most gracefully.

The good subject has, finally, an appropriate form. This means simply that when we have finished the article or the book we feel a sense of completion. We have been given enough information to fulfill the author's promise implied by his point of view toward the subject. The author who has achieved a good subject has found the proper dimensions of his writing. He is not too brief nor too windy for he has built an appropriate vehicle for carrying his meaning to the reader.

If we accept these elements of a good subject, then we must accept their implications for the teaching of writing. Our students must have a point of view towards their subject. They must write opinion, opinion they can document on the page. They must be taught to be critical of their subject matter and to be honest in their conclusions.

Herman Melville, **Billy Budd.** By permission of the Harvard College Library.

Next, if they are to give us information, they must write papers on subjects with which they are familiar. They must write out of their own experience. Their experience, however, should include scholarly experience—information they have experienced in the library or the laboratory. In school we usually ask students to write on subjects on which they are not informed and about which they do not care. No writer, student or professional, can create a good subject unless he has something to say.

Finally, the student must find the appropriate dimensions of his piece. He may limit or expand his subject, or he should be allowed to decrease or increase the length of his paper. Much of the unsuccessful writing in school comes from the fact that the student is trying to say too much in too short a paper or too little in too long a paper. We must allow him to fit the dimensions of his subject to the dimensions of his assignment.

First, we must teach the student writer to become aware of his world. He must become conscious of the potential for writing in what he sees and in what he reads.

This can be done, at first, by talking about the writer's unique awareness. Elizabeth Bowen has said, "Experience is the reaction to what happens, not the happening itself."[1] Tying this together with the famous Socratic statement that the unexamined life is not worth living, the teacher may make the student see an event as a writer sees it. A father, for example, lectures his son on cheating and then, at the same dinner table, brags about the snow tires he hid on the expense account. Is the experience what happened, or is it the son's reaction to his father's contradictory statements?

The teacher should bring into class, conversationally and casually, the mention of things which happened to him on the way to school, or last week-end, or when he was a student himself. He should demonstrate his own awareness of the world and encourage his students to examine their world spontaneously. He should listen to what they have to say and not be critical of their vision of the world, or of their own world. Instead he should get them to look critically at their world, by asking good questions about it.

Elizabeth Bowen's marvelous short essay "The Roving Eye" explains how the writer sees.

"The Roving Eye"

How, and why, does the writer find the subject—*his* subject—which germinates into play or story, poem or novel? Is this a matter of chance, or of expert calculation? The question, natural enough, is not easy to answer in natural terms—hence the growth around literary art of a myth or mystery. Writers are not secretive, but they are shy—shy behind the facade they learn to put up, and most shy about what is most simple to them. The fact is, they are of childishness which could seem incredible, and which is more than half incredible to their thinking selves. The childishness is necessary, fundamental—it involves a perpetual, errant state of desire, wonder, and unexpected reflex. The writer, unlike his non-writing adult friend, has no predisposed outlook; he seldom observes deliberately. He sees what he did not intend to see; he remembers what does not seem wholly possible. Inattentive learner in the schoolroom of life, he keeps some faculty free to veer and wander. His is the roving eye.

[1] *Seven Winters and Afterthoughts.*

By that roving eye is his subject found. The glance at first only vaguely caught, goes on to concentrate, deepen; becomes the vision. Just what *has* he seen, and why should it mean so much? The one face standing forward out of the crowd, the figure in the distance crossing the street, the glare or shade significant on a building, the episode playing out at the next table, the image springing out of a phrase of talk, the disproportionate impact of some one line of poetry, the reverberation after a street accident or tiny subjective echo of a huge world event, the flare-up of visual memory or of sensuous memory for which can be traced no reason at all—why should this or that be of such importance as to bring all else to a momentous stop? Fate has worked, as in a falling in love—the writer, in fact, first knows he has found his subject by finding himself already obsessed by it. The outcome of obsession is, that he writes—rationalization begins with his search for language. He must (like the child who cannot keep silent) share, make known, communicate what he has seen, or knows. The urgency of what is real to him demands that it should be realized by other people.

It might, it appears, be said that writers do not find subjects: subjects find them. There is not so much a search as a state of open susceptibility. Can, and still more should, the state deliberately be maintained? At the outset it is involuntary, unconscious; when it is less so it loses some of its worth. "Relax, become blank, be passive"—should one advocate that? No, surely: nothing can happen to an inactive man; life shuns and experience forsakes him. Temperamentally, the writer exists on happenings, on contacts, conflicts, action and reaction, speed, pressure, tension. Were he a contemplative purely, he would not write. His moments of intake are inadvertent; not only that, but they may occur in what seems the very heart of the mêlée. How, then, and in what sense is he to pull out? How shall he sip unstaled his peculiar inner faculty for experience, his awareness of *the* experience, his susceptibility?

The essential is, that he be not imposed upon. He must know his own—that is, when it comes to subject. Truth is in his eye, in that roving eye: there are, and should never cease to be, unmistakable moments of recognition. Yet such moments may be daunting and inacceptable—"*Must* this be my subject?" the writer sighs. He is not so young, perhaps; he foresees with dismay endless demands and challenges, a required break with all he knows of technique, a possible inadequacy of his powers, cold critics, a baffled public, a drop in sales. Can there be no alternative? There are, of course, a dozen: lively, factitious, tempting—the deflected writer writes with sinister ease: what he had lost, or that he is lost himself, he may if he is fortunate never know. But the true, abandoned subject takes its revenge.

The outward, apparent, tie between writer and subject is not fortuitous. Background, origin, circumstances, the events of life, may be found to account, clearly enough, for a writer's trend and predispositions—his choice of scene, his pitch of mood, or his view of persons. A man's whole art may be rendered down, by analysis to variations upon a single theme. A novelist's cast of characters may, from book to book, seem to be repetitions of one another. Or, regional colour lends a sort of rich, enchanted monotony to an entire output. Recurrence of images, the shape and blend of style, give to individual writing a sort of signature. But all that is not *subject:* subject remains apart—an inexplicable factor, an inner choice for which no external can yet account. The child, almost any child, is born with the hope that the universe is somehow to be exploited: It may be the writer does not outlive that hope—here and there the eye passes, from clue to clue. Through subject, he offers his explanation. But can he say so—how be as simple as that?

It is for the critic, perhaps, to perceive, and say. Concentration on any one writer's work almost always ends by exposing a core of naïveté—a core which, once it has been laid bare, seems either infantile or august. There is little *inner* complexity, after all: the apparent outer complexity of the art has been little more than the effort towards expression. Somewhere within the pattern, somewhere behind the words, a responsive, querying innocence stays intact. There is, there must be, always the husk of thought. Intellectually, the writer ought to desire and must expect to confront in his critic one who is his intellectual match; it may be, his intellectual senior. Mind meets mind: style must stand up to hard analysis; structure at once reveals and defies its faults; method is there to sustain query; imagery is to be sifted through. All the same, there comes a point in the judgment process when intellect brings itself to a natural stop: the final value is rated by intuition. The vital test is, the sense of truth in the vision—its clearness, its spontaneity, its authority. In the case of the giant writer, here is no doubt; though there lingers an element of surprise—Balzac and Tolstoi, Faulkner and Mauriac, confound as well as command us by their discoveries. Unsuspected meaning in everything shines out; yet, we have the familiar resheathed in mystery. Nothing is negative; nothing is commonplace. For is it not that the roving eye, in its course, has been tracing for us the lineaments of a fresh reality? Something has been beheld for the first time.

The artist Ben Shahn in *The Shape of Content* describes the education of an artist in a fine piece of specific writing.

From The Shape of Content

Attend a university if you possibly can. There is no content of knowledge
He is specific that is not pertinent to the work you will want to do. But before you attend
a university work at something for a while. Do anything. Get a job in a
He develops his point potato field, or work as a greasemonkey in an auto repair shop. But if you
out of specifics do work in a field do not fail to observe the look and the feel of earth and
of all things that you handle—yes, even potatoes! Or, in the auto shop, the
smell of oil and grease and burning rubber. Paint, of course, but if you
Senses have to lay aside painting for a time, continue to draw. Listen well to all
conversations and be instructed by them and take all seriousness seriously.
Discrimination Never look down upon anything or anyone as not worthy of notice. In
college or out of college, read. And form opinions! Read Sophocles and
Note: except reviews Euripides and Dante and Proust. Read everything that you can find about
Pogo—surprise art except the reviews. Read the Bible; read Hume; read Pogo. Read all
specific kinds of poetry and know many poets and many artists. Go to an art school,
or two, or three, or take art courses at night if necessary. And paint and

This piece of writing by a "non-writer" might be examined by a class

Talk but listen

Again, listen

Why does an artist listen?

Relationship of writer's mind, eye and hand

Artist's involvement in life—his commitment

Standards

paint and draw and draw. Know all that you can, both curricular and non-curricular—mathematics and physics and economics, logic, and particularly history. Know at least two languages besides your own, but anyway, know French. Look at pictures and more pictures. Look at every kind of visual symbol, every kind of emblem; do not spurn sign-boards or furniture drawings or this style of art or that style of art. Do not be afraid to like paintings honestly or to dislike them honestly, but if you do dislike them retain an open mind. Do not dismiss any school of art, not the Pre-Raphaelites nor the Hudson River School nor the German Genre painters. Talk and talk and sit at cafes, and listen to everything, to Brahms, to Brubeck, to the Italian hour on the radio. Listen to preachers in small town churches and in big city churches. Listen to politicians in New England town meetings and to rabble-rousers in Alabama. Even draw them. And remember that you are trying to learn to think what you want to think, that you are trying to coordinate mind and hand and eye. Go to all sorts of museums and galleries and to the studios of artists. Go to Paris and Madrid and Rome and Ravenna and Padua. Stand alone in Sainte Chapelle, in the Sistine Chapel, in the Church of the Carmine in Florence. Draw and draw and paint and learn to work in many media; try lithography and acquatint and silkscreen. Know all that you can about art, and by all means have opinions. Never be afraid to become embroiled in art or life or politics; never be afraid to learn to draw or paint better than you already do; and never be afraid to undertake any kind of art at all, however exalted or however common, but do it with distinction.

The content of the art course is not the mathematics of perspective, and the content of the writing course is not the semicolon, it is what is happening in the minds of the students. For anything to happen in the mind of the student he must first be in a state of susceptibility. He must be seeing, hearing, thinking, reacting. The student should be aware of the writer's twenty-one senses. It is the writer's tough sensitivity and seeking receptivity which fills his days with ideas for writing.

The Writer's Twenty-one Senses

1 *Sight* The writer notices high school students are vulnerably aware of each other by the revealing way they try not to show how much they are watching each other. The boys roughhousing on the stairs ignore the girls, but make sure the girls are watching, and the girls flouncing up the stairs make sure that they ignore the boys while they are certain the boys are watching them. Here's an idea for an essay, "I'm glad I'm old," or an examination of the real anxieties of the adolescent.

2 *Hearing* The writer sees a student come into the classroom, which is busy in a workshop discussion. The student looks around and says loudly, "Is anyone here?" Everyone looks up, puzzled, and the student starts to leave, although the classroom is filled with people. Then he spots a gray head

and says, "Oh, I see someone's here." He goes over to ask the teacher permission to borrow the dictionary. The students aren't shocked but the writer is, for the scene is an invitation to wonder if we treat students as people or things, or if students have any identity at all in school.

3 *Touch* The writer will leave the stands and walk across the field after the football game, and in the touch of the spongy earth of the playing field, unfamiliar to his middle-aged feet, he will receive a feeling of youth and know what it is like to be waiting for the kickoff.

4 *Taste* The writer in the high school cafeteria will taste American chop suey and realize that is a taste—hard granules of meat, slimy elbows of macaroni, lukewarm tomato, thin transparent skin of grease—he need never "enjoy" after he has graduated from high school. But then he may wonder if that is a pleasant taste for students who eat their only hot meal in the school lunch program.

5 *Smell* The writer will smell the new-car odor in the fourth-hand car a student has bought, and by questioning used car dealers find out that they spray old cars with a new-car smell. There's an idea for a story: how do used car dealers make an old dog appear new?

6 *The Sense of the Specific* The writer has the sense of the specific, the revealing detail which opens the door of meaning to him and will do the same for the reader. He sees a teacher ignore a question when the bell rings at the last class on Friday and beat his students out of the room, and then he sees that same teacher wearing large cuff links engraved with the letters TGIF. Later, he discovers they are an abbreviation for "Thank God It's Friday," and he feels he knows that teacher.

7 *A Sense of the General* The writer not only sees those specific, revealing details about the teacher who waits to escape, but he also begins to make a generalization about all institutionalized people—the attendants in the mental hospital who look like their patients; the high school teachers who, if they don't escape on Friday and re-enter an adult world, begin to act like their students. His criticism of the teacher turns to understanding through perception, thoughtful seeing.

8 *A Sense of People* The writer doesn't think in generalizations, he thinks in terms of individuals. He doesn't talk about school administrations but talks and thinks very quickly in terms of Bill Randolph, Uriah Sneed, Wyn Pinkerton. His world is populated with individuals—lively, contradictory, quirky people to whom he reacts and to whom other people will react.

9 *Skepticism* The writer is not cynical, saying there are no answers to the questions intelligent man must ask, but he is skeptical, always asking and re-asking good, tough questions. The writer is society's doubter, the one who says, for example, "Just why *do* we teach English every year?" The writer is the person who listens to the English teacher complaining that "my students are no good, none of them, they never ask interesting ques-

tions, they never pay attention, they never write good papers." And the writer wonders if the teacher ever realizes why the students who come to his class, all the students, react the same way.

10 *History* Most people have no historical memory; they cannot look back beyond the shadowy days of their own childhood. The writer generally sees back beyond his own birth. He sees the big regional high school, with all its faults, in a line of schools back to the local high school, back to the one-room school, back to a nation which decided that one of its most important jobs was to educate its young, all of its young.

11 *Implication* The writer sees ahead. Having looked back across the development of the high school, he wonders what the implications are of the contemporary developments in education. Are the universities forcing the high school to become the general college? Is the idea of forcing everyone to receive an education a good one? Are our schools ignoring the general student? Has the new math in particular forced youngsters who want to be engineers to make career decisions as early as the seventh or eighth grade, decisions which are irrevocable? The writer is constantly looking about him and seeing the implications of things.

12 *Problems* The writer often sees what is going on around him as a problem. Many English teachers accept as a condition of life the fact that the student is taught the same rules of writing in the seventh, eighth, ninth, tenth, eleventh and twelfth grades without being able to practice them. The writer sees this not as a hopeless condition, but as a problem which can be identified, isolated and treated.

13 *Solutions* The writer has an eye for the teacher who is successful in producing writers. He has a sense that the person who is doing something well is solving a problem which other people must face.

14 *Self* The writer is self-centered. This does not mean that he is selfish. It does mean that he keeps putting himself in the center of the world and looking about him. "What if I were a teacher or a principal or a superintendent or a parent?" he asks. He looks out on the world from many windows, seeing with his emotions and his mind.

15 *Reader* The writer not only has things to tell, he has someone to tell them to. He is aware that there are things that the teacher wants to know, the student needs to know, the administrator thinks he knows and doesn't. He has a sense of audience, of somebody waiting for his information.

16 *Involvement* The writer is involved. The middle-aged writer sitting on a bench in the high school office waiting to see a school administrator, watches the school secretaries—busy ignorers—greet the message-bearing students the way all civil servants treat penitents. The writer feels the students' terrible sense of abandonment; he is involved in the students' loss of identity. The writer lives, for a moment, the students' hopelessness.

17 *Detachment* The writer often gets his ideas out of his own contradictory relations with the world. He is more involved than the normal person, and, simultaneously, more detached. He is inside the student waiting on the bench and inside the school administrator, who must deal with a repetitive stream of people within an unchanging, complex framework of rules and regulations whose reasons for being have been lost but whose existence is real.

18 *Curiosity* The writer who gets many ideas is forever astonished at the obvious. Each time he goes to the school he sees with wonder the process of education taking place; he spots those moments of eagerness, of asking, which are at the heart of education. He sees, feels and hears the excitement of a good teacher explaining an old idea to a new audience.

19 *Language* The writer is delighted with language. He toys with words as a cat plays with a mouse—*Up The Down Staircase*. He comes laughing to class because he has passed the superette, and he explains the joke to the students, who then think of other ridiculous words. He asks, as Barbara Tuchman has, why the non-fiction writer is always described in the negative. Because he deals with reality should he be called the realator? He laughs at and with words, enjoying them as a way of leading him to meaning.

20 *Form* The writer has a hunger for form, which is his way of discovering meaning. He has to put his specific insights into some pattern—a poem, a paragraph, an essay, a newspaper article. He wants to bring the discussion to a close at the end of class, rounding it off or at least ending it with the best question which can be asked, so that there is a sense of continuity. The writer wants to build something, to make something out of the fact that three boys have been arrested in one week for vandalism in this school. What does it mean? Is it just coincidence, or is it all part of a pattern? What do they have in common? Why did they do it?

21 *Irony* Finally, the writer has a sense of irony. Irony is the most intelligent form of humor, and the writer has it to an extraordinary degree. He is both an idealist and a realist. Irony is what makes it possible for him to live with what ought to be and what is. He sees the irony in the fact that a nation which says it believes in educating individuals finds the numbers of individuals to be educated demand a mass education, which denies individuality. In such an irony he may see an essay, an editorial, a speech, a poem, a text, a novel.

Does the writer really have twenty-one senses, not nineteen, or eight, or twenty-three? That's something for you to decide, for you and your class to decide. The class should develop its own list of senses and then go out looking for sensations, for ideas. The writing student should be forced to come to class with a list of specifics, a collection of perhaps fifty, or one hundred fifty, revealing details which might lead to a subject. The student should be stimulated through photographs, film strips, phonograph records. He may even poke a hole in a paper, holding it three inches from his eye to see what is important in that artificially limited world. The student should be made to describe what happened in assembly, or what happened a few minutes before in the classroom. He should look out the window with the teacher to see the infinity of colors. He should sit quietly in the classroom and listen to discover how much he can know about what is going on in the rest of the school by hearing. He may want to focus on one sense for a moment by putting a bandage over his eyes and exploring the world of the blind man. Perhaps he will keep a journal of what events have occurred in his world, so that later he can turn them into experience by reacting to them.

How much can you tell from how little? Here's a poignant piece of writing by one of my students, Mrs. Louise Farrockhrooz, who lived in an apartment above an elderly faculty member. How well she knew him from a few contacts; how well she is able to make us know him by a few revealing details.

"A Neighbor"

Tone

Specifics establish scene, writer's authority

Quiet humor, a bit of a bite

Show, don't tell

He's revealed some more

We moved into our sixth apartment in two years. Once again we had smudgy walls and a smelly refrigerator to clean and boxes of books to lug around with boxes and boxes of stuff we felt more and more tied to. This new place was in an old New England house with two large chimneys. We were renting one quarter of it and one of its four fireplaces, its main endearing characteristic. Soon a problem revealed itself; the bath tub refused to drain. We went to the downstairs tenant, Professor Harris, to borrow a plunger. Unable to resist the opportunity to see the condition the apartment had been left in or to inspect my housekeeping efforts, he climbed the stairs, plunger in hand. Because of his extensive experience he insisted on sitting in the bathroom and demonstrating plunging techniques. He bent attentively over the tub murmuring, "Just plain ordinary dirt," again and again. After recommending Draino and leaving his plunger he went downstairs. A few minutes later he returned with a bag of curtains which he offered for our use and was then off to correct exams.

Motionless—just the right word

Specifics

That was not my first acquaintance with him. Almost three years before I had glanced into his open apartment door while on my way to visit a friend upstairs. The living room had been motionless with antiques, a golden carpet, a Chippendale highboy in the corner and a yellow stuffed couch piled high with newspapers and magazines—neatly piled newspapers and magazines.

Note build-up to this point: show, then tell

Reader says, of course

Several months before moving in we saw the Professor to make arrangements for subletting an apartment. He did not own the house but after twenty years of residence managed it with no objections from the owner. I sat in a yellow chair and observed things remained as they were in my three-year-old impression. I looked for dust. There was none. The room was comfortable, beautifully furnished and immaculate. He was a bachelor.

That was the only time I was actually in his apartment. From then on our association was an occasional greeting from the doorway, if his door was open, and a jar of homemade preserves I gave him. Each time I hovered at the doorway looking at the dark floor boards bordering the rug and saw no dust.

Repetition of specific

I knew he was writing a book and that he saved the boxes his laundered shirts came in. He ate his meals out. Most evenings as we ate supper and looked at the passing traffic he was to be seen crossing the street. Standing at the curb's edge he looked both directions several times. Then, slowly rotating his head back and forth, quickly walked in smooth rhythmic strides to the opposite curb. He always wore a hat.

See him in action
Proper tone, pace continues

Every two weeks Professor Harris went to the "farm" and took his old Chevrolet out of the garage for the journey. These were the only times he drove and the car was in good condition. He did not have faulty parts repaired; they were replaced. In winter he rinsed it underneath before padlocking it back in the garage. Before each overnight excursion he instructed us at least twice to lock the front door as a protection from vandalism. Once, during a week long vacation, he came down on Thursday to be sure the house was locked tight.

Remember this detail; it will be used at the end
Specific

Most of his days were spent at his office and after passing the empty apartment on my way upstairs I viewed our living room with thoughts of his elegant, little known rooms below.

Anything else I learned about him I learned from sounds. At first the noises were a meaningless jumble, but gradually the half-conscious process of detecting neighbors' activities began. Each morning at seven as the whistle blew the [1] water downstairs would almost simultaneously begin to run. At twelve every night his door [2] opened, the front door [3] lock clicked, and his door [4] shut. Again [5] running water. Every week-end the [6] vacuum quietly hummed from room to room. Rarely, we heard sounds of conversation as we passed the door on the way upstairs.

Use of sense

Several months later he was taken to the hospital. He recovered more rapidly than was expected and soon went to his sister's for more rest. The water had stopped running at seven and the door no longer clicked at twelve. As soon as he felt well enough, he came back to check the house and leave the snow shovel. The next day he died.

Then a fine twist—the sounds unheard
She never says he was lonely—we discover it for ourselves from her revealing details
Repetition of details not heard

We attended the memorial service. They praised the life of what was now a jar of already buried ashes. The unfinished book was not mentioned.

Now voices are more frequently to be heard behind the door; his plants are carried away and the elegant rooms gradually dismantled. Today the car was towed away.

She gets out of the way and allows an action to conclude piece

Mrs. Farrockhrooz had something to say and she knew how to say it. The student writer must be held back from writing until he has something to say. The student must appreciate the importance of seeing before saying. He should, for example, be told to light a candle at home and to describe in 200 words just what he sees. Then, the next day, he should be made to compare what he has seen to what the famous scientist, Michael Faraday, saw before he wrote, in *The Chemical History of a Candle,* "You see, then, in the first instance, that a beautiful cup is formed. As the air comes to the candle it moves upward by the force of the current which the heat of the candle produces, and it so cools all the sides of the wax, tallow, or fuel, as to keep the edge much cooler than the part within; the part within melts by the flame that runs down the wick as far as it can go before it is extinguished, but the part on the outside does not melt. If I made a current in one direction, my cup would be lopsided, and the fluid would consequently run over—for the same force of gravity which holds worlds together holds this fluid in a horizontal position, and if the cup be not horizontal, of course the fluid will run away in guttering. . . . You see now why you would have had such a bad result if you were to burn these beautiful candles that I have shewn you, which are irregular, intermittent in their shape, and cannot therefore have that nicely-formed edge to the cup which is the great beauty in a candle. I hope you will now see that the perfection of a process—that is its utility—is the better point of beauty about it."

It is worth a class period or more to compare the student descriptions to Faraday's description. Few of them, if any, will have made generalizations about "the same force of gravity which holds worlds together," "the better point of beauty." But the student should understand that these generalizations are rooted in observation, in experience and in knowledge. Faraday first saw before he spoke, and he understood what he saw.

Wallace Stevens said, "The tongue is an eye,"[2] and the student should understand that we have to see before we say.

But observation is not enough. The writer must not only see, but also understand. To move from an idea, which really is a hint of a subject, to a subject, he must develop a thought, a coherent whole which develops and restrains the idea. This difference between idea and thought, between real life and drama, was shown most effectively in a column by Howard Taubman in *The New York Times.*

"Life's a Stage"

One of the most poignant dramatic scenes I have seen in years occurred several weeks ago, not on a stage but in the subway.

It was after 7 p.m. when the Eighth Avenue local heading downtown from the Central Park area has that tired, ravaged look, as if armies had recently marched and struggled through it and had left their detritus of newspapers, paper bags and cellophane wrappings.

There is usually a deserted, dispiriting air about the subway at this hour, even to a critic on his way to something new and, hopefully, exciting in a Greenwich Village theater. On this evening, however, the last car in the train, though it held a thin scattering of passengers, was full of animation.

A small boy and girl, unmistakably brother and sister, were playing a wild game of circling a central metal pole. They were both dark-skinned. His eyes beamed happily out of his round face, and with the tight curls of his abundant hair he looked like a grinning, colored amorino. The sister seemed to be about six, a year or two older than the boy. Her face was leaner, her eyes just as bright, and her leadership unquestionable.

[2] *Opus Posthumous.*

Their energy was unflagging, and their powers of invention apparently unlimited. In the few minutes it took to approach the 59th Street Station, they circled the pole a score of times at breakneck speed, tumbling over each other and rising hilariously to resume the jostling chase. Somehow they also found time to clamber over a seat, jar it loose, restore it carefully, like thoughtful citizens, to its place and take another whirl around the pole.

Their laughter was contagious, feeding upon itself and upon the smiles of the few strangers who were watching them. Their faces, knees, and clothes were getting dirtier as they played, and there seemed to be no one to expostulate. Did they belong to any one in the train? Or had they found their own way into the subway on a forbidden binge?

As the train was rolling into the 59th Street Station, the answer appeared. An older lad of about eight or nine gathered the little ones by the hands and took them to the seat where he had been sitting, his back to us, with a woman presumably the mother.

The older boy, who wore a striped tee shirt, jeans, sneakers, and a sober expression, pulled at the woman's arm as the subway doors opened. She could not be budged. Her body was like a dead weight, and her head hung limply against the window.

The lad tugged frantically, and a look of panic came into his serious young face. The doors closed. The younger children ran back to their scramble of games around the pole. The older boy sat down beside the woman—slowly and fearfully.

At 42nd Street the older boy made another desperate try to move the inert figure beside him, though this time he did not even attempt to collect the younger children first. His effort was vain, and as he sat down, tears began to run down his cheeks.

A kind-faced Negro passenger who happened to be sitting not far from the inert woman and distressed lad spoke to them. The boy nodded and shook his head, but his responses seemed listless.

The little ones, who seemed unaware of the trouble, had now slowed down. The amorino, eyes still shining, sat on the filthy floor, trying to rub away a sticky smudge on his palm. The more he rubbed the stickier and more diffused it became, and presently there were streaks on his face. His sister sat down beside him, and she too had hands and face patched with grime.

The last of the passengers left the car at 4th Street. As I walked slowly along the platform and the train began to move toward its final stop at Chambers Street, I looked through the window. The unstanched tears were white rivulets on the older boy's cheeks. He stood over the immobile woman —her impassive face, I could see, looked young—like a child on a cross.

That family haunts me. Unanswered questions pile up.

Who were they? What ailed the woman—was she drunk or just sick? Where were they going? Did they ever get there?

What about the children? And what especially about the older boy? Having tried to act with responsibility, would he continue to have the courage to do so? What would become of him? Anything could happen to him; he could become a man with a mission or a murderer.

Who was responsible? There must have been a father; where was he? Who was the villain—the man, the woman, society? Was this the price of individualism, which conferred freedom of opportunity and growth as well as unobstructed paths to despair and decay?

Why didn't the passengers intervene? Why didn't I try to help?

Excuses are always ready to hand. To interfere might be an impertinence and an intrusion. Furthermore, we were enroute to obligations of our own. I had to be on time for the rise of a curtain.

Perhaps there would be some answers in the theater. Possibly the playwright would raise questions of his own, probing and insoluble. But even at its most searching, life on the stage would not be so painful as it had been in the subway that evening.

For art, though it delves into chaos, seeks measure and order. At its greatest, drama faces unflinchingly the truth of the heart and the world that has shaped, enlarged or corroded it. At its greatest, drama has the grace to purge and exalt.

There is no shred of comfort in the memory of the little drama in the subway.

A good subject is something the writer knows, cares about, and can communicate. He must get his ideas from awareness, but he must develop them by gathering and applying knowledge and thinking about the meaning of the knowledge. Good writing is never vague. The student must see that when he writes:

> Life is that wonderful thing we all have when we are living here on earth, for everything in the earth which moves lives, and I see the wonder of having only one life to live so you'd better take advantage of it.

That student has a problem in syntax, but more than that, he has a problem in seeing, and he must be taught to see before he can straighten out his syntax. If he is taught to see he may be able to write about life in this way:

> The ant scurries in front of my foot, and while I continue talking to my friend I reach out idly and kill the ant. "Why did you kill that particular ant?" he asked. Quickly I answered, "Because I am God," and we laugh at my joke. But later that night I am very quiet at dinner. When my father asked, "Why are you so quiet?" I answer without thinking, "Because I killed an ant." My family laughs and I try to explain and fail. Then I go upstairs where I hear them laughing about a dead ant.

At least now he has limited the subject, life and the wonder of life, to one specific incident. Every subject lives within its limitations. The subject is limited by how much the author knows or can learn about it, by how much space he has, by his own limits of language, intelligence, observation and perception. The student writer must learn to accept and use these limitations which the writer has had to discover. George F. Kennan, diplomat turned historian, wrote the following about his experiences in limiting subject matter*:

"I just want to make a few very informal observations about the nature of history as a subject and about the condition of the historian. My excuse for doing so is simply that I came to this work unusually late in life, after a quarter of a century, in fact, in a wholly different sort of occupation. . . .

"One of the first things that dismayed me, as I tried to put pen to paper with a view to relating historical events, was to discover the hopeless open-endedness of the subject of history itself: its multi-dimensional quality, its lack of tidy beginnings and endings, its stubborn refusal to be packaged in any neat and satisfying manner. I was soon brought to realize that every beginning and ending of every historical work is always in some degree artificial and contrived. No matter what you told, there was always something that had gone before, or came afterward, which you didn't have time to tell about, or which you didn't know about, and which was nevertheless essential to the completeness of the tale.

"This open-endedness of the historical subject applied, I was brought to realize, not just to the longitudinal dimension of related subjects and related happenings. No matter what field of human activity you selected for treatment, there were always a dozen other fields that had something to do with it, which you couldn't treat. And wherever you tried to draw the boundary between what you could write about and what you couldn't, it was always an artificial boundary, doing violence in some degree to the integrity of the presentation itself.

"The perfect historical work, in other words, could not be written. If you were a great enough historian, if you were sufficiently learned in the environment of your subject as well as in its central core, then you might be able to do a good job of concealing from all but the most perceptive of your readers the untidiness of the outer limits of your presentation. But the untidiness would be there, nevertheless. There would always be a border, however well concealed, beyond which the firmness of your knowledge trailed off into the obscurity of your ignorance, or where the obvious limits on the patience of publishers and readers made it impossible for you to tell all you knew.

"In addition to this diffuse quality of the subject, I was startled to discover how rigorous, when you stopped to think of it, were the limitations of perspective. History, it seemed, besides being open-ended, partook also of the nature of a sphere. You couldn't see it from all directions at once. You could see it only from some tiny, fixed point in its ample stratosphere. This point was always arbitrary in relation to the subject. An infinite number of other points could conceivably have been selected. Each would have re-

* Reprinted from "The Experience of Writing History" in the Spring 1960 issue of the *Virginia Quarterly Review* by permission of the *Review* and the author.

vealed something which you, from the perspective of your particular point, were unable to reveal. Every point was, therefore, severely limited in its possibilities. Not only that, but there was a real question as to what latitude you really had in selecting the point you were going to use—whether, in fact, it was not already substantially selected for you.

"This brought up, as you will readily see, the whole perplexing question of subjectivity. I had naively supposed, before I tackled this work, that there was a body of unrevealed or unappraised historical fact lying scattered around, like so many archeological fragments, in the archival and bibliographical sediment of the ages, and that the historian's task was only to unearth these fragments, to order them, to catalogue them, and to arrange them in a manner that would permit them to tell their own tale. I was soon to learn that it was not this simple. These fragments were there, all right; but they had, it seemed, no single, definitive tale to tell. They could be arranged in an infinite number of ways, and each had its specific implications. Much was left to the powers of insight of the arranger. He had to do this arranging on the strength of his own good conscience, and to take personal responsibility for the product. This was the task of analysis and interpretation. And this meant that the fixed point from which one viewed history was actually none other than one's own self—one's self in the most intimate personal sense.

"The describing of historical events, in other words, was partly an act of the creative imagination of the writer. You might know the bare skeleton of circumstance: that such and such occurred on such and such a day. The fact remains: you weren't there; you didn't see it. To arrive at its true significance—to understand its atmosphere, its meaning for those who experienced it, its relation to other events—you had to put yourself in the place of the people who were there; you had to apply to the historical record something which, however you tried to make it informed and dispassionate, was still an act of the imagination."

The writer develops his subject by putting things in focus, by developing a point of view. It may be his own point of view about the subject or it may be the point of view within the subject. And he may discover this subject by switching his point of view, moving around the subject the way a photographer moves around his subject. If the student is writing about his parents, he may discover the subject by switching roles. How does he appear to his parents when he comes in two hours late from a dance? How does he appear to his father? to his mother? What are his parents like to his younger sister? to his married brother? Are they different people? How do they appear to his brother's wife? What do his parents think of their parents? How are his parents as children today? How do his parents act when they come home late from a dance and he has been babysitting? How does his grandmother treat his mother? What is his father like at church? in the office? on the sidewalk downtown? behind the wheel of the family car? at the family picnic? The student must work with point of view. He must see that the football game is different to the coach, to the young player on the bench, to the old drunken star in the stands, to the boy who is playing quarterback or defensive tackle or end or halfback, to the sports writer, to the cheerleader, to a father and to a mother. The game varies; it is a different game depending on where you sit—high up in the stands, at the end zone or at home in front of the television.

The student writer is engaged in the most fundamental human intellectual activities when he is on a search for a subject. He is examining life—observing it and trying to understand it. When he has seen something significant and is able to understand its significance, he has found a subject.

16 The Student Senses an Audience

The writer may write for himself in the sense that he is true to himself, but he does not write to himself. The act of writing is not complete until the writer has a reader who understands what he has to say.

The student writer must be given the opportunity to achieve a reader. At first this reader is the teacher, a good listener who can go more than half the way to see what the writer has to say, and then show him how to say it more effectively so that he can attempt to reach a larger and less sympathetic audience. The teacher of writing must be a critic, but not in the beginning. The teacher of writing should be a most sympathetic reader. He encourages the writer to find his own voice. He helps him the way we help a baby walk, holding on to him and protecting him from the falls he is sure to suffer, and then later staying just ahead of him, just out of fingertip reach. So it is for the teacher of writing. He is an audience for the writer, demanding but not too demanding, sympathetic without being sentimental, who encourages the writer to write a bit better than he has written before.

Still, the student needs other audiences. He needs to see the difference an audience makes by writing a paragraph as it would appear in the local newspaper, or on the television news show, in a school paper, in *The New Yorker* or *Life* or *Atlantic* or *Playboy*. The student must understand that he should do with calculation in his writing what he does naturally in his speech. The student speaks one way to his mother, another way to his best friend, still another way to his best girl, a fourth way to his teacher, and a fifth way—going back to the Anglo-Saxon roots of his language—when he's in the locker room. This is not hypocrisy, although it can be a technique of the hypocrite; the student is speaking in a manner, in a tone and with a language appropriate to the audience. He does this because he wants to communicate, and he must do the same thing in his writing.

The writer must write for the other students in the class. They will be much more critical than the teacher, although the student usually thinks that his classmates will be sympathetic and the teacher critical. He should write for other teachers. The writing teacher should work out ways in which the student's history or science papers can pass through the writing course.

It will be helpful for the writing student to edit his classmates' papers, or perhaps to edit the papers from a different class. He may read the papers from the senior class when he is in the seventh grade, or vice versa, then have the students from those classes read his papers and criticize them. It is important that he does not just write for one teacher. It is too easy for the student to learn what the teacher wants and to give it to him; the student of writing, if he is to be an effective writer, must be able to reach many audiences, each in an appropriate tone. He, himself, must experience the problem of writing for different audiences in a way which will make them accept what he has to say, and believe it.

17 The Student Searches for Specifics

The student must realize he does not write with words, he writes with ideas, with facts, with solid materials which he has to gather. He must be shown that the revealing detail makes all the difference. For example, when the student writes, "He told her casually that he loved her," the casually really doesn't say very much. We don't know what he means and we don't care much about it. The same thing can be written, "Hubert said, 'Marianne, I love you,' glancing at his wristwatch." In that single specific we see—and feel—Hubert's casualness.

Show, don't tell, we repeat, because it is important in all kinds of writing to get out of the way of what we have to say. The most effective writer is the one who can make you see the facts so that they become your own facts and, knowing them, make you come to your own conclusion. To speak with the facts and to get out of the way, you first have to have them. To show students the value of using specifics rather than vague generalities, you may take a student paper and have the class analyze it. Here is one:

> He was a very unpleasant person. Sam True was not what I would call an honest person, with anyone. His family didn't seem to care for him and I didn't like much to look at him. He wasn't very pretty. As a boss he left a great deal to be desired. His actions with his customers defied the laws of good business and it was hard to see why they returned except that he allowed them to charge things and they lived beyond their means mostly.

The class can be told to forget the problems of syntax. They should see that the problem with the paper is that the reader doesn't care about Sam True. The reader doesn't see him; he is merely told about him in a rather vague and general way. The class might rewrite the paper on the board, correcting the grammar, but without any additional facts. For example:

> Sam True was very unpleasant. He did not have a reputation for honesty and he was not physically attractive. He was an inadequate employer and the way he treated his customers indicated he was not an effective businessman. The only advantage his business had was that he offered credit.

It should be obvious to the class that there is no way that Sam True can be made a lively person unless the writer has the specifics which allow him to write the piece in the following way.

> Sam True ate cigars. He'd roll his thick lips back from his teeth, mean little teeth, yellow and sharp, and you'd see them grinding away at the wet rope of tobacco. That was the first thing

I noticed when I went to work for him--the way he chewed his cigars. After a week in Sam True's butchershop, I realized he treated his customers the way he treated his Corona Corona. He gave everyone credit and once he got his teeth into them he ground away at their self-respect. When Jack McAdams' new widow came in with their three boys and asked for "a pound of hamburg, please, on credit," I watched Sam raise his lips to receive a new cigar and saw his teeth snap down. I knew she'd get the hamburg and Sam his bite of pride.

That's a crude portrait, but an effective one, for the reader has the specifics which make him see Sam True, and be repulsed by him.

The student should take a piece of good, lively writing and remove the concrete details from it to see what happens. For example, you can read the column on the left in the following excerpt and then the one on the right to see the difference specific details can make.

That winter, the old General moved to Sixth and D. Streets. His new quarters, situated on the ground floor were convenient for a man who walked slowly; and Cruchet was one of the best cooks in Washington.

In spite of his increasing infirmities, the General was addicted to the pleasures of the table. His servant brought out the wines and liqueurs. The old man had refined his palate in the best restaurants in Paris; and liked, too, duck, and the hams of his native Virginia. Yet nothing, to his taste, equaled the delicacy he called "tarrapin."

That winter, the old General moved from the rooms he had rented from the free mulatto, Wormley, in I Street to Cruchet's at Sixth and D. Streets. His new quarters, situated on the ground floor—a spacious bedroom, with a private dining-room adjoining—were convenient for a man who walked slowly and with pain; and Cruchet, a French caterer, was one of the best cooks in Washington.

In spite of his nearly seventy-five years and his increasing infirmities, the General was addicted to the pleasures of the table. Before his six o'clock dinner, his black body servant brought out the wines and the liqueurs, setting the bottles of claret to warm before the fire. The old man had refined his palate in the best restaurants in Paris; and woodcock, English snipe, poulard, capon, and *tête de veau en tortue* were among the dishes he fancied. He liked, too, canvasback duck, and the

From his prime, the General had retained, not only a discriminating palate, but the defects suitable to a proud and ambitious nature. He had always been vain, pompous, exacting, jealous and high-tempered. Now he was irritable and petulant. His love of flattery had grown, and he often spoke of the great commanders of history, and matched with theirs his own exploits. Near his desk stood his bust in marble and the walls were brilliant with his portraits at various ages. They were arresting figures those generals on the walls; handsome, slender, heroic. He pointed to the bust, to the portraits, to show what he had been.

hams of his native Virginia. Yet nothing, to his taste, equaled the delicacy he called "tarrapin." He would hold forth on the correct method of preparing it: "No flour, sir—not a grain." His military secretary could saturninely foresee that moment, when, leaning his left elbow on the table and holding six inches above his plate, a fork laden with the succulent tortoise, he would announce, "The best food vouchsafed by Providence to man," before hurrying the fork to his lips.

From his splendid prime, the General had retained, not only a discriminating palate, but the defects suitable to a proud and ambitious nature. He had always been vain, pompous, exacting, jealous and high-tempered. Now that his sick old body could no longer support the racking of its wounds, his irascibility had dwindled to irritation, and his imperiousness to petulance. His love of flattery had grown, and he often declared that at his age compliments had become a necessity. While taking a footbath, he would call on his military secretary to remark the fairness of his limbs. In company, he spoke of the great commanders of history, and matched with theirs his own exploits at Chippewa and Lundy's Lane, at Cerro Gordo and Chapultepec. Near his desk stood his bust in marble, with shoulders bared; classical, serene and idealized. The walls were brilliant with his portraits at various ages, from the young General Winfield Scott who had been victorious over the British in 1814 to the already aging General-in-Chief who had defeated the Mexicans in 1848. They were arresting figures, those generals on the walls; handsome, slender, heroic, with haughty eye and small, imperious mouth. Gold gleamed in spurs, in buttons and embroidery and huge epaulettes, in the handle of the sword which had been the gift of Virginia; and one portrait showed the superb cocked hat, profusely plumed, that had earned for Scott the sobriquet of "Fuss and Feathers." He stood six feet, four and a quarter inches in height, and had been wont to insist on the fraction. But, swollen and dropsical, he spoke no longer of his size. He pointed instead to the bust, to the portraits, to show what he had been.

Such was the commanding general of the Army of the United States in December of 1860, but not so did his compatriots see him. In epaulettes and sash he was still his country's hero. Europe might celebrate the genius of Napoleon; the New World had its Winfield Scott. For nearly half a century the republic had taken pride in his achievements and, if he now lived in a glorious military past, so did his fellow-countrymen.

Such was the commanding general of the Army of the United States in December of 1860, but not so did his compatriots see him. His eye had lost its fire and he could no longer sit a horse, but in huge epaulettes and yellow sash he was still his country's hero. Europe might celebrate the genius of Napoleon; the New World had its Winfield Scott. For nearly half a century the republic had taken pride in his achievements as soldier and pacificator; and, if he now lived in a glorious military past, so did his fellow-countrymen. He was the very figure to satisfy a peaceful people, fond of bragging of its bygone belligerence. The General was as magnificent as a monument, and no one was troubled by the circumstances that he was nearly as useless.

The student must be able to seek his own details. They may be the specific quotations from a novel which document his interpretation of the work, they may be the economic statistics which illustrate a paper in history or the laboratory observations which precede an effective laboratory report. He can be taught to see these details; he can be made to look critically and accurately at the world around him.

The historian Barbara Tuchman makes a strong case for the importance of corroborative detail, the significant little facts which make history come alive.[3] G. B. Harrison, professor of English and world authority on Shakespeare, wrote in *Profession of English*[4]: "The most effective elementary

[3] See "History by the Ounce," *Harper's Magazine,* July 1965.

[4] *Profession of English* (New York: Harcourt, Brace & World, Inc., 1962).

training I ever received was not from masters at school but in composing daily orders and instructions as staff captain in charge of the administration of seventy-two miscellaneous military units. It is far easier to discuss Hamlet's complexes than to write orders which insure that five working parties from five different units arrive at the right place at the right time equipped with proper tools for the job. One soon learns that the most seemingly simple statement can bear two meanings, and that when instructions are misunderstood the fault usually lies with the working of the original order."

Students can learn to write specifically by writing orders. None of Terence Ortwein's students at Hanover (New Hampshire) High School will ever forget the mess—or the lesson—when he brings bread, butter, jelly and peanut-butter to class and follows instructions the class has written on how to make a peanut-butter-and-jelly sandwich.

The teacher can show students how to develop the abundance of specific detail necessary for good writing by writing on the blackboard a list of descriptive details of something with which they are familiar—their town, the Fourth of July celebration, the high school cafeteria. The teacher begins by soliciting the ingredients of that description. The students decide to describe the high school in one paragraph. The teacher tells them to list what should go into the description. In the beginning the students will talk like school administrators. They will tell the teacher to put on the board such phrases as "the school building," "the academic curriculum," "the teaching staff," "extracurricular activity." As the teacher puts ten or twelve vague words and phrases on the board, the whole exercise slows, and the teacher ends the exercise by telling them to write a description that night using their list.

The students go home and face the raw material they have. Here it is:

the school building
the curriculum
the teaching staff
parking lot
new building
the lawn
sports
an auditorium
cafeteria
the principal's office
students
classrooms
extracurricular activities

The students return with this typical paragraph:

My high school consists of a new building, my friends who are students, and we walk or some drive to the school where we go to class with the teachers, or have extracurricular activities. Sometimes a person gets sent to the principal's office. The school also has a cafeteria, parking lot, auditorium, and sports.

The class should discover that the paragraphs are poor because they had poor raw material. The teacher should read his own paragraph to the class and describe his own desperation at writing with the few vague generalities given him. The teacher should *not* emphasize the grammatical or rhetorical problems in the paragraph; it cannot be a good paragraph no matter how correctly written because there is no raw material there. The writer has nothing to say. The students will share with the teacher the same familiar hopelessness of writing the "theme." Now the teacher can show them how to find the ingredients of a lively, specific description.

The process of drawing out the concrete details is slow and painful at first. There are long pauses. The students do not know what the teacher is hunting. It may take an hour to begin a workable list. No matter. This is a course, first of all, in seeing, in having something to say, in finding the subject. It does not matter if the students write in the beginning. They must be taught how to see specifics.

A student suggests the dramatic club, the teacher refuses to put that on the board. A student suggests the class play, the teacher encourages him, "That's better." Then someone says, "Brigadoon," the teacher puts it on the board. Another student shouts out, "Grades." The teacher waves that off, until finally a student says with a grin, "F-minus-minus-minus." That goes on the board. "The Watusi," "pizza at Frank's," "Tolkien," "Miss March." At the end of the class the student is asked to list forty or fifty more specifics beofre the next class. The class votes informally on each specific, and when there are a hundred or more concrete details describing the high school the class knows it is ready to look for patterns.

Here is a partial list of the class's specifics:

Brigadoon
F-minus-minus-minus
pizza at Frank's
Tolkien
Miss March
echoes in empty gym
lonely sound of slamming lockers
friendly morning sound of slamming lockers
geography book with a map out of date
initials gouged in desks
beating Center High 21 to 17
Miss Harp's wig
green blackboards
12th grade English
getting up for school at 6:45
getting up for school at 8:04
dress and run
coke for breakfast
a date for the Junior Prom
brown orchids
waiting to get a job
factory
father's factory
we're on an assembly line to graduation

When the class has a hundred more it is ready to select those details which may be ordered into a meaningful description. The students may feel the need for a dominant impression and the need for discipline and control. The class has too much to say and it has to limit its abundant raw material.

The students must be reminded that the same technique is appropriate to all student writing. When he writes an analytical article on a Frost poem, the student needs the ability to reach for a specific quotation, to refer accurately to a word or a line. There is a basic relationship between good observation and good scholarship. This is just as true of the vocational student who is writing down instructions on how to make a chair leg as it is for the science student describing how to make an atomic space ship. The scientific paper and the descriptive composition are both marked by their concrete documentation based on observation of the world. The poet is a person, as is the scientist, who sees with precision and speaks with precision. If students are expected to use the language with accuracy, they must be taught to see with accuracy.

When the students have their list they are ready to work on a piece of writing. The teacher should also work from this rich list of specifics. This can be a class exercise on the board, or it can be a homework exercise. Here is an example of one paragraph which could have been written from that list.

> Every morning my father goes to his factory, and I go to mine--East High School. Our brain factory looks just like his, a long, low building with a flat roof, lots of glass and a huge parking lot. But inside there are students waiting to get out so they can go to the state university or to the other factory and the teachers waiting for summer vacation. The clatter of the lockers, the calls about lunch, jokes, and last night's date and the last bell. We have "green" blackboards, old worn books, and the initialed desks from the old high school. But we're waiting for the intercom to tell us to go back to our home room at 2:50. We can't wait to get out of school, to graduate, so we can go to the other factory. All but the teachers, they have to stay until 3:30 because this is their factory, too.

There's a great deal wrong with that rough first draft of a descriptive paragraph, but it does have an idea and vitality. It is capable of being rewritten and polished into a fine paragraph. The class can be made to see the advantages of seeing, of having an inventory of concrete details when they sit down to write.

If a student is taught to write with specifics he will never turn in a paper such as this one, which begins:

> She was a very pretty girl of five years with pretty hair put up in pigtails. She always wore the finest clothes and had the best toys and came from the finest home. . . .

The student who is taught to be specific will write, as these students of John Harris of Conard High School, West Hartford, Connecticut, have written.

Sunday Dinner

Sunday dinner at 94 Ledgewood Road always includes Julia Child and Clarence Darrow on the guest list. When Julia herself can't make our Sunday afternoon fete, at least one of her recipes is present. In honor of our guests, the dining room is set for dinner, instead of the kitchen, and a white linen tablecloth usurps the position of the plastic placemats. If our Sunday dinner were announced over the P.A., Mr. Morin would say, "Attendance is mandatory." So, at 1 P.M., we join Julia, from Quiche Lorraine to Salsbury steak in Bordelaise sauce (hamburg soaked in red wine), for Sunday dinner. Julia's French recipes are delicious delicacies, once translated, but those sauces! They usually complete the dining-room decor by stippling the white tablecloth, when one of us, trying too hard to be neat, flips, drops, or slops some off his plate. But, as long as I'm not the first to defile the linen cloth, I don't blush to a fire-cracker red.

Though our whole family assembles uniformly at 1 P.M., their attire is hardly uniform. At our Sunday dinner, it doesn't matter what we wear, though it does matter what we don't wear, and dad comes in his golf shoes, Cathy in her pajamas, I in my tennis dress, mom in her church outfit, and Missy-dog in her fur coat.

At precisely 1 P.M., EST. dad, as Clarence Darrow, sits down and begins an interrogation about my date the night before. "Who, when, where, how, and what time did you finally get home, young lady?" Then he puts my sister on the stand with, "Have you done any of your homework yet, and why not?" Then, mom adeptly puts Clarence, himself, on the witness stand, asking, "Have you fixed all the things on your list yet, and why not?" At last, Clarence and Julia excuse themselves and we all depart from the freckled tablecloth, our destinations determined by our outfits.

Sunday Dinner

Whenever my mother answers, "You'll see" to the question, "What's for dinner?" we know that we're having one of those dinners that no one in the family likes, but that my mother feels she should make for "variety." Last Sunday we had a perfect example of one of these meals: glazed corned beef and sweet potatoes. The meat was salty and none of us particularly liked it but we were faced with the problem of making some kind of comment to my mother. We couldn't tell her that we didn't like the meal because she'd probably become hurt or offended, and we couldn't praise her for fear that she'd make the awful meal again. We all ate slowly, each of us wondering if anyone at the table would have the nerve to say anything, and fearing that my mother would come right out and ask us. Finally my eight-year-old sister, being able to stand it no longer, said, "Yech, this tastes terrible. Can I make a peanut butter-and-jelly sandwich?"

It may be helpful for the students to submit their lists of specifics to show the teacher the research they have done. Perhaps they can be assigned as reporters to report on the local teen-age hangout, to find out how to buy a motorcycle or how to write a term paper. One teacher assigned groups of students to explore a topic. Three students decided to write on "different ways of committing suicide." They started their paper, "There are many ways of committing suicide these days. 1) overdose of pills, 2) stabbing or shooting yourself, 3) jumping off a high object." That is as far as they got. They realized that they didn't know about suicide, and they started out to investigate the subject.

We tell our students to write from abundance, to select the significant details from among the many, and then we assign them papers on subjects which they find remote and on which they cannot possibly be informed. We must give them the direction and the time so that they can assemble the specifics from which they can design good papers.

18 The Student Creates a Design

Writing is thinking. The student must discover that writing is not the dainty arrangement of superficialities, it is the solid construction of thoughts. Writing is rarely spontaneous. The writer is a calculator, a schemer, a designer; he builds. Notice the notes on page 52 I have written for a paper on creativity. What I am trying to do as a writer is to create a design, a pattern, an order, and you can see this process going on on the page.

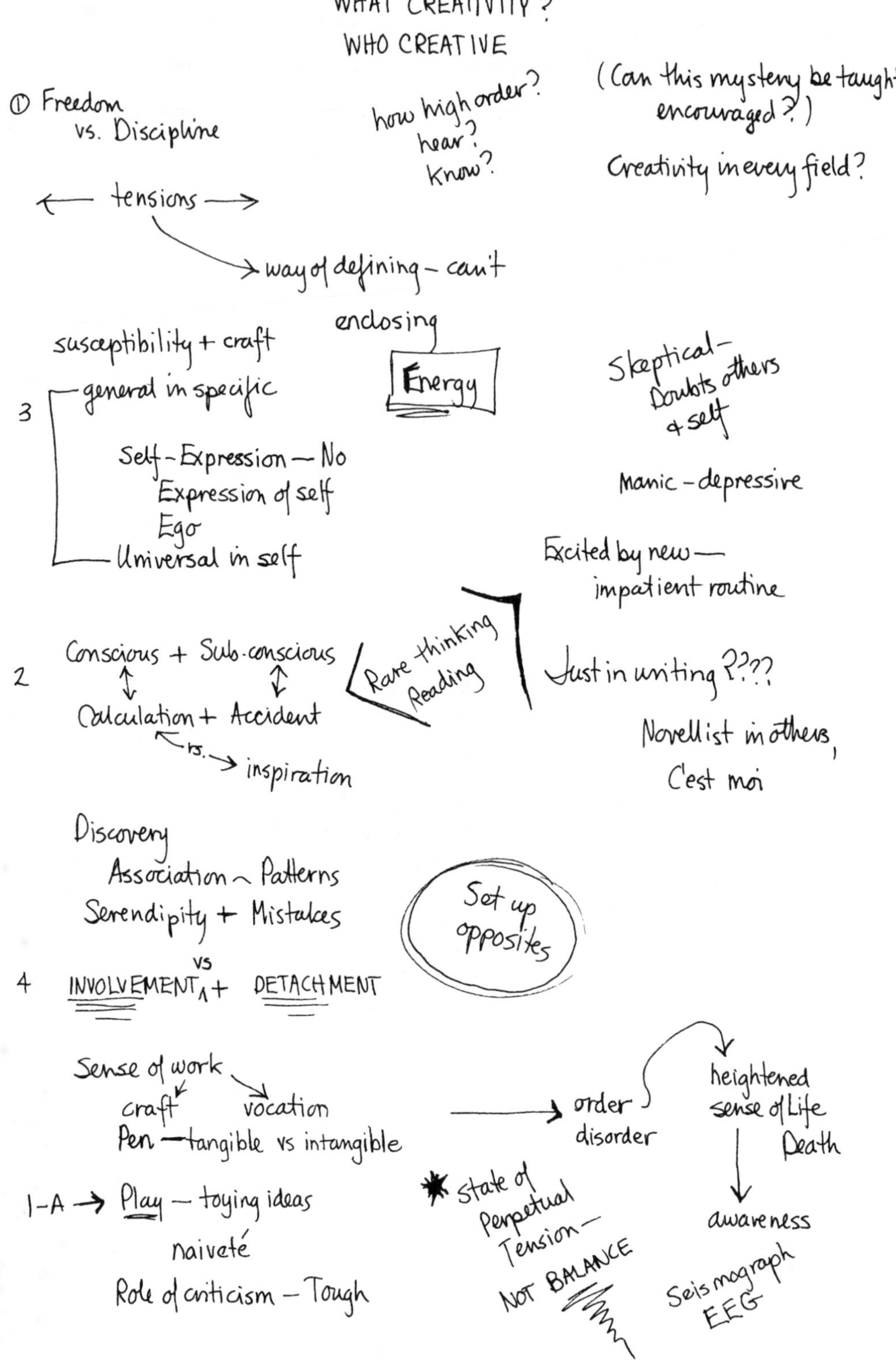
WHAT CREATIVITY?
WHO CREATIVE
(Can this mystery be taught? encouraged?)
how high order? hear? know?
Creativity in every field?
① Freedom vs. Discipline
tensions
way of defining – can't enclosing
Energy
susceptibility + craft
3 general in specific
Self-Expression — No
Expression of self
Ego
Universal in self
Skeptical – Doubts others & self
Manic – depressive
Excited by new – impatient routine
Rare thinking
Reading
Just in writing????
2 Conscious + Sub-conscious
Calculation + Accident
vs.
inspiration
Novellist in others, C'est moi
Discovery
Association ~ Patterns
Serendipity + Mistakes
Set up opposites
4 INVOLVEMENT vs + DETACHMENT
Sense of work
craft
vocation
Pen — tangible vs intangible
order
disorder
heightened sense of Life
Death
awareness
1-A → Play — toying ideas
naiveté
Role of criticism — Tough
state of Perpetual Tension – NOT BALANCE
Seismograph
EEG

The writer is the person who is seeking order. He may do this with a subconscious outline that stays in his head, or he may scribble down an outline on a piece of paper. This outline may be extremely formal, or it may be casual; it is not important. The important thing is what results from the outline. The student should see the advantage of making an outline even for a paragraph. The place to begin to teach a sense of structure is within the paragraph. For example, here is the diagram of the paragraph.

Special Problems:

A) Opening Paragraph (lead)
B) Concluding Paragraph

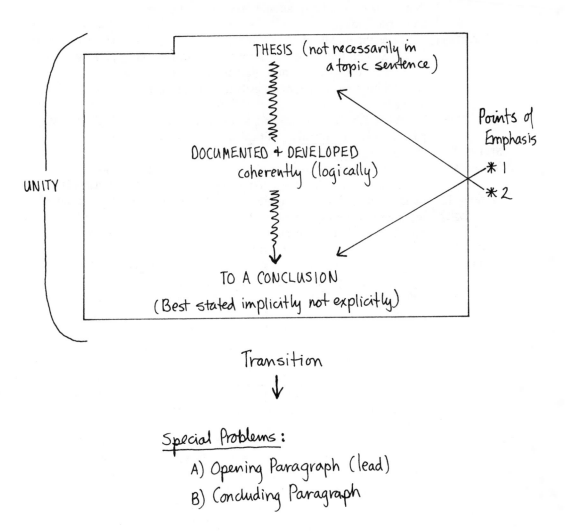

The student should be shown that an essay is built from a series of paragraphs—an opening paragraph, developing paragraphs, and a concluding paragraph—which are held together by the devices of unity, developed by the techniques of coherence and made effective by the use of emphasis.

Exterior Relationship of Paragraphs

Interior Development of Paragraphs

Unity

"Why I Write"

Is this an effective title? Why?

From a very early age, perhaps the age of five or six, I knew that when I grew up I should be a writer. Between the ages of about seventeen and twenty-four I tried to abandon this idea, but I did so with the consciousness that I was outraging my true nature and that sooner or later I should have to settle down and write books.

What are the problems of any lead? How can they be solved?

What is the point of view?

Transition

I was the middle child of three . . .

What are the points of emphasis in any paragraph?

. . . And the more one is conscious of one's political bias, the more chance one has of acting politically without sacrificing one's esthetic and intellectual integrity.

Thesis

Topic or thesis sentence

What I have most wanted to do throughout the past ten years is to make political writing into an art. My starting point is always a feeling of partisanship, a sense of injustice. When I sit down to write a book, I do not say to myself, "I am going to produce a work of art." I write it because there is some lie that I want to expose, some fact to which I want to draw attention, and my initial concern is to get a hearing. But I could not do the work of writing a book, or even a long magazine article, if it were not also an esthetic experience. Anyone who cares to examine my work will see that even when it is downright propaganda it contains much that a full-time politician would consider irrelevant. I am not able, and I do not want, completely to abandon the world-view that I acquired in childhood. So long as I remain alive and well I shall continue to feel strongly about prose style, to love the surface of the earth, and to take a pleasure in solid objects and scraps of useless information. It is no use trying to suppress that side of myself. The job is to reconcile my ingrained likes and dislikes with the essentially public, non-individual activities that this age forces on all of us.

What are the unifying devices?

of thought? (logic)

of language? (rhetoric)

Conclusion—thesis repeated

Point #1

How is thesis developed?

Does he turn a corner here or make a step forward?

Point #2

How do the ideas in the paragraph fit together?

What makes this an unusually effective sentence?

How does the end relate to beginning and middle of paragraph?

Transition

It is not easy . . .

. . . I have not written a novel for seven years, but I hope to write another fairly soon. It is bound to be a failure, every book is a failure, but I do know with some clarity what kind of book I want to write.

Transition — Looking back through the last page or two, I see that I have made it appear as though my motives in writing were wholly public-spirited. I don't want to leave that as the final impression. All writers are vain, selfish and lazy, and at the very bottom of their motives there lies a mystery. Writing a book is a horrible, exhausting struggle, like a long bout of some painful illness. One would never undertake such a thing if one were not driven on by some demon whom one can neither resist nor understand. For all one knows that demon is simply the same instinct that makes a baby squall for attention. And yet it is also true that one can write nothing readable unless one constantly struggles to efface one's own personality. Good prose is like a window pane. I cannot say with certainty which of my motives are the strongest, but I know which of them deserve to be followed. And looking back through my work, I see that it is invariably where I lacked a political purpose that I wrote lifeless books and was betrayed into purple passages, sentences without meaning, decorative adjectives and humbug generally.

What are the problems of a concluding paragraph. How can they be solved?

Unity

What is the role of tone in achieving unity?
What is his tone?

Where is Orwell specific? general? Why?

Simile

How are his points woven together?

Lively?

What does this mean? Is it true?

What is his point of emphasis?

Students should chew at and attack papers which are badly designed and well designed to see what makes one fail and the other work. They should go through the process of critical analysis as it will be shown in Chapter Six, and they should go back to their own lists of specifics with two or three students looking at the same one and showing the alternate ways in which that list can be developed. The student should not think that there is just one way to write anything. He should learn that there are many ways of approaching the same set of facts as is shown in the following exercise.

Here are the facts—cold, clean, and apparently indisputable.

Name: Wallace Randale Sheldon
Position: United States Senator seeking third term. Chairman of the Policy Affairs Subcommittee.
Physical description:
age—64 years
height—six feet, two inches
weight—223 pounds
appearance—white-haired, pink-cheeked
Background: Clerk in hardware store who rose to be millionaire manufacturer of plumbing supplies.
What he said in Washington: "I oppose the President's tax proposal."
Where he campaigned: Thompson Falls, Woodstown, Beaver City, Badger, Black City.
How he travelled: In a 1956 Ford.
How his audience reacted: They cheered.

What he said back home: "Some of my colleagues complain about campaigning. I don't. I think it is our duty to talk to the people and to listen. Because of what you've told me about how you feel and why, I'm going to change my position and vote for the tax bill."

Here are some of the variations with each note true and each tune different.

Badger, August 15—Senator Wallace R. Sheldon announced here today he would vote for the tax bill. Campaigning for re-election, the Senator told cheering audiences in Thompson Falls, Woodstown, Beaver City, and Black City that he had listened to the voice of the people and changed his mind. In Washington last week Senator Sheldon had announced he was opposed to the President's tax proposal.

• • •

A millionaire in a 1956 Ford visited the sticks this week and wowed 'em from Beaver City to Badger and back. He was Senator Wallace R. Sheldon and he told cheering audiences he had heard the voice of the people and was now for the tax bill. What he heard was the death rattle in the ballot box.

• • •

It takes a big man to change his mind, and Senator Wallace R. Sheldon—six-feet-two and 223 pounds—has the stature for the job. In Washington he was opposed to the tax bill, but on a campaign swing in his home state he heard the voice of the people. "I think it is our duty to talk to the people and to listen," Senator Sheldon told the small towners bluntly. "I'm going to change my position and vote for the tax bill."

• • •

"Some of my colleagues complain about campaigning. I don't," Senator Wallace R. Sheldon told audiences back home last week. He was frankly perspiring. "I think it is our duty to talk to the people and listen. Because of what you've told me of how you feel and why, I'm going to change my position and vote for the tax bill."

• • •

The image of the American businessman is that of a big, bluff, hearty guy who stares facts right in the eye and Senator Wallace R. Sheldon looks the part. But last week Senator Sheldon revealed another side of the businessman's character—the customer's always right. In Washington he had studied the tax bill and said forthrightly he was against it. This week he came home, listened to the customers and said, "I'm going to vote for the tax bill."

• • •

Burly U.S. Senator Wallace R. Sheldon, who met many a payroll before he went to the Senate, knows how to face a fact. Last week he told the people what they wanted to hear, that he would change his position and vote for the tax bill.

• • •

Last week Senator Wallace R. Sheldon demonstrated why, for all the hoopla and howdies, American campaigns are an essential part of democracy. He came back home from Washington and listened to the voice of his people. In Badger he announced, "Because of what you've told me about how you feel and why, I'm going to change my position and vote for the tax bill."

• • •

Democracy's strength, and weakness, lies in its elections. Last week the United States suffered an attack of democratic indigestion. In Washington Senator Wallace R. Sheldon, a businessman who understands the real meaning of taxes, studied the President's proposals and said, "I oppose the President's tax proposal." Then he came back to Badger and rediscovered the first law of politics is to get elected. On the hustings he promised, "I'm going to vote for the tax bill."

• • •

Even in a jet age Washington seems a long way from Beaver City, but it was shown last week that the people still rule in America. Senator Wallace R. Sheldon, chairman of the powerful Policy Affairs Subcommittee, went back home and heard the voice of the people. He announced he would change his position and vote for the tax bill.

• • •

A ruddy-faced bruiser of a man, Senator Wallace R. Sheldon showed reporters last week that at 64 he can still campaign with the best of them. Seeking his third term in the Senate, the Senator was running hard in Thompson Falls, Woodstown, Beaver City, Badger, and Black City. He showed reporters more than energy, he demonstrated why the small-towners respect him—he's honest enough to change his mind. "Some of my colleagues complain about campaigning. I don't," Senator Sheldon said bluntly. "It is our duty to talk to the people and listen. I'm going to change my position and vote for the tax bill."

• • •

In Beaver City Senator Wallace Randale Sheldon showed his age last week. He's 64, weighs in at 223 pounds, and it was hot, very hot. Perspiring, he told an audience that "because of what you've told me about how you feel and why," he would change his position and vote for the tax bill.

• • •

Wallace Randale Sheldon has everything an ex-hardware clerk could want —the largest chunk of stock in a firm that manufactured 700,000 toilet bowls last year and a seat in the United States Senate. He has a reputation for vigor and statesmanship as chairman of the Policy Affairs Subcommittee, but last week he showed he was still just another politician who wants re-election above all. "I'm going to change my position," he told an audience in Badger. "I'm going to vote for the tax bill."

The writer will discover just what he wants to say as he writes, but he must have some idea of where he is going before he decides to write. What is his approach, what is his point of view? In general, there are four ways of documenting and developing a piece of writing, as the following diagrams show.

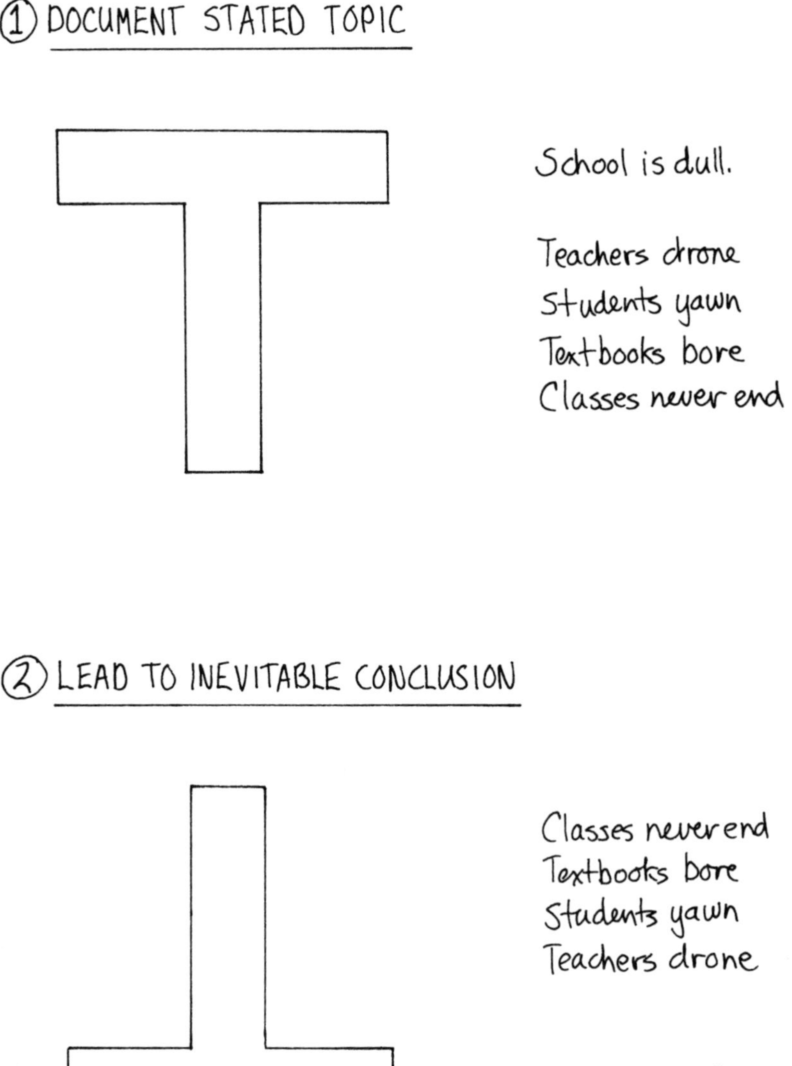

① DOCUMENT STATED TOPIC
School is dull.
Teachers drone
Students yawn
Textbooks bore
Classes never end
② LEAD TO INEVITABLE CONCLUSION
Classes never end
Textbooks bore
Students yawn
Teachers drone
School is dull.

③ LEAD TO CONCLUSION AND DOCUMENT IT

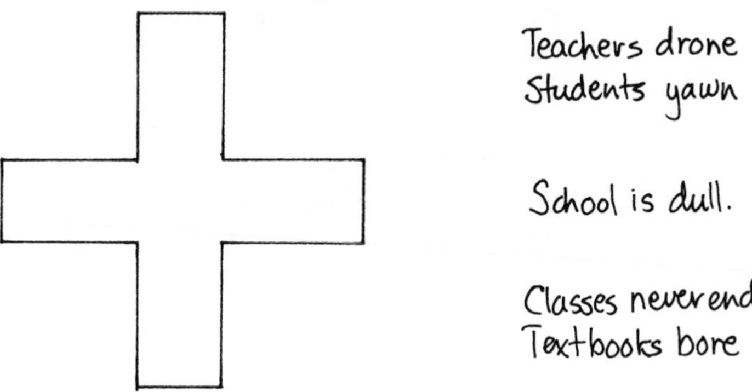
Teachers drone
Students yawn
School is dull.
Classes never end
Textbooks bore

④ STATE TOPIC, DOCUMENT IT AND LEAD TO CONCLUSION

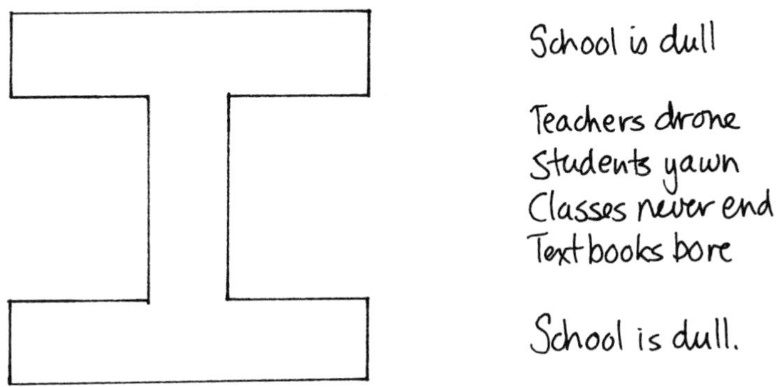
School is dull
Teachers drone
Students yawn
Classes never end
Textbooks bore
School is dull.

The student writer should be taught to work on leads, those first few lines which are so important to the journalist. The magazine writer often spends approximately eighty-five per cent of his time in writing an article sharpening, shaping, and developing his lead. It is the lead which establishes his tone and his hold over his subject. Once the writer has written his lead he has control over his subject. The lead gives a similar control to the reader. The lead tells him if he wants to read the piece. The lead both informs and entices him.

The technical skill of writing leads is indeed important. There are a few writers who will write the middle of a piece first, but most writers find they have to have the beginning right before they can write on. The man who has completed his lead has stepped off the high diving board, and once both feet have left the diving board it is very hard to step back. Students of writing should be brought to delight in leads. The writer appreciates what Orwell has done again and again when he picks up *A Collection of Essays by George Orwell*.[5] Here are some of the leads from his most famous essays:

> Soon after I arrived at Crossgates (not immediately, but after a week or two, just when I seemed to be settling into the routine of school life) I began wetting my bed.
>
> In Moulmein, in lower Burma, I was hated by large numbers of people —the only time in my life that I've been important enough for this to happen to me.
>
> Saints should always be judged guilty until they are proved innocent . . .
>
> As the corpse went past the flies left the restaurant table in a cloud and rushed after it, but they came back a few minutes later.
>
> First of all the physical memories, the sounds, the smells and the surfaces of things.
>
> As I write, highly civilized human beings are flying overhead, trying to kill me.

The writer will collect his own leads, and the student should be sent on a lead-hunting expedition so that he will see their importance. In fact, for a while the student should write only the lead, and then outline his essay. He should also write different leads for different audiences. Instead of writing five essays, he might write a lead a day for the same essay for five days. In practicing lead writing he will begin to see how the beginning of a piece of writing shapes the entire piece of writing, and how the writer has made a conscious, calculated choice when he writes.

Here are some more leads to demonstrate to the student the way in which the writer practices his craft.

> The biggest shadow in the world—235,000 miles high, 105 miles wide, and 75 miles thick in its densest part—fell across San Diego today, the shadow of the moon as it crossed the face of the sun. (Magner While, "Eclipse of the Sun," *San Diego Sun,* September 10, 1923—a story which won the Pulitzer Prize.)
>
> The problem of aerial navigation without the use of a balloon has been solved at last. (*Norfolk Virginian Pilot,* December 18, 1903.)
>
> Calvin Coolidge believed that the least government was the best government; he aspired to become the least president the country ever had; he attained his desire. (Irving Stone, *They Also Ran.*)
>
> The old man puffed into sight like a venerable battlewagon steaming up over the horizon. First a smudge of smoke, then the long cigar, then the

[5] *A Collection of Essays by George Orwell* (New York: Doubleday & Company, Inc., 1954).

familiar, stooped-shoulder hulk that a generation had come to know as the silhouette of greatness. Prime Minister Winston Churchill scowled as he emerged from the Queen Mary . . . (*Time,* January 13, 1952.)

At Brooks Brothers, Manhattan clothiers to men, there are things that one seldom hears mentioned. One of them is vests; Brooks Brothers calls them waistcoats. Another is ties; they're scarves. Still another is profits; they're vulgar. (*Time,* April 1, 1946.)

Snow, followed by small boys on sleds. (Routine weather forecast in the *New York World Telegram* by H. Allen Smith)

In recent months there has been much comment about the decision to use atomic bombs in attacks on the Japanese cities of Hiroshima and Nagasaki. This decision was one of the gravest made by our government in recent years, and it is entirely proper that it should be widely discussed. I have therefore decided to record for all who may be interested my understanding of the events which led up to the attack on Hiroshima on August 6, 1945, on Nagasaki on August 9, and the Japanese decision to surrender on August 10. No single individual can hope to know exactly what took place in the minds of all of those who had a share in these events, but what follows is an exact description of our thoughts and actions as I find them in the records and in my clear recollection. (Henry L. Stimson, *Harper's Magazine,* February 1947.)

In the beginning God created Heaven and earth. (Genesis 1:1)

At the height of Harlem's nighttime fury a white police officer stood in the litter of glass and garbage that had come crashing down from the darkened rooftops and raised a bullhorn to his mouth. "Go home," he pleaded with the glowering Negro mobs that clustered along Seventh Avenue and atop the shabby tenements. "Go home," "Go home." From a man in the mob came a shout: "We are home, Baby." (*Time,* July 31, 1964.)

And first, of ye occasion and inducements thereunto, the which, that I may truly unfould, I must begine at ye very roote & rise of ye same.

The which I shall endeavor to manefest in a plaine stile, with singuler regard unto yet simple trueth in all things, at least as near as my slender judgments can attaine the same." (Governor William Bradford, *Of Plimoth Plantation.*)

There is something to be said for a bad education.

By any standards mine was deplorable; and I deplored it for years, in private and in public. I flaunted it as if it were a medal, a kind of cultural Purple Heart which both excused my deficiencies and lent luster to my mild achievements. But as time goes on I murmur against it less. I find that even ignorance has its brighter side. (Phyllis McGinley, "The Consolations of Illiteracy," *The Province of the Heart.*)

When I wrote the following pages, or rather the bulk of them, I lived alone, in the woods, a mile from any neighbor, in a house which I had built myself, on the shore of Walden Pond, in Concord, Massachusetts, and earned my living by the labor of my hands only. (Henry David Thoreau, *Walden.*)

In the morning mail of January 8, 1962, the Supreme Court of the United States received a large envelope from Clarence Earl Gideon, prisoner No. 003826, Florida State Prison, PO Box 221, Raiford, Florida. Like all correspondence addressed to the Court generally rather than to any particular justice or Court employee, it went to a room at the top of the great marble steps so familiar to Washington tourists. There a secretary opened the envelope. As the return address had indicated, it was another petition by a prisoner without funds asking the Supreme Court to get him out of jail —another, in the secretary's eyes, because pleas from prisoners were so familiar a part of her work. She walked into the next room and put the envelope on the desk of an assistant clerk of the Supreme Court, Michael Rodak, Jr. (Anthony Lewis, *Gideon's Trumpet.*)

"Isn't disloyalty as much the writer's virtue," asks Graham Greene, "as loyalty is the soldier's?" (Elizabeth Bowen, "Disloyalties," *Seven Winters and Afterthoughts.*)

The New York Giants, who overwhelmed two opponents at football last year, underwhelmed ten and whelmed two . . . (Red Smith, *New York Herald Tribune.*)

Dam Doi, Viet Nam—This jungle town went through a blood bath Tuesday and the generals called it a victory. Perhaps it was. But it was not the kind of victory this shattered town can endure very often. (Malcolm W. Browne, Associated Press.)

I often feel drawn to the Hudson River, and I have spent a lot of time through the years poking around the part of it that flows past the city. I never get tired of looking at it; it hypnotizes me. I like to look at it in midsummer, when it is warm and dirty and drowsy, and I like to look at it when it is stirred up, when a northeast wind is blowing and a strong tide is running—a new-moon tide or a full-moon tide—and I like to look at it when it is slack. It is exciting to me on weekdays, when it is crowded with ocean craft, harbor craft, and river craft, but it is the river itself that draws me, and not the shipping, and I guess I like it best on Sundays, when there are lulls that sometimes last as long as half an hour, during which, all the way from the Battery to the George Washington Bridge, nothing moves upon it, not even a ferry, not even a tug, and it becomes as hushed and dark and secret and remote and unreal as a river in a dream. (Joseph Mitchell, "The River Men," *The New Yorker,* April 4, 1959.)

For more than half an hour thirty-eight respectable, law-abiding citizens in Queens watched a killer stalk and stab a woman in three separate attacks in Kew Gardens.

Twice the sound of their voices and the sudden glow of their bedroom lights interrupted him and frightened him off. Each time he returned, sought her out, and stabbed her again. Not one person telephoned the police during the assault; one witness called after the woman was dead. (Martin Gansberg, *The New York Times,* March 27, 1964.)

I suppose that the first thing that a District Judge tries to learn but never succeeds in learning is not to talk too much from the bench. The reason that most of us chatter so much is not because we suppose ourselves to be more competent than counsel, we fear that we shall go to sleep on the bench. (Judge Charles E. Wyzanski, Jr., *The New Meaning of Justice.*)

From legal poppy fields in Turkey, by camel across the sands of Syria, to the not-so-legal laboratories in Lebanon, then by ship to southern France for final refining, back to Italy and, courtesy of the Mafia, to New York's docks and airports—heroin comes to Harlem. (James Mills, "The World of Needle Park," *Life,* February 26, 1965.)

Walpurga Hausmannin, evil and wretched woman, now imprisoned and in chains, has, under solicitous questioning as well as torture, confessed her witchcraft and made the following admission. (Quoted from a newsletter of 1587 by Louis L. Snyder and Richard B. Morris, in *A Treasury of Great Reporting.*)

On any person who desires such queer prizes, New York will bestow the gift of loneliness and the gift of privacy. It is this largess that accounts for the presence within the city's walls of a considerable section of the population; for the residents of Manhattan are to a large extent strangers who have pulled up stakes somewhere and come to town, seeking sanctuary or fulfillment or some greater or lesser grail. The capacity to make such dubious gifts is a mysterious quality of New York. It can destroy an individual, or it can fulfill him, depending a good deal on luck. No one should come to New York to live unless he is willing to be lucky. (E. B. White, "Here is New York," *Holiday,* April 1949.)

I began my history at the very outbreak of the war, in the belief that it was going to be a great war and more worth writing about than any of those which had taken place in the past. (Thucydides, *The Peloponnesian War.*)

The writer is fascinated by the way things begin, partly because he has such a strong sense of design. The student should study the opening chapter of *Great Expectations* or *Bleak House* by Dickens, Hardy's *Return of the Native* and the foreshadowing description of Egdon Heath, the first chapter of *A Farewell to Arms* which Hemingway is supposed to have rewritten several hundred times, the beginning of Graham Greene's novels, any of them, Forster's *A Passage to India,* Marquand's *A Point of No Return,* in which he tells so much in one opening page, the beginning of Flaubert's masterpiece, *Madame Bovary,* Tolstoy's opening sentence in *Anna Karenina* —"Happy families are all alike; every unhappy family is unhappy in its own way." The student writer who has studied leads may come to write, as Miss Wendy Hagstrom of Conard High School in Hartford, Connecticut wrote, "There are no skinny babies," as a lead to a fine essay.

The teacher of writing must spend a great deal of time on design. It is a good idea to go back to the old device of précis writing to show a student how he can compress a piece of writing to a paragraph and get at its essence. He should play *Reader's Digest* editor; the teacher may take a *Digest* article and the original so that the class can cut the original and then compare their versions with what the *Digest* editors have done. When you cut an article to a quarter or a fifth of its original size, you have to discover and analyze its structure.

The teacher may take a statement, such as the one by Barbara Tuchman in the February 25, 1967, *Saturday Review:* "The integrating idea or insight then evolves from the internal logic of the material, in the course of putting it together. From the gathering of the particulars one arrives at the general, at that shining grail we are all in search of, the historical generalization," and then have students write variations on it:

The writer should have a game plan, but the quarterback is always prepared to call an automatic when he goes up to the line or to change tactics in the huddle. His purpose is to win, and what he's looking for is a winning strategy.

The writer, the scientist, the teacher all seek the same thing--the skeleton which will hold a series of observations together.

The interrelating perceptualization is evolved from the internal structure or the conceptualization of the content. From the collectivization of the data one can structure a program, creating a model or idealized thesis which one can plug into while involved in the learning situation.

The writer is an explorer, he has a dream and travels towards it, mapping his course until he has charted a new country.

There is a misconception encouraged by teachers who do not understand scholarship that the student should take an empty wineskin of an idea, such as "revolution must be preceded by expectation" and pour it fat with facts, statistics, quotations, the entire academic apparatus. The student should be encouraged first to discover the solid facts of his subject; only when he has mined many hard nuggets of truth should he be allowed to build a generalization.

The historical insight is not inspired by ignorance. It develops slowly, the way a picture is discovered in a dark-room, first vague shadows, then an outline, and at last the final definition.

Specific details are the writer's raw materials. He works slowly with them, seeking their natural pattern. His ideas are hand-crafted, and you can see on his manuscript pages the way he has fitted and shaped his specifics. When he is a good craftsman he learns he cannot force them. He must discover the inherent shape of his subject, the natural structure of his materials.

The writer is an executive who makes thousands of executive decisions in each piece he writes. He chooses what to say and how to say it in a series of important and vital decisions. One way to make the student see these decisions is to have him write a brief essay in a column down the left-hand side of the paper, and then on the right-hand side have the student tell, paragraph by paragraph, what he was doing in his own essay and why he did it. Another variation, taught me by a student, Miss Robin Snodgrass, is to have a student tear her own essay apart, perform a sentence by sentence criticism, and then rewrite it.

The student should be asked to examine the following two paragraphs and decide which one is the more effective, which one is well-built.

Mr. Braxton was the first person I hated. He leaned against the blackboard and, smiling, answered questions with questions. He was a doubter and a disbeliever and he delighted in contradictions. He laughed at the important things and was serious about details--the number of feet above sea level and the capital of South Dakota. The prime disturber of my life, I cursed Mr. Braxton and went to bed plotting his destruction only to wake up early so I could look up more facts in the encyclopedia before class. I hated Mr. Braxton and feared him and finally escaped him only to find myself, years later, in front of a class, leaning against a blackboard smiling, answering questions with questions.

The good teacher doesn't answer questions, he asks them. He is a student who keeps studying his subject, looking for the structures which hold it together. He doesn't so much teach a subject as a way of looking into things. When he passes you on to the next grade he hopes you will have an appreciation of the importance of a fact and perhaps the ability to ask a few hard, tough questions. Perhaps even some day, the good teacher thinks, you will be able to stand in front of another class, asking his questions. I hated him but I'm glad I had him now. He made me see that most subjects have a structure, an underlying organization, the skeleton he was always seeking.

And he should read student papers, such as the well-built paragraph written by a student at Sanford (Maine) High School on dribbling.

Position is the key to good dribbling. The knees should be bent, the body weight should be carried low, and the head should be up, with the eyes not watching the ball. The ball is kept in front of and slightly to the side of the body; the side depending on which arm is used to dribble. The ball is handled with the finger tips and not with the entire hand. A smooth downward motion of the fingers and wrist must push the ball down with enough force to bring it back up. For good control the ball should be met by the fingers before it has reached the maximum point of its bounce. The ball should never be batted or slapped. Developing a "feel" for the ball makes dribbling come easy. To help develop this "feel" beginners usually bounce the ball while kneeling with their eyes closed. This short dribble is easy to control. After developing this "feel" and learning the correct position, dribbling should be known, but nothing beats good hard practice.

The writing student must understand he does not just sit down and write, that before he writes he attempts to solve as many problems as possible off the page. He is a general who cannot predict what will happen in a battle, but still he tries to develop his strategy, his knowledge of the enemy, and his tactics before the opening gun is fired. Here are the steps a writer might go through before he writes.

You Should Know What You Want To Write

How Do You Find Something to Say?	How do you find something to say on education?
Be aware—use all your senses, read, listen, be receptive to new ideas.	Look at what goes on in class, listen to what teachers and students say. Read Conant, Bruner.

Be honest—see with your own eyes, hear with your own ears, evaluate with your own mind.

Don't look at education through your teacher's eyes, your classmates' ears, your parents' opinions. What really goes on?

Be curious—seek answers to your questions, do research.

Ask your teacher what he's trying to do. Ask your classmates why they don't learn. Look up articles on teaching and learning.

Be informed—accumulate a body of knowledge.

Read newspapers. Listen to television and radio news. Read periodicals and books. Create an inventory of facts and ideas about education.

See relationships—have a sense of historic trends and future implications.

Why do we think everyone should have a grammar school, a high school, a college education? What does this mean today, next year, in 1980; to your children, grandchildren?

Be concerned.

If you don't care about education you won't be able to write about it.

Be skeptical—doubt, question, evaluate, be critical.

Am I learning anything? Am I learning the wrong thing? Does the pattern of my education make any sense?

Develop a sense of irony—perspective, humor.

Why does my teacher think it is virtuous for me to do what is difficult when he does what is easy for him—teaches English? Why does he preach questioning and "zap" me when I question him?

What Is a Subject?

Limit the subject—focus on something you can see, deal with something you can control.

Education depends on the teacher. A good teacher is important. What is a good teacher? Howard Smuggs is the best teacher I've ever had.

Have something to say—what information do you have, what opinion do you have?

Why is Smuggs a teacher teacher?

Be able to document your case—can you complete the research?	What evidence do you have he's a good teacher—quotations from other teachers, testimony from students, achievements of alumni?
Reach a conclusion.	Smuggs is a good teacher because he. . . . There might be more education in our schools if more were like Smuggs.

How Do You Test Your Subject?

Play the devil's advocate—examine your subject critically, present it to a critical audience.	Is Smuggs really such a great teacher? Does he just have good students? What do the students he flunked think of him?
How must you qualify your subject?	Smuggs is too impatient to teach in junior high school. He makes too many puns. He is prejudiced about modern poetry.
Does your subject make sense—are you logical?	So Smuggs' classes are fun, does that make him a good teacher?
Are you being honest?	Do you really think Smuggs is a good teacher? Do you really think others should follow his example?

How Do You Fill Out Your Subject?

Go to written sources.	How do Barzun, Highet, Bruner, and others define a good teacher? What written evaluation standards does your school system have?
Go to live sources.	Sit in on Smuggs' classes. Interview Smuggs, his colleagues, his students, his graduates, his supervisors.

What Do You Do When the Subject Changes?

Accept change as a condition of writing—writing is a process of discovery.	Smuggs is relaxed in class because he's unrelaxed outside of class—spends hours preparing, has doubts about his ability to teach.

Recognize that invention comes after orderly investigation—the conscious primes the unconscious.

I'll bet it's lonely to be a teacher—maybe I'll write a short story about that.

You Should Know Whom You Want To Reach

Will this article be read by teachers? I'd like other teachers to learn from Smuggs.

What Questions in the Reader's Mind Must I Answer?

I have 159 students in English, two study halls a day, and I have to coach the field hockey team? What's Smuggs' load?

Speak in Terms Your Reader Will Understand

Don't pander, don't change your subject, but present your subject in terms the reader will understand.

For the student—"The notes I take in Smuggs' class make sense. They help me write papers in college." For the teacher—Smuggs spends a great deal of time seeking the structure, or the internal order of the subject matter, and he tries to present it so the student will see it.

Be Your Own Audience

Be critical—would you read this article, would you believe it?

If I were a teacher I'd be bored by the end of the first page. How can I interest the reader, establish authority, document my case?

You Should Know How You Want To Say It

What Form is Appropriate?

I'll try to write this for the state teachers' magazine.

What is the *natural* order?

I'll show Smuggs being a good teacher, then I'll document the fact he is a good teacher, show why he's a good teacher, conclude that others could be good teachers if they were like Smuggs.

What are my space limitations?

1500 words.

What is my tone?

I want to persuade other teachers. I must be objective—give my readers evidence, show them Smuggs in action, lead them to their own conclusions.

The writer does not write until he has a feeling of subject, audience and form. He needs to know his destination, the route and the vehicle he will use, the fuel he will need, the obstacles he will encounter, the time it will take him to get there.

The writer knows his subject and his form will evolve as he writes. He will rediscover what he has to say. He will limit and refine his topic. He will reveal holes in his own argument which will require reorganization (re-limiting) or research. He will not begin to write, however, until he has an idea he wants to express, a potential audience, a possible form. He must have a conscious or subconscious sense of structure, a written or mental outline, a unifying idea or thesis he will attempt to support or explore in writing before he writes.

19 The Student Writes

The most inexperienced student writer shares with the most experienced writer the terror of the blank page. You may lecture the student and tell him he ought to write, but the fact is that most students know or soon discover it is hard work to write. We cannot make it easy for the student to write, for there is nothing easy about the kind of revelation which happens when you put yourself on the page. The writer exposes what he is to the reader, and that is the problem.

The drama critic Walter Kerr has written, "Creative writing is a harrowing business, a terrifying commitment to an absolute. This is *it,* the writer must say to himself, and I must stand or fall upon what I have put down. The degree of self-exposure is crucifying. And doubt is a constant companion. What if I am not as good as I thought? is a question that always nags, and can cripple. Where, for whatever combination of reasons, there is a beginning of failure of faith, a flagging of self-assertion, the writer quite naturally looks for a possible way out. . . ."[6]

It is not only the creative writer, the dramatist or the poet, who feels this way. The man who publishes a scientific theory exposes himself to his colleagues, the person who writes a memorandum to his boss proposing changes in factory procedures reveals himself, the person who writes a love letter exposes himself to an answering affection—or to ridicule.

"Get black on white," said de Maupassant. Good advice, but not so easy to follow; for once the black is on white, the vision which is in the head is exposed to the eye. This feeling of apprehension about the blank page and how it can be solved may best be shown by the experience of one great writer, Winston S. Churchill, who took up painting in middle life*:

"Having bought the colors, and easel, and a canvas, the next step was *to begin.* But what a step to take! The pallet gleamed with beads of colour; fair and white rose the canvas; the empty brush hung poised, heavy with destiny, irresolute in the air. My hand seemed arrested by a silent veto. But after all the sky on this occasion was unquestionably blue, and a pale blue

[6] "How Playwrights Lose," *Harper's Magazine,* September 1966.

* Reprinted from *Amid These Storms* (1932) by permission of Charles Scribner's Sons, and by permission of Odhams Press Limited, publishers of the British edition (*Thoughts and Adventures*) and proprietors of the copyright.

at that. There could be no doubt that the blue paint mixed with white should be put on the top part of the canvas. One really does not need to have an artist's training to see that. It is a starting point open to all. So very gingerly I mixed a little blue paint on the pallette with a very small brush, and then with infinite precaution made a mark about as big as a bean upon the affronted snow-white shield. It was a challenge, a deliberate challenge; but so subdued, so halting, indeed so cataleptic, that it deserved no response. At that moment the loud approaching sound of a motor-car was heard in the garage. From this chariot there stepped swiftly and lightly none other than the gifted wife of Sir John Lavery. 'Painting! But what are you hesitating about? Let me have a brush—the big one.' Splash into the turpentine, wallop into the blue and the white, frantic flourish on the pallette—clean no longer—and then several large, fierce strokes and slashes of blue on the absolutely cowering canvas. Anyone could see that it could not hit back. No evil fate avenged the jaunty violence. The canvas grinned in helplessness before me. The spell was broken. The sickly inhibitions rolled away. I seized the largest brush and fell upon my victim with berserk fury. I have never felt awe of any canvas since.

"Everyone knows the feeling with which one stands shivering on a springboard, the shock when a friendly foe sneaks up behind and hurls you into the flood, and the ardent glow which thrills you as you emerge breathless from the plunge."

Every writer feels the same terror of the blank page. That is one reason writers get what they call writer's cramp, and it is why so many people who are supposed to publish don't. It is a terrible commitment to reveal yourself on the page, to reveal how much or how little you know, to reveal your inadequacies as a writer. You just have to plunge in. It never gets any easier. The writer has to suspend his critical judgment to accomplish a first draft and the student writer, as well, has to suspend his critical judgment, even if it is only the opinion "that there English ain't for me." His inadequacy will make learning impossible unless he is encouraged to write a first draft without subjecting it to the red pencil. That will come later.

The journalist, J. D. Ratcliff says, "When I finish a first draft, it's so bad it wouldn't get 'D' in a high school English course. Then I rewrite, usually about six times. It's a tedious process, but I finally get the words that say what I want."

Each publishing writer has his formula for getting to work, and his ways of avoiding work. He knows it is important not to write too soon, that he cannot write until he knows that he has something to say, but he also knows that he must bring himself to his writing desk. Usually he establishes a ritual of work, a place and a time. We should do the same thing for the student by forcing him to write frequently, at a regular time and place. The student usually finds that a short paper required every day is easier than longer papers which must be passed in at greater intervals of time. Everyone puts writing off until the last minute. The professional does this, and there is no reason the amateur should not. But if the student is to learn to write we must force him to commit himself to the page. He must get in the habit of writing.

We should allow the student the first draft. He should try to make it as good as he can, but that may not be very good. He may still be discovering his subject. We should not criticize his spelling or grammar in the first draft. We may even allow him to scribble the first draft; the paper does not need to be neat the first time around. The important thing is that he pushes on, that he writes regularly on almost a daily basis, knowing that some of his papers won't be corrected. The student will be willing to write papers that are not corrected if the reasons are explained to him. He should be told that the professional writer writes many drafts, that rewriting is not punishment but merely the process of writing. There comes a time when the subject is right and it must be committed to the page. There is nothing final about the draft. It is merely a way of discovering the subject, of finally getting it down on paper, of turning it from a sketch into a draft of a finished form. In the draft he may indicate things that he has to look up; there may be holes that he knows will have to be filled, but he should attempt to push on to a completed piece of work.

There should be only one requirement, that the deadline is met. Late papers do not exist. They must be in on time, with monotonous regularity, so that the writer develops a habit of production. There is always an excuse not to write, but those excuses must rarely be accepted. The student should be allowed to write in his own way, at home or at school, with pen or typewriter, on subjects of his choice, and in lengths and forms which are appropriate to his subject. Some students will produce a first draft which is final. That is good. If this rare paper is as good as it can be the first time around, then that should be accepted. But most students committing themselves to writing will find that the first draft is not adequate, that the first draft is the beginning, not the end, of writing. And as terrifying as it is to write, it is a relief to find that a draft is done and the writer can begin to write.

The student should understand that he learns to write by writing. I have posted on the wall of my classroom the Chinese proverb I found on the wall of the Children's Museum in Boston:

> I hear . . . and I forget.
> I see . . . and I remember.
> I do . . . and I understand.

20 The Student Develops a Critical Eye

The student lives in a plastic, mass-produced world. The writing course can give him a chance, perhaps his only chance, to be a craftsman. When he writes he has the opportunity to take his time to do the job right. If we are to give him this craftsman's chance, then he must be allowed to write drafts and subject them to his own scrutiny.

How can you teach a class to do this? You can't. You can show a class that writers have always taken the time to reconsider what they have written, to change and develop it, but you cannot teach a class to go through this process. You can, however, teach individuals to do this. When a student has something he wants to say and he has tried to say it and he hasn't quite succeeded, then you can give him the opportunity to do the job right. In class and in conference a student should be urged to ask himself four crucial questions:

What have I said?

Does what I have said make sense?

What additional information do I need to know?

Does my form fit my new content?

The writer must go back to the original question of subject and see if he has the subject that he thought he had. Then he must make sure he is speaking appropriately for the audience he expects to reach, then regather the raw materials he needs, filling in the holes that have become apparent from the first draft, and finally he has to redesign the piece of writing.

The student may decide that his piece of writing is entirely different. His draft may have posed the argument that Hemingway was a great writer, but when he rereads his draft and reads some more Hemingway, he may decide that he no longer admires Hemingway's style, or his subject matter, or his philosophy of life, and the student may recast his paper. He may start writing a profile of his father and end up writing a profile of his mother. He may switch his point of view towards the American Revolution or his conclusions about the physics experiment in inertia. At all times he should be encouraged to work back and forth through the seven skills, finding his way to his own subject.

The student writer should realize he already owns an extensive rhetorical toolbox. When he looks at the beginning of his piece of writing he should know why it has a beginning—to give it form, to give him control over it, and to give the reader a chance to recognize his subject. Once the writer knows why he is beginning his piece of writing, he can reach for the appropriate tool. It is a helpful device to have the student list on the board and in his notebook the many tools that he already possesses.

It should be clear to him that some tools are very common—the usual hammer or screwdriver—while others are more obscure—a rare chisel, or a special buffer or a shaper. But they are all in his toolbox ready to be used.

What tools does he have in his rhetoric box with which he can shape a beginning of an essay? You should encourage him to list them on the board. He starts it with an anecdote, a quotation, a statement, a question, a description of a place or a person, a definition of a problem. You should be able to lead the class by listing perhaps fifty or sixty ways of starting an essay, and the same procedure should be gone through for the development of the essay, and the conclusion. The average secondary school writer has at his command more than a hundred rhetorical tools which he is capable of using. They should be identified and shown to him.

If he still does not understand how to make a choice, then exercises should be developed which will show him this. He may go through an anthology or a number of magazines, picking out the various ways somebody has started, developed, or ended articles. He may be asked to write twelve five-line definitions of a good teacher, a stimulating exercise which may reveal more than you wanted to know about your own teaching. The student should never feel he *has* to rewrite, but he should rarely feel a sense of satisfaction with the first draft.

As he works on with his piece of writing he should discover the inspiration of the writing desk. It is possible that inspiration will come to him when he is walking in the woods or sitting in a drive-in theater, but the writer knows that the best inspiration comes when he is putting pen to paper, that the happiest spontaneity comes while he is working, trying to say it as well as he possibly can.

And the student should see the work of the other members of the class develop. He should have a chance to follow, edit, criticize and encourage classmates' articles. If the class is rewriting, not in harness but each one at his own pace, it will begin to see that pieces of writing improve with rewriting, that the best things are not lost but are developed and shaped in the process of rewriting. Every student should be familiar with the case histories of paragraphs such as the following one. The paper was written for a vague, general assignment—"Just write a paragraph"—by an average student at the beginning of the tenth grade.

<u>I Think Sports Car Racing Is A "Drag"</u>

My parents are members of the Cape Cod Sports Car Club. Ever since they joined we have had nothing but foreign cars, and at present they own a Volvo station wagon and a B.M.W. 1800 T.I. The station wagon belongs to my mother, but she races the B.M.W. in gymkhanas set up by different sports car clubs in different counties and states. Usually my parents do very well in their class and sometimes in the Club. I myself find these races very exciting and fortunately there are very few accidents and all of which are very minor. I have the feeling that in not to long a time I to will become a member of the club.

Most teachers will groan with recognition. It's an above-average paper, full of problems—"a Shakespeare he ain't." The paragraph, however, has specifics: the names of the cars, some actual details of what they do. There is some development, there is a relationship between the first sentence and the last, and the pun in the title at least shows he is aware of words and has some willingness to play with them, an ingredient of an above-average writing student.

It would be easy, however, to fall all over the writer. The paragraph is rich with technical errors—awkward constructions and very badly misspelled words. He does not use the language with accuracy; he is not correct in his usage; his style is graceless. If the teacher wants to convince this boy that he is not a writer and has little potential for writing, the paper could be covered with red.

If the teacher wants to teach writing, he should make the student realize the theme is not yet ready for careful correction or polishing. There is absolutely nothing that polishing or editing will do to make this an interesting paragraph. It says very little. Indirectly, at least, it indicates something about the economic background of the child's parents, but so what? There is nothing in the paragraph to distinguish it. It hasn't been anywhere and it isn't going anywhere. It is not the result of any probing thought.

The student doesn't need to be told that this piece is a bland, plastic paragraph that doesn't say very much. He should be shown how to discover a real subject which will stand up to extensive rewriting and editing. There should be class discussion of subjects, an attempt to define the good subject which has specificity, movement, containment—which has something to say. There is something said by the article with a good subject, something worth-while communicated to its reader.

At this stage it may be a good idea for the teacher to have a conference with the student. This would be a quick conference, only a minute or two, and he would merely tell the student his paragraph has possibilities, but that it doesn't really dig into the subject. The teacher might suggest that the student write a little bit more about how a race is organized or focus on one race. He might point out to the student that there is something to talk about in the accidents, and that why he feels he wants to do this is a possible subject. What is the excitement? What is it like to see his mother out racing an automobile? The teacher might indicate by these questions that there are a number of possibilities for more lively pieces.

That's one way to go about it. A much more productive method is to make the student put this piece aside and to list many specifics—fragments in which he may discover the elements of a good theme. In the beginning those fragments will be rather generalized, but as he feels the need to put down many specific, concrete details, then he may come up with solid raw material. This method is exactly, of course, what the scholar uses when he researches a paper. What we are demanding from students are specific details, what the scholar also has to collect. When the student is made to follow the scholar's method, that is when he, instead of listing the details on a single piece of paper, uses a separate card for each quotation and for the biographical facts of, let us say, Hemingway's life, for some critical opinions of what he has done, some reactions to stories, a précis of each important work, the student can be led away from the subjective approach to the most objective research program.

The professional writer spends a very small percentage of his working time in writing. He spends a great deal of his time researching, thinking, mining his specifics and perceiving the patterns in them. We must have the student write frequently, but we must count the list of specifics as a piece of writing, the first draft as a piece of writing, the outline as a piece of writing; each is part of the process that will eventually give us a draft which can be polished.

Can you guess the age and the grade of the following student writer? Her teacher, Miss Hava Kane, had been working on specifics by having her students list their specifics on the right-hand side of the page and then write a short piece from the list. The only instruction she gave the class was to write about something that had happened to them that morning—an incident, an adventure, an experience—and she reminded them to be specific. While the students were writing, Miss Kane moved about the room, working with each of the students individually. Here is one of the papers, a first draft as it was written in class.

In The Morning-at home	list
On Thurs day, Feb. 1, at my house there was a "buzz, buzz," and my mother came in and shut off the alarm clock. She went into the Kitchen to make breakfast while I got up and dressed. Then I went into eat and when I finished went to my room.	Wake up alarm clock get dressed called to breakfast hear scream baby brother
Suddenly I heard a scream, and a cry, and footsteps-my mother ran into get the screaming baby. The doorbell rang, time to go to school.	went in room hear doorbell get on coat boots and mittens go across street for ride To school

Miss Diane Siegel developed her specifics well, so that a short, concrete and well-formed piece of writing grew out of them. She entered into the process of writing as it is experienced by the professional writer. Diane Siegel is an unusual young lady, but she is not considered an exceptional student at the Bridlepath School in West Hartford, Connecticut. In case you didn't guess, Diane is seven years old and in the second grade.

Here is a list of specifics that the high school student who wrote the dull paragraph on page 74 was made to turn in.

1. Cape Cod Sports Car Club.
2. B.M.W.
3. Volvo station wagon.
4. A real "drag."
5. Alfa-Romeo.
6. A rally.
7. Four carburetors--four cylinders.
8. Fast curve.
9. Fifty-mile-an-hour curve.
10. Sports car slalom.
11. Race on the beach.
12. Stay home, heard accident on radio.
13. Dad brings a new car home.
14. Wheels leave road on turns.
15. Charlie's car tips over.
16. When I get a Honda.
17. Mother wins trophy.
18. Dad's first trophy.
19. "Three years and $9000 later."
20. Seagull broke windshield.
21. When I drive at Indy.
22. Radial tires.
23. Blow-out at 80 mph.
24. Trip to Connecticut rally.
25. No room for my knees in sports car.
26. Sports cars are safe.
27. I steered the car.
28. Cars blur going by.
29. Eating your dust is true.
30. Disk brakes are better than American.
31. What a tachometer tells you.
32. Maps.
33. Will Dad get his Porsche?
34. Will Mother be mad when he does?
35. Racing on frozen lake.
36. Racing at air base.
37. Seeing a jet take off.
38. When I manned check-point.
39. Working a stop watch.
40. The sound of a B.M.W.
41. The sound of a Rover.
42. Other kids in the club.
43. One year, 11 months, 3 weeks, 4 days, 26 hours, 53 minutes, 8 seconds until I can drive.
44. Spray of sand when cars skid.
45. Boring hours waiting.
46. The smell of exhaust.
47. Roll bar.
48. Hill climb.
49. Ending up in a ditch.
50. Dad's ears get red.
51. Jack races with bare feet.
52. I get thirsty watching races.
53. Dad likes to get scared.
54. Dad likes to scare me and Mother.
55. My coke and sandwich kit at race.
56. Dad comes back from rally at 4:07 a.m.
57. "Coasting" the curves.
58. A car worth $6000.
59. Dad's left arm is tanned.
60. Our first sports car--a VW.
61. Thirty-seven trophies in the study.
62. Third oldest sports car club in America.
63. Why I like sports cars.
64. How Dad walks when he loses.
65. How to get lost on a rally.
66. I rode in a skid.
67. We started going backwards.
68. The sound of cars revving up.
69. My stomach says I'm excited.
70. We get 8 sports car magazines a month.
71. I want to be a pilot.
72. I'm going to go to the Air Force Academy.
73. I'll fly a jet.
74. What's a sports car nut?
75. The nut behind the wheel.

76. How to shift down.
77. The antique cars I saw.
78. How to drive fast and safely.
79. Other kids' parents drink, mine race sports cars.
80. The smell of burning rubber.
81. The scrunch of brakes in a skid.

The list is rambling and repetitive. It lacks focus or direction, but it was hard work. For the first time this student had to look at the subject carefully—and examine his life. He kept walking away from his list and coming back, complaining it was an outrageous assignment. "List seventy-five specific concrete details about my subject indeed!" His details were neither specific nor concrete in many cases, but he was looking at the subject with a critical eye, trying to remember in his mind's eye what was important, what he knew about car racing, what his subconscious mind remembered, and what it meant. Students should write their own lists of specifics, seeing their own subjects with their own eyes.

If the student writing about sports cars had worked on this list in class, it would have been very helpful for the teacher during workshop class to walk by his desk, look at three or four specifics and say, "That's a good one," about the seagull that broke the windshield. The teacher might have pointed out that "trip to Connecticut rally" doesn't say very much. The student must see what the teacher means by a concrete detail.

Students, of course, are too often con men, taught well to find out what the teacher wants and then to give it to the teacher. The teacher must, in such lists as this, begin to encourage honesty, to have the student look into himself and into his subject with candor and vigor.

The list also gives the teacher a chance to defeat the cliché and the vague generalization by saying to the student, "What does that mean? Can't you be more specific?" The teacher should praise a student when he gets a good concrete detail which has the ring of reality. The student should not feel, at this stage, that he is being subjected to criticism. At first he must develop a rambling, questioning, seeking mind; at first he should run off at the head and put down the specifics from which he will build an article.

The sports car subject is one that may not interest most English teachers. That isn't the point. The point is that this is a subject that the student is interested in, it is something that he knows quite a bit about, he can make a list of details, and he can write from abundance. If it is an indication that he lives in a barren home, then the teacher should be even more willing to have him look into the subject. Maybe he will see the limitations of the subject. The teacher should be an ideal listener. The teacher, in fact, should be a student and encourage the student to teach him about sports cars. The student should want to tell this teacher in writing something that is important about sports cars.

The teacher can go over the list with the student in conference or by marking on the paper. In any case, he should emphasize these points: What do you think the best subject is for a paragraph? What do you think you should be writing about? What are the items on your list that are related?

It may be possible for the student to list or organize the different things that go together in the list. There may be natural topics in the list. Once the student has seen those four, or five, or six potential pieces, each collected with specific facts, then he can begin to rearrange those facts into a pattern. And perhaps as he goes along he will add other specifics that he will be reminded of by what he is writing. He will be discovering his subject and its dimensions.

The specifics are the student's raw material. In the future he may learn how to develop better raw material, but at the moment this is what he has. He should be made to study this list to look for patterns. It is perfectly all right if he wants to add more specifics, but he should be reminded of the definition of a subject, "a good subject is something the writer cares about, knows, and can communicate." If he has put his specifics on individual pieces of paper he may be able to group them. Otherwise he can copy them on little papers, or make lists. He should begin to see the force of specifics and be attracted to them himself. His first list is:

```
Wheels leave road on turns.
Seagull broke windshield.
One year, 11 months, 3 weeks, 4 days, 26 hours,
   53 minutes, 8 seconds until I can drive.
```

The student must be told that he can't fit in all the specifics he wants; he has to select. He may like that marvelous anecdote about the seagull's breaking the windshield, but unless it relates to the subject he chooses, it must be left out. This is the way he comes to understand something about unity. If it doesn't belong he must leave it out.

The student must find his subject by grouping his specifics. Once he does this he may discover his subject is something that doesn't even appear there. He may see, for example, that he really wants to write about the fear he feels when racing and the fact he knows he is a coward. Or he may want to write about the day that the family went to the air base and he got a ride in a jet instead of going to the race.

The student should write out several possibilities for paragraphs. He doesn't need, at this stage, to form his paragraphs. He just needs to put together in either a shorter list form or in a paragraph list the specifics which he has. He will, for example, probably want to write about sports cars. So, let him see what happens when he writes down those specifics that he has about sports cars.

```
Cape Cod Sports Car Club
B.M.W.
Volvo station wagon.
Alfa-Romeo.
Four carburetors--four cylinders.
Wheels leave road on turns.
Radial tires.
No room for my knees in a sports car.
Sports cars are safe.
Disk brakes are better then American.
What a tachometer tells you.
The sound of a B.M.W.
The sound of a Rover.
Roll bar.
A car worth $6000.
Our first sports car--a VW.
```

He should see that actually he's pretty vague, he's using proper nouns, yes, but he really doesn't have very much to say. He doesn't know a very great deal about cars, and what he does know is difficult to communicate. You may ask him what a tachometer is, what disk brakes are. He may see that he has to define these. You may make him write one definition, and in general you may make him see that he cares about the subject, but he doesn't really know enough, and he cannot really communicate it because there is so much that he will have to tell the reader that will not fit in a short paragraph. Another paragraph he may try is "When I Drive." He will list:

```
When I get a Honda.
When I drive at Indy.
I steered the car.
One year, 11 months, 3 weeks, 4 days, 26 hours,
   53 minutes, 8 seconds until I can drive.
I want to be a pilot.
I'm going to the Air Force Academy.
I'll fly a jet.
How to shift down.
How to drive fast and safely.
```

In this case he may see that—he hasn't driven yet—if he writes this he must write about what he wants in the future, and it's hard to tell what he has done in the future. A more vigorous subject he may choose is one about skids.

```
Fifty-mile-an-hour curve.
Wheels leave road on turns.
Spray of sand when cars skid.
Coasting the curves.
I rode in a skid.
The scrunch of brakes in a skid.
```

He must see that this subject has more vigor and promise, for he can take the reader along with him on a skid. What is it like to feel the car going out of control? He can't write about it from the point of view of the driver, because he has not been a driver, but he can write about it from the point of view of a passenger, if it is a fearful experience or if there is some point to it. He also may find as he groups his specifics that there are a large number of items about his father, and that he may have the makings of a biographical profile.

```
Dad brings a new car home.
Dad's first trophy.
"Three years and $9000 later."
Will Dad get his Porsche?
Will Mother be mad when he does?
Dad's ears get red.
Dad likes to get scared.
Dad likes to scare me and Mother.
Dad comes back from rally at 4:07 a.m.
Dad's left arm is tanned.
How Dad walks when he loses.
Other kids' parents drink, mine race sports cars.
```

The student should look at one of those paragraphs and decide which he wants to write about. Then he should examine it and see for himself what it needs. He should be led to see the virtue of the dominant impression and eventually be able to solve in the paragraph the problems of unity, coherence, emphasis (which is, in a sense, dominant impression). He should study the paragraph and see what it lacks and what it needs.

Will this process take time? Of course, it may take weeks. But the writer knows that it takes a very long time to research his subject and find his focused subject. The actual process of writing does not take place until his subject is ripe, until he has many specifics from which to choose. The school system too often makes the student write when he doesn't know anything about the subject, when he doesn't have anything to choose from, and when he doesn't care about the subject. No wonder the student can't write. Under those conditions even Shakespeare couldn't write.

Here is the student's first draft now that he has listed his specifics, grouped them, and thought about his subject.

My father's left arm is more tanned than the other. He spends all his spare time in his sports car, and when he won his first rally last week a friend said it cost him "three years and nine thousand dollars." The man across the street resents Dad's sports cars and thinks he wants to show off his money. I don't think he's right. Other kids' parents drink, mine race sports cars.

Again the paragraph could be covered with red. If it had to have a grade, the mark would be far short of what it might be after a rewrite or two. The teacher should show the student that he has good specifics, and that his reaction to the neighbor's criticism was quite perceptive. The teacher might suggest he rewrite the paragraph, telling the reader exactly why his father races sports cars.

My father's left arm is more tanned than his right, but that isn't the reason he races sports cars. He really loves the sound of a well-tuned engine, he needs to relax after a hard week's work and he does sell to some of the people he meets racing. But those aren't the reasons my father races sports cars. Once he took me along on a rally run and I saw the way he looked when the inside wheels left the road as he coasted a turn. I was scared, but he laughed. I still didn't understand why he raced sports cars until he let me stay up late one night to see an old movie about the war. I guess I really knew, but I asked him where he'd been in the war and he said in school and he sounded very sad, as if he'd lost something. I think I may know why Dad races sports cars.

The theme has a long way to go, but at last he has found his subject. The professional writer could roll up his sleeves and go to work. Now, at last, he has a beginning. The student has found something important to say. He should work on another draft—and perhaps another and another—which will develop the subject he has discovered, building an even more solid structure which has coherence, unity, and emphasis. He may, in several more versions, achieve the following paragraph.

My father is a normal American businessman. He's the first one up in the house and the first man to arrive at his office building. He always wears a fresh white shirt and he never wears a sport jacket to work. People buy insurance from my father because he is dependable and reliable. They know my Monday through Friday father. I know my father on weekends, when he gets up early but puts on a sports shirt, sunglasses, his rally cap, and races sports cars. Once I asked him why he races, but he just mumbled something about "appreciating a well-made car." I'm not sure he knows the reason he races, but I may have discovered it last Saturday night when the two of us sat up late to watch a war movie. I asked him if he'd been in school during the war. He nodded yes, and I said he was lucky. He looked surprised and then sad, as if he'd lost something, and he went to the kitchen to get another beer.

21 The Student Rewrites

"The difference between the right word and the wrong word is the difference between lightning and a lightning bug," Mark Twain growled. After the student has discovered what he has to say and the form in which he can say it, he engages on the final search for the right word. Now he can speak with precision. He will be allowed to make his piece of writing as good as he possibly can; to work it over, paragraph by paragraph, line by line, word by word.

To show the student how important a word is, you might hand out this excerpt from an article by Stewart Alsop in *The Saturday Evening Post* of May 21, 1966, which shows what a difference just one *letter* can make.*

". . . According to [McNamara's] current estimate, a full nuclear exchange in which the Soviets struck first, at the present level of U.S. defense,

*Reprinted from "Robert McNamara: His Business Is War," by permission of Stewart Alsop.

would kill between 130,000,000 and 135,000,000 Americans. 'Even these gruesome estimates,' he told this reporter, 'are almost certainly conservative.'

" 'They're based on AEC computations involving blast and radiation,' he explained. 'These factors are measurable in terms of experience in Hiroshima and Nagasaki and control tests, the tethered animals, and so on. But they do not include thermal effects—there is simply no way to measure thermal effects in advance—fire storms, for example. And they do not include fatalities resulting from chaos, disease, and so forth after an attack—again there is no way to measure these effects. So even given a considerable damage-limiting effort, it's extremely important to realize that a full nuclear exchange could destroy both sides.'

"To be sure it was accurate this reporter submitted the above paragraph to McNamara. The last sentence in the paragraph came back with one deeply significant correction. The word 'could' was changed to 'would.' . . ."

President Franklin Delano Roosevelt was a superb editor. When a World War II directive came across his desk, it read in part, "In those establishments where suspension of labor is possible, direct those parties of management to the termination of the illumination." He is reported to have crossed it out and written, "In buildings where work may be stopped, tell the managers to turn out the lights."

Students should be shown the care this writer-President took when he spoke to and for the United States. A great playwright—and an influential ghost writer—the late Robert E. Sherwood described in detail how Roosevelt wrote his speeches.*

". . . this was the process that Rosenman and I watched over and over again in the preparation of the speeches and messages in which Roosevelt made known his policies to the nation and to the world. The work that was put in on these speeches was prodigious, for Roosevelt with his acute sense of history knew that all of those words would constitute the bulk of the estate that he would leave to posterity and that his ultimate measurement would depend on the reconciliation of what he said with what he did. Therefore, utmost importance was attached to his public utterances and utmost care exercised in their preparation. . . . The important speeches sometimes required a week or more of hard labor, with a considerable amount of planning before the intensive work started. I don't know what was the record number of distinct drafts of a single speech but it must have been well over twelve, and in the final draft there might not be one sentence that had survived from the first draft.

"When he wanted to give a speech for some important purpose, whether it was connected with a special occasion or not, he would discuss it first at length with Hopkins, Rosenman and me, telling us what particular points he wanted to make, what sort of audience he wished primarily to reach and what the maximum word limit was to be (he generally put it far too low). He would dictate pages and pages, approaching his main topic, sometimes hitting it squarely on the nose with terrific impact, sometimes rambling so far away from it that he couldn't get back, in which case he would say,

* From pp. 212–217 (hardbound edition) *Roosevelt and Hopkins* by Robert E. Sherwood. Copyright 1948, 1950 by Robert E. Sherwood. Reprinted by permission of Harper & Row, Publishers, and by permission of Eyre & Spottiswoode Ltd.

'Well—something along those lines—you boys can fix it up.' I think he greatly enjoyed these sessions, when he felt free to say anything he pleased, uttering all kinds of personal insults, with the knowledge that none of it need appear in the final version. When he stopped dictating, because another appointment was due or it was time to go to bed, we would go to the Cabinet Room in the West Wing and start reading through all the assembled material. The President kept a special 'Speech Folder' into which he put newspaper clippings that he had marked, indicating either his approval of some sentiment expressed or indignation that such falsehood should get into print (he could not always remember what the marking signified). There were also all sorts of letters from all sorts of people, known and unknown, containing suggestions as to what he should say, and there were random bits of his own dictation, thoughts that had suddenly occurred to him during preceding days and weeks which might be useful sometime. All of this material was sifted, and added to the newly dictated material with the aid of scissors and paste and a few connecting clauses, until something resembling a coherent speech was put together and fair copies of it made. It was generally two or three times too long. When the President was free to see us again, we handed him this draft and he looked immediately at the last page to see its number, whereupon he announced that at least ninety-two per cent of it must be cut. He then started to read through it, pausing frequently to dictate 'Insert A,' 'Insert G,' etc. . . .

"When he had finished dictating inserts, the speech was far longer than it had been and farther from any coherent form. We then returned to the Cabinet Room and started a second draft. This process went on day and night. . . .

"On the final two days of preparation of a speech Roosevelt would really buckle down to serious work and then what had seemed a formless, aimless mess of words would begin to assume tautness and sharpness. He studied every implication for its effect on various groups in the nation and on allies and enemies and neutrals. He paid a great deal of attention to the punctuation, not for its correctness but for its aid or hindrance to him in reading the speech aloud. Grace Tully liked to insert a great many commas, and the President loved to strike them out. He once said to her, 'Grace! How many times do I have to tell you not to waste the taxpayers' commas?' He liked dashes, which were visual aids, and hated semicolons and parentheses. I don't think he ever used the sonorous phrase, 'And I quote—.' If he had to have quotation marks, he did not refer to them, knowing they would appear in the printed version.

"In the final draft of a speech, every word was counted and Roosevelt finally decided the precise number that he would be able to crowd into thirty minutes. His sense of timing was phenomenal. His normal rate was 100 words a minute, but he would say, 'There are some paragraphs in this speech that I can take quickly so I can handle a total of 3,150 words'—and that did not mean 3,162. At other times, he would feel that he had to be deliberate in his delivery and the words would have to be cut to 2,800. This cutting was the most difficult work of all because, by the time we had come to the ninth or tenth draft, we felt sure the speech had been boiled down to the ultimate monosyllable. Roosevelt's estimates were rarely off more than a split second on his broadcasts. . . ."

Every teacher of writing should examine the actual evidence of how President Roosevelt's editorial hand improved one of the most famous speeches in history.

DRAFT No. 1 December 7, 1941.

PROPOSED MESSAGE TO THE CONGRESS

Yesterday, December 7, 1941, a date which will live in ~~world history,~~ the United States of America was ~~simultaneously~~ and deliberately attacked by naval and air forces of the Empire of Japan, ~~without warning~~.

The United States was at the moment at peace with that nation and was ~~continuing the~~ conversations with its Government and its Emperor looking toward the maintenance of peace in the Pacific. Indeed, one hour after Japanese air squadrons had commenced bombing in ~~Hawaii and the Philippines,~~ the Japanese Ambassador to the United States and his colleague delivered to the Secretary of State a formal reply to a ~~former~~ message, ~~from the Secretary.~~ This reply ~~contained a statement~~ that diplomatic negotiations ~~must be considered at an end, but~~ contained no threat ~~and no~~ hint of ~~an~~ armed attack.

It will be recorded that the distance ~~of Manila, and especially~~ of Hawaii, from Japan make it obvious that the attack ~~were~~ deliberately planned many days ago. During the intervening time the Japanese Government has deliberately sought to deceive the United States by false statements and expressions of hope for continued peace.

DRAFT NO. 1

-2-

The attack yesterday on ~~Manila and on the Island of Oahu have~~ the Hawaiian Islands has caused severe damage to American naval and military forces. Very many American lives have been lost. In addition American ~~[illegible]~~ ships have been torpedoed on the high seas between San Francisco and Honolulu.

Yesterday the Japanese Government also launched an attack against Malaya.

Last night Japanese forces attacked Guam.

Japan has, therefore, undertaken a surprise offensive extending throughout the Pacific area. The facts of yesterday speak for themselves. The people of the United States have already formed their opinions and well understand the implications ~~these attacks bear on~~ to the very safety of our nation.

As Commander-in-Chief of the Army and Navy I have~~, of course,~~ directed that all measures be taken for our defense.

Long will we remember the character of the onslaught against us.

(A) No matter how long it may take us to overcome this premeditated invasion the American people will in their righteous might win through to absolute victory.

DRAFT NO. 1 -3-

I speak the will of the Congress and of the people ~~of this country~~ when I assert that we will not only defend ourselves to the uttermost but will see to it that this form of treachery shall never endanger us again. Hostilities exist. There is no mincing the fact that our people, our territory and our interests are in grave danger.

I, therefore, ask that the Congress declare that since the unprovoked and dastardly attack by Japan on Sunday, December seventh, a state of war has existed between the United Statew and the Japanese Empire.

****

Harry S. Truman Library

Another author, Arthur Schlesinger, in his history of the Kennedy Presidency, *A Thousand Days,* describes the important process by which language was used—and misused—in Washington.*

"The intellectual exhaustion of the Foreign Service expressed itself in the poverty of the official rhetoric. In meetings the men from State would talk in a bureaucratic patois borrowed in large part from the Department of Defense. We would be exhorted to 'zero in' on 'the purpose of the drill' (or of the 'exercise' or 'operation'), to 'crank in' this and 'phase out' that and 'gin up' something else, to 'pinpoint' a 'viable' policy and, behind it, a 'fall-back position,' to ignore the 'flak' from competing government bureaus or from the communists, to refrain from 'nit-picking' and never to be 'counter-productive.' Once we were 'seized of the problem,' preferably in as 'hard-nosed' a manner as possible, we would review 'options,' discuss 'over-all' objectives, seek 'break-throughs,' consider 'crash programs,' 'staff out' policies—doing all these things preferably 'meaningfully' and 'in depth' until we were ready to 'finalize' our deliberations, 'sign on to' or 'sign off on' a conclusion (I never could discover the distinction, if any, between these two locutions) and 'implement' a decision. This was not just shorthand; part of the conference-table vocabulary involved a studied multiplication of words. Thus one never talked about a 'paper' but always a 'piece of paper,' never said 'at this point' but always 'at this point in time.'

"Graceless as this patois was, it did have a certain, if sometimes spurious, air of briskness and efficiency. The result was far worse when the Department stopped talking and started writing. Whether drafting memoranda, cables or even letters or statements for the President, the Department fell into full, ripe, dreariness of utterance with hideous ease. The recipe was evidently to take a handful of clichés (saying something in a fresh way might create unforeseen troubles), repeat at five-minute intervals (lest the argument become clear or interesting), stir in the dough of the passive voice (the active voice assigns responsibility and was therefore hazardous) and garnish with self-serving rhetoric (Congress would be unhappy unless we constantly proclaimed the rectitude of American motives).

"After the Bay of Pigs, the State Department sent over a document entitled 'The Communist Totalitarian Government of Cuba as a Source of International Tension in the Americas,' which it had approved for distribution to NATO, CENTO, SEATO, the OAS and the free governments of Latin America and eventually for public release. In addition to the usual defects of Foggy Bottom prose, the paper was filled with bad spelling and grammar. Moreover, the narrative, which mysteriously stopped at the beginning of April 1961, contained a self-righteous condemnation of Castro's interventionist activities in the Caribbean that an unfriendly critic, alas! could have applied, without changing a word, to more recent actions by the United States. I responded on behalf of the White House:

> It is our feeling here that the paper should not be disseminated in its present form. . . .

* From pp. 417–420 and pp. 689–691 of *A Thousand Days* by Arthur Schlesinger, Jr. Reprinted by permission of Houghton Mifflin Company, and by permission of Andre Deutsch Ltd.

Presumably the document is designed to impress, not an audience which is already passionately anti-Castro, but an audience which has not yet finally made up its mind on the gravity of the problem. Such an audience is going to be persuaded, not by rhetoric, but by evidence. Every effort to heighten the evidence by rhetoric only impairs the persuasive power of the document. Observe the title: 'The Communist Totalitarian Government of Cuba . . ." This title presupposes the conclusion which the paper seeks to establish. Why not call it 'The Castro Regime in Cuba' and let the reader draw his own conclusions from the evidence? And why call it both 'Communist' and 'totalitarian'? All Communist governments are totalitarian. The paper, in our view, should be understated rather than overstated; it should eschew cold war jargon; the argument should be carried by facts, not exhortations. The writing is below the level we would hope for in papers for dissemination to other countries. The writing of lucid and forceful English is not too arcane an art.

"The President himself, with his sensitive ear for style, led the fight for literacy in the Department; and he had the vigorous support of some State Department officials, notably George Ball, Harriman and William R. Tyler. But the effort to liberate the State Department from automatic writing had little success. As late as 1963, the Department could submit as a draft of a presidential message on the National Academy of Foreign Affairs a text which provoked this resigned White House comment:

This is only the latest and worst of a long number of drafts sent here for Presidential signature. Most of the time it does not matter, I suppose, if the prose is tired, the thought banal and the syntax bureaucratic; and, occasionally when it does matter, State's drafts are very good. But sometimes, as in this case, they are not.

A message to Congress is a fairly important form of Presidential communication. The President does not send so many—nor of those he does send, does State draft so many—that each one cannot receive due care and attention. My own old-fashioned belief is that every Presidential message should be a model of grace, lucidity and taste in expression. At the very least, each message should be (a) in English, (b) clear and trenchant in its style, (c) logical in its structure and (d) devoid of gobbledygook. The State Department draft on the Academy failed each one of these tests (including, in my view, the first).

Would it not be possible for someone in the Department with at least minimal sensibility to take a look at pieces of paper designed for Presidential signature before they are sent to the White House?

It was a vain fight; the plague of gobbledygook was hard to shake off. I note words like "minimal" (at least not "optimal") and "pieces of paper" in my own lament. I can only testify with what interest and relief the President and the White House read cables from ambassadors who could write—Galbraith from New Delhi with his suave irony, David Bruce from London with his sharp wit, Kennan from Belgrade with his historical perspective and somber eloquence, John Bartlow Martin from Santo Domingo and William Attwood from Guinea with their vivid journalistic touch.

"Theodore H. White summed it all up in a letter he sent me from the Far East in the summer of 1961—a dispatch the President read with great interest. 'The State Department and its competitive instruments,' White wrote, 'have in the years since I worked with them become so tangled as to be almost unfit for any policy-making purpose or decision. . . . Somewhere there exists in the State Department a zone, or a climate, or inertia, which prevents it from thinking in terms of a new kind of politics, new departures in technique, an inertia which binds it rigidly to the fossil routine of conferences, negotiations, frozen positions. What must be changed must be changed first in Washington, at the center."

• • •

"Dean Acheson once said of presidential addresses, 'This is often where policy is made, regardless of where it is supposed to be made.' The presidential speech was automatically a declaration of national intent, addressed not only to Congress, the country and the world but also (sometimes equally important) to the executive branch of the government.

"Kennedy's speeches covered a whole range of occasions from greeting delegations of foreign students to warning the world of the perils of nuclear war. Though he was a perfectly competent writer, he rarely had time to compose his own speeches any longer (except when he spoke extemporaneously, as he very often did). Ted Sorensen was, of course, his main reliance. They had worked closely together for a decade, and on these matters their minds rolled in unison. I do not know which of them originated the device of staccato phrases ('We shall pay any price, bear any burden, meet any hardships, support any friend, oppose any foe to assure the survival and success of liberty') or the use of balanced sentences ('Never have the nations of the world had so much to lose or so much to gain. Together we shall save our planet or together we shall perish in its flames'); but by the time of the Presidency their styles had fused into one.

"Next to Sorensen, Richard Goodwin was Kennedy's best writer. After Goodwin's departure to the State Department, I found myself increasingly involved in speech drafting. The President somewhat mistrusted my efforts, however, as 'too Stevensonian,' by which he meant too complicated in syntax and fancy in language. He felt that his voice had too narrow a range to permit rhetorical flight and used to envy Stevenson his greater inflection of tone. Actually his own range steadily expanded during the Presidency, and he rapidly became an orator of unusual force and eloquence.

"He would begin work on a speech by calling in the writer and sketching out his ideas. When the occasion was serious, he would read the draft with intense care, scribble illegibly on the margin and then go over the result with the writer. Like most politicians, he had little sense of the structure of a speech. He also was an uncertain speller; nor was his grammar infallible. In his impromptu remarks, for example, he often bobbled his compound objects.* But he was an excellent editor, skilled at tuning up thoughts and eliminating verbal excess. Above all, he loved pungent expressions. Early one Sunday in December 1962 he woke me to read aloud two sentences from a Khrushchev speech in the morning newspapers. One began, 'At the climax of events around Cuba, there began to be a smell of

* One can find even in his *Public Papers* a reference to the 'tremendous landslide that swept the Vice President and I into office by one-tenth of one per cent.' (1963, 444)

burning in the air.' The other went: 'Those militarists who boast that they have submarines with Polaris rockets on board, and other surprises, as they put it, against the Soviet Union, would do well to remember that we are not living in mud huts either.' Kennedy remarked with admiration, 'Khrushchev certainly has some good writers.' (I said that we could do as well for him if he would only give two-hour speeches.)

"If the occasion was political or festive, he would approach the speech with greater casualness, quite often using the prepared text only as a point of departure or, as he had done so often in the 1960 campaign, abandoning it entirely. He gave one of his most sparkling talks at a luncheon in October 1961 marking the publication of the first four volumes of the John Quincy Adams papers. I had prepared a draft. Then his rather detailed suggestions led to a new draft, at which he glanced half an hour before the lunch while conducting conversation with other staff people on unrelated topics. In a few moments we went over to the Statler-Hilton Hotel. During lunch he went calmly over the manuscript, crossing out paragraphs and writing inserts. When he rose to speak, the first half of his remarks was absolutely new (including the felicitous opening: 'I want to say to Mr. Adams that it is a pleasure to live in your family's old house'). The second half was a free (and improved) adaptation of the text he had brought with him.

"The speech process often brought his miscellany of curious knowledge into play. In September 1962 he asked me to prepare something for a talk he had to make at Newport at the dinner before the America's Cup races. He suddenly said, 'I understand that there is about the same amount of salt in the human blood as there is in sea water, and that is a proof of our origin in the sea.' This sounded like an old wives' tale to me, but I said I would check into it. I called one of Jerome Wiesner's specialists, who was skeptical too but agreed to look further. In an hour he called back, rather excited, and said, 'It seems as if you have got on to something there.' Apparently blood does have a certain amount of salt, almost as much as sea water, and Claude Barnard and others had speculated that the need of cells for a salt solution might be related to man's primal origin in the sea. When I later asked Kennedy where in the world he had heard this, he said he couldn't remember. In Newport he converted it into poetry: 'All of us have in our veins the exact same percentage of salt in our blood that exists in the ocean, and, therefore, we have salt in our blood, in our sweat, in our tears. We are tied to the ocean. And when we go back to the sea—whether it is to sail or to watch it—we are going back from whence we came.' "

The student writer must learn to take a similar care with his own work as historians and Presidents take with theirs. For example, here are two paragraphs written by students of Mrs. Miriam Moody in Sanford (Maine) High School and then rewritten and edited by the class.

~~It all started with~~ Scaccia's first [first shot hit the] basket in the third quarter. Suddenly, their plays began to click. The cover came off the basket as ~~the Sanford five found the range.~~ [with Scaccia's first shot in the 3rd quarter.] There was a player in red leaping high for every rebound and a more regular swish of the Sanford basket. Portland seemed to sense the difference too, as in desperation they fouled again and again, giving the Redskins free chances to make up their deficit. As the seconds flashed by, the score evened up and Sanford finally gained a lead which they held to the end. ~~The Redskins are on their way to Bangor and All State.~~ On to Bangor.

[Everything was going wrong.] ~~In the first half of the Sanford versus Portland game things look unfavorable for Sanford.~~ ~~It looks as though it will be one of those games where everything goes wrong.~~ Sanford's big center, Nick Scaccia, was having what looked like an off night. ~~For a while it looked as though~~ ¶ Portland couldn't miss. ~~a basket.~~ Things were running smooth for Portland while Sanford was fighting to keep up. The beginning of the second half brought on a complete change. A few three-point plays encouraged Sanford and there was no stopping them. ~~Portland began to miss and Sanford began hitting.~~ ~~The breaks started coming for Sanford.~~ From the second half on it was Sanford all the way. ~~With Portland playing one of the finest games Sanford took the title by a decision of three points.~~ ~~A margin of three points decided the title.~~

11 sentences
-5
6 sentences

Here is another example of what Mrs. Moody was able to do with two paragraphs which were edited in class and then rewritten by the author. Here are the original two paragraphs.

Yesterday I had my first experience with death. ~~One of our family's closest friends died of a fall down stairs.~~ I ~~have~~ remember other people dying, even relatives but never before did death hit me as hard as this one. ~~Perhaps it's because I'm older and see things in a different sense. Yet I can seem to think that it is something more.~~ I've always felt very close to this lady and took for granted that she would always be here. ~~People talk of having a second mother and if anyone ever did, this is~~ She was what people might call a second mother to me. And I can't imagine life without her.

If she had been ill for some time or if she had died of a heart attack I might have been able to face her death easier. But she died of an accident that seems to me so needless and I question why it happened at all. I don't think that I ever had such a complete feeling of desperation as I've had for the last two days. ~~Everywhere I go,~~ All through the house I see her familiar face where she had been so many times. Even in other places ~~where I hadn't~~ she is on my mind and I see her as she was, not believing that I'll never see her again.

After the class had gone over this piece and made the changes which are written in, the author was able to write a new version.

Yesterday I had my first experience with death. Never before even when relatives died, have I felt this way. I even find myself questioning why she died, which I suppose I shouldn't do. It seems so unnecessary and I wonder why some feeble person couldn't have gone in her place. I always felt very close to this lady and took for granted that she would be here forever. She was what people might call a second mother to me and I can't imagine life without her. Everywhere I go in the house I see her familiar face in the places that I had seen her so often before. I almost think that the house is haunted by her presence. Even in other places I see her as she was and can't believe that she is gone.

It would have been possible to go on and edit this again. The teacher had to decide how much editing the student could take on a particular piece, and she had to bring the student to the point where she could do the editing herself. This is what might have happened by further editing of the revision.

Yesterday I ~~had my first experience with~~ met death. ~~Never before~~ even when relatives died, before, ~~have~~ I ~~felt this way.~~ never met this dark visitor. I ~~even~~ find myself questioning why ~~she died;~~ he came, which I suppose I shouldn't do. ~~It seems so unnecessary and~~ I wonder why some feeble person couldn't ~~have gone~~ have been taken in her place. I ~~always felt very close to this lady and~~ took it for granted that ~~she~~ (use name?) would be here forever. She was ~~what people might call~~ a second mother to me and I can't imagine life without her. Everywhere I go ~~in the house~~ I see her familiar face, ~~in the places that I had seen her so often before.~~ ~~I almost think that~~ the house seems ~~is~~ haunted. ~~by her presence.~~ ~~Even in other places~~ I see her as she was and I can't believe that she is gone.

It may be a good idea to take the student into the writer's workshop by using some of the books listed in "The Writing Teacher's Library," page 247. The student must realize that it is not a punishment to re-write, but that editing and rewriting are the way writers write. It may be helpful to take the student through the process which created the first paragraph in the Preface of this book. I do not write every paragraph this way, but this is the way I work on a tough paragraph. In this case the paragraph was difficult because it was starting the Preface, and beginnings are always difficult for me. It was also hard because I wanted to say enough but not too much—I didn't want to give the book away—and I had a number of technical problems to solve. I had the outline of the book before me when I started to write, and I knew what I wanted to do in the Preface: I wanted to indicate the need that caused this book to be born.

I thought I would sit down and write this paragraph easily, but actually I worked on it off and on for six days, and then when I revised the book I changed it some more.

PREFACE

(Outline – need seen)

What is preface trying to do?
Establish Nesdec's role
author's authority

This book is the direct result of a need to improve the teaching of composition which was seen by the English teachers and their Administrators whose school systems were members of the NESDEC. They felt...

This book is based on need experience

This book ~~has been~~ was built in answer to a ~~need~~

need on
from
out of experience
from the materials of experience

The ~~built~~ book ~~was~~ is built in answer to a need ~~from~~ with the materials of experience.

NEED –
– expressed by NESDEC

EXPERIENCE – Teachers of Teachers
also a writer
– other teachers
– tested in 200 schools

ACKNOWLEDGEMENTS etc.

This book is built from (teaching? writing) experience is answer to a need for ~~an~~ a more effective ~~way~~ method of teaching composition in the SECONDARY schools.

(then reverse to need?)

¶ TITLE was built in answer to a need

For a more effective method of teaching composition in the secondary school

(grr) Extensive (combined)

from the experience of — ~~TEACHERS~~ / ~~WRITERS AND TEACHERS~~ / TEACHERS + WRITERS.

tested & retested

The classroom experience of

The writing desk (~~practiced~~ x-experience of writers

?
men who are ~~able~~ to write
and others ~~who are~~ able to teach writing

---

it distils the methods of writing practiced by the professional writer into an approach (essence) which has been (proven) (proved) effective in the classroom

Need seen (NESDEC)

Experience — Teacher of teachers also writer + distill — believe synthesis
— other teachers
— read, practised, edited, tested

Acknowledgements

~~After Ack~~
Way book may be read

Classroom exp.
Writing desk exp.

PREFACE

TITLE was built in answer to a need for a more effective method of teaching composition in ~~a~~ the secondary school from ~~the~~ ~~experience~~ classroom experience of teachers ~~and~~ the BLANK experience of writers. and the It distills the ~~methods of~~ ~~approach to~~ composition practiced by the professional writer into ~~a method of~~ an approach to teaching composition which has proved effective in the classroom.

~~The purpose of TITLE is to teach the English teacher how to teach writing.~~

Need as seen by NESDEC

Experience

Acknowledgements

Publishing – Editorial

Practical

Personal – Private

Writing board – Typewritten ms.

Cut classroom?

PREFACE

The need for a more ~~effective method of teaching composition in the secondary school in~~....

=

TITLE was built from the experience of publishing writers and practicing teachers to create a more effective method of teaching composition in the secondary school.

The book (first) reveals ~~shows~~ how the professional writer works and then shows how the methods (steps) ~~lessons he~~ follows ~~has taught himself~~ can be applied in the classroom. (to students who do not intend to become prof. writers) ???

Pt. out writer (who he?) has taught himself. Has a skill — para.

The need for combining experience of writers and teachers ~~such an approach~~ was (first) seen by the New England.... This organization of X school systems

Don't write first chapter here

Need to bring in writer who a teacher

Synthesize | Details — Study + Experience
Test in Classroom |

Book can be read A + B

Way of studying + a desk book — source reference

Acknowledgements — name by category

Preface

TITLE was written to give English teachers an effective method of teaching composition based on the experience of professional writers. book was tested by experienced teachers in 100's of classrooms to show how the steps the publishing writer follows can be applied in classroom.

This does not mean that students will be trained to be professional writers. It does mean students will be encouraged (motivated) to teach themselves the lessons that professional writers have taught themselves.

[add transition] writing is a skill, it is not given so much as it is developed. This book will show the teacher how to help the student develop the ability to communicate in writing with others--in a business letter, a poem, an engineering report, a news story--whatever his ability and need.

- in school
test
scholarly
essay
paper
- after school

Need

Experience (method book written)

How to use – variety

Acknowledgements

PREFACE

WRITING CAN BE TAUGHT was written to give English teachers an effective method of teaching composition based on the experience of professional writers. The book was tested by teachers in hundreds of classrooms to ~~adapt~~ show how the steps the publishing writer follows ~~so they~~ can be applied to the needs of the student. This does NOT mean that students will be trained to be professional writers. It does mean, however, that writing is more a skill than a gift, it is not so much given as it is developed. This book will show the teacher how to help the student develop the ability to communicate in writing with others--in school, on an essay test, a term paper, an examination, a book report; ~~after~~ beyond school in a business letter, a scholarly paper, an engineering report, a news release, a corporate memo, a poem--whatever ~~his~~ the student's individual ability and need. Through the method in this book students will be encouraged to teach themselves the lessons that professional writers have taught themselves. The student will write, and his writing will improve.

(If you will turn back to the Preface which actually appears at the beginning of this draft you will see that when the book was dictated and then edited again further changes were made in this single paragraph.)

The process of editing is a continuation of the process of discovering. The student chooses the right word by looking back at what he has to say, and then he chooses the most effective way of saying it. He may not follow the rules of grammar rigidly, but he will rediscover them for himself as he tries to say what he has to say in a way that other people can understand. If his pronouns do not relate to the correct subject, his writing will make no sense; if his parallel clauses are not parallel, his sentences will fall apart. If he drops into the passive voice when it is unnecessary, his writing will become dull. Martin Mayer in *The Lawyers* (Harper & Row) quotes James B. Minor, a lawyer who reduced the bulk of the Federal Aviation Agency regulations, as saying ". . . Now we try to clarify the regulations. We avoid legalese, avoid the passive voice, use the present tense."

The professional writer and editor will use the present tense whenever possible, and he will use the simple past or future tense only when necessary. He will avoid the verb "to be" (is, was) when it is used as a helping verb, and he will try to speak in the active voice. "Joe was hit by John," is flabby and wordy compared to "John hit Joe." The first sentence is in the passive voice, the second in the active. The first sentence has sixty per cent more words than the second. The passive voice reverses the natural order of speaking. It is natural to say "the journalist uses the active voice" and unnatural to say "the active voice is used by the journalist."

The student, when he is writing, may find it helpful to keep before him the rules for newspaper writers from the *Bulletin* of the Minnesota Newspaper Association.

1. Don't use no double negative.
2. Make each pronoun agree with their antecedent.
3. Join clauses good, like a conjunction should.
4. About them sentence fragments.
5. When dangling, watch your participles.
6. Verbs has to agree with their subjects.
7. Just between you and I, case is important too.
8. Don't write run-on sentences they are hard to read.
9. Don't use commas, which aren't necessary.
10. Try to not ever split infinitives.
11. Its important to use your apostrophe's correctly.
12. Proofread your writing to see if you any words left out.
13. Correct spelling is absoluteley essential.

At first the student may become bored with the process of editing, but if he sees its necessity, if he understands that people will not know what he is saying unless he has edited it well, he will begin to develop a pride in the work of shaping and fitting words to meaning.

will go on all night by fits and starts. I must take my chance to get off during a quiet interval. You dont mind my waiting just a minute or two, do you ?

RAINA Oh no. I am sorry you will have to go into danger again. (Motioning towards ottoman) Won't you sit -- (shies like a frightened horse).

MAN Dont frighten me like that. What is it ?

RAINA Your pistol! It was staring that officer in the face all the time. What an escape !

MAN Oh, is that all ?

RAINA (sarcastically) I am sorry I frightened you. (She takes up the pistol and hands it to him) Pray take it to protect yourself against me.

MAN (taking the pistol) No use, dear young lady : there's nothing in it. It's not loaded. (drops it disparagingly into his revolver case).

RAINA Load it by all means.

MAN I've no ammunition. What use are cartridges in battle ? I always carry chocolate instead ; and I finished the last cake of that yesterday.

RAINA Chocolate ! Do you stuff your pockets with sweets, like a schoolboy, even in the field ?

MAN Yes. Isnt it contemptible ?

~~RAINA (Going to the table R., and taking a box of sweets from it)~~

RAINA Allow me. I am sorry I have eaten them all except these (offers him the box).

MAN (Ravenously) You're an angel ! (gobbles them) Creams! Delicious ! Bless you, dear lady. You can always tell an old soldier by the inside of his holsters and cartridge boxes. The young ones carry pistols and cartridges ; the old ones, grub. Thank you. (hands back box. She snatches it contemptuously from him and throws it away. Ugh ! Dont do things so suddenly, gracious lady. Dont revenge yourself because I frightened you just now.

RAINA Frighten me ! Do you know, sir, that though I am only a

Four The Climate for Writing

In the usual classroom the teacher speaks and the students listen. In the writing class, the students speak and the teacher listens.

The climate of the writing workshop must encourage individual students to bring their own content to the course. During the class the students should not be passive receivers of information. They must be doers, writing and rewriting—discovering what they have to say, discovering what they need to know to say it effectively—until the students complete the act of writing by reaching a reader who understands what they have written.

The writing teacher should create a lesson plan which is flexible, disciplined, free, and demanding, all at the same time. Each student must be able to fail and try and fail and try again as he practices what he has come to understand is the normal process of the writer. Each student must face the lonely discipline of the empty page, the unsuccessful draft and the unknowing reader. The class environment must place the responsibility for learning on the student so that he feels the obligation and the opportunity to teach himself. The teacher must search for methods which prevent him from interrupting the natural progress of his students. The writing teacher who teaches least usually teaches most if his students work in an environment which allows them to teach themselves.

22 Why Writing Isn't Taught Effectively

Most American high school graduates do not know how to write. This is one of the few statements on which most educators agree, and it is an opinion they share with employers and parents. Writing—the vital ability to express one's self with clarity and grace—is not taught in our schools.

Most students pass through twelve years of English courses, but few students ever have an intensive, concentrated opportunity to learn to write. They do write papers and their grades often depend on papers but the students are rarely taught how to write papers or given the chance to practice and develop composition skills.

There are many reasons writing is not taught in school. In the first place there are few writing teachers prepared to teach writing. English teachers are trained to be teachers of grammar or educated to be teachers of literature—if indeed they are prepared at all. A study by the National Council of Teachers of English revealed that only half of the English teachers majored in that subject at college and only a handful of English teachers had courses in composition beyond Freshman English. There are many who never took that course.

George Bernard Shaw, **Arms and the Man.** By permission of the Harvard College Library and The Public Trustee and the Society of Authors.

We cannot say that our teachers of English are incompetent or irresponsible because they do not teach composition, when they are never educated to be composition teachers. They do not teach writing because they do not know how to teach writing, and it is the purpose of this book to attempt to help correct this lack.

There is another reason the English teacher simply does not attempt to teach writing, and that is because the English Department is a complicated collection of contradictory disciplines.

The English teacher each year is expected to teach or review the mechanics of the language. The approach may be through traditional grammar, transformational grammar, structural linguistics, the history of the language or a combination of all methods, but the result is the same. The teacher is expected to be an expert on the science of language, and he is expected to teach his students how language has been used in the past. This is a fine scholarly discipline but there is little evidence it has any relation to the student's ability to write. The study of language as language too often isolates language from meaning or use, and the experience in many classrooms shows that students who excel at analysis of the language cannot write, and students who can write do not necessarily have a scientific understanding of their language.

This situation is compounded by the fact that our students move from one method to another within a single school system and, of course, in a mobile society they move from one school system to another. The student is generally subjected to a confusing variety of grammatical approaches during his twelve years in school. The wise student attempts to forget these contradictions when he sits down to write. Many students who attempt to follow the contradictory language rules they have been taught are soon lost in a jungle of syntax. Most are never rescued.

The English teacher is also expected to be a reading teacher. In the beginning he teaches the students to recognize that black squiggles on the page are symbols for meaning. Eventually he teaches the students critical reading. Most of our students today are demonstrably better readers because of the time they have spent in careful analysis of a text. The ability to perform an act of critical analysis, however, does not mean that the student can write well. I can analyze a football play or a sonata but I can't score a touchdown or perform in Lincoln Centre.

The English teacher not only teaches reading, he teaches literature. He is expected to make his students familiar with the historic context of English, American, and, frequently, world literature. He is supposed to introduce his students to the great writers and to the most common forms of literature. He may develop units on the myth, the lyric, the tragedy, showing how an attitude towards life has been expressed in many centuries and in many cultures.

In many school systems the English teacher is expected to design and operate courses in the humanities which integrate literature with history, philosophy, art and music. The teacher who can do this—and there are a surprising number of them—is indeed a Renaissance man. He is not often, however, a writing teacher. He is properly interested in great ideas and in illuminating humanistic visions of man's experience. He may be an exciting teacher but he is not, by training or temperament, prepared to coach his students in the fundamental skills of composition.

The English teacher often has other chores ladled into his curriculum by his supervisors. He may be expected to teach oral expression—public speaking, debate and even how to answer the telephone. He may teach business letter writing, advise the school paper, drive the debate club, lay out pictures for the yearbook, direct the school play and write school press releases. The English teacher must choose among the many demands placed on him and since he is not trained to be a writing teacher, he will rarely choose to emphasize writing.

In a survey of high school education, James Bryant Conant proposed that half the time spent in English courses in high school be spent on composition.[1] The College English Examination Board states that one-third of the time should be spent on writing. To a layman these proposals seem reasonable, even conservative. They are actually radical, for a United States Office of Education and National Council of Teachers of English survey of 168 high school English departments in forty-five states reported that composition was emphasized only 15.7 percent of the class time.[2]

The English teacher is not only the victim of his preparation and an overcrowded curriculum, he also suffers from a system which has made him believe—and made his supervisors believe—that a person is teaching only when he stands before a class talking. The role of preacher may be appropriate when you are lecturing on the history of a language, explicating a text, or synthesizing a century's literature. It is certainly not appropriate to the teaching of writing. There are a few things which need to be said about writing but once said, the student must spend his time in the lengthy process of discovering and solving his own writing problems. The teacher must be the student's most effective reader. When the English teacher is forced to stand before the class, period after period, day after day, talking, talking, talking, his students will not learn to write.

There are many other reasons students are not taught to write. Some of them may be summarized in ten myths which have been passed on by generations of English teachers as articles of faith.

Myth One: Correct usage comes first For generations most English teachers have given first priority to correct usage. They feel compelled to mark every error on every draft, constantly focusing the student's attention on grammar and spelling rather than on content and form. Most students, and all writers, disagree with this emphasis. Language should be used correctly but the final, careful editing cannot take place until the writer has discovered, by writing, what he has to say and how he wants to say it.

Myth Two: Each student paper must be corrected by the teacher The English teacher is the faculty martyr. He lugs home, night after night, a cross of papers, all of which he believes have to be marked in red, the symbol of his own blood. He never escapes from the burden of papers to be corrected, and his students, who glance only at the grade, never learn to write. Belief in the myth that the teacher must correct each student paper interrupts the necessary process of writing. The student must correct his own paper by drafting, rewriting and editing his own work until he is prepared to face the reader's stern evaluation of what he has said.

[1] James Bryant Conant, *The American High School Today* (New York: McGraw-Hill, 1959).

[2] *National Study of High School English Programs,* Cooperative Research Project No. 1994.

Myth Three: Students should write a few papers but write them well As long as writing is an unnatural act which is performed rarely and only for an extremely critical audience, students will not learn to write. Writing must become the students' normal method of disciplined thinking. Students will not begin to write well until they are writing prolifically. The great writers have not hoarded their talents, but produced with a rich prodigality. Literature is the distillate of enormous failure.

Myth Four: Students do not want to write Writing is hard work and man is often lazy, so that students are not likely to write unless writing is required. But if students are both required and encouraged to write and if their teacher is a constructive reader, then students will frequently write more than is required. Man's drive to communicate is basic; he will write for a reader who will listen to what he has to say. He will seek criticism from an editor who is not attacking him but who is attacking the page with the clear, constructive purpose of trying to help the writer express himself more effectively.

Myth Five: A good reader will become a good writer Every student should be trained to be a perceptive reader, but it simply does not follow that the skillful reader will automatically become an effective writer. There are writers, both student and professional, who read relatively little and write very well. There are also many people, including English teachers, who read very well and write very poorly. The English curriculum in most secondary schools assumes that an emphasis on reading will produce effective writers. The ability to read well does not lead inevitably to the ability to write well. Because of the paperback revolution, students in English may be reading far more than in the past, but student writing has not greatly improved.

Myth Six: The best subject is a literary subject It is a matter of dogma in many English departments that students have nothing to say until literature is poured into their heads. We cannot assume that literature is the primary interest of our students—or even that it should be. We must realize that the writing of literary analysis is but one form of writing. If we evaluate our students only on their ability to write literary analysis we will over-reward a minority and penalize a majority.

Myth Seven: Grade levels are significant in teaching writing The English teacher should glory in the individual diversity of man. Too often, however, he falls into the fallacy that there is a group writing problem peculiar to the tenth grade, the seventh grade, or the twelfth grade. Students cannot be taught writing in a military manner, herded together by age, grade, height, or the development of secondary sexual characteristics. Students must be taught individually. Each student, when he meets a problem in his own writing, should have a teacher who is prepared to help him solve that problem. The order in which he strikes problems in writing will not correspond to his classmate's, and the time he takes to solve his problems will vary. That is not important. What is important is that the student solve his writing problems so that his writing becomes effective. The order in which he does this and the methods he uses are not the test of the course. The test of the writing course is the student's ability to write with clarity and grace when he graduates.

Myth Eight: Students learn best by imitating models of great writing The rhetorical teaching method used by the ancients is particularly attractive to the contemporary teacher who wants to make a science of composition. We do not, however, have a modern rhetoric which identifies and isolates the forms of discourse appropriate in modern society, with its diversity of rhetorical purposes, tones, appeals and audiences. And we have not yet found a method of applying the classical techniques of teaching oral discourse to mass education. Most students find isolated paragraphs, neatly labeled by rhetorical type, remote from their own writing problems. A student's ability to recognize his teacher's rhetorical classifications has little effect on the student's own writing.

Myth Nine: You can teach writing by talking Some English teachers lecture about writing day after day, period after period, and become discouraged because the students listen but do not practice what their teachers preach. Other instructors feel guilty or inadequate because they do not know what to say about writing in hour-long classes. Both categories of teachers should understand there is not a great deal to say about writing. There are only a few skills, but it will take the students many years to master them. There is no content in the writing course in the conventional academic sense. And in the usual class period the student should not listen to lectures but write, rewrite, edit, or respond to student writing through individual conferences and small group discussions.

Myth Ten: You can't teach writing There is a romantic belief, shared by too many English teachers, that writing is a mystical act, and that the ability to write is granted by God to a few students. This is an easy evasion of the teacher's responsibility. There is indeed a mystical element in great art, but writing is first of all a craft. It becomes an art when someone else places value on the product of the writer's craft. Writing can be taught to students if they are given the opportunity to discover for themselves the basic skills which each writer has to learn and practice while he aspires to art.

Finally, writing isn't taught in our schools because English teachers have the excuse of numbers. The majority of English teachers have a student load which makes it difficult and even, apparently, impossible to teach composition. Many English teachers have five or six class periods five days a week, in addition to study hall, lunchroom, and library monitoring duty. When parents, college administrators, and employers call for more instruction in writing they are answered with the English teacher's lament: "I have too many students."

Most English teachers agree that students should write a paper each week (they think of it as a maximum standard, while I believe it is a minimal one). If they correct a paper in the way they have been taught, identifying each grammatical and spelling error as well as marking it for logical thought, appropriate diction, tone and all the other ingredients of a good piece of writing, it is an intensive, exhausting task. One study has shown it takes at least 8.3 minutes to correct the average short high school composition. Ten minutes is more likely, and perhaps five papers an hour is possible under this system. Remember, that includes not only identifying all the student's problems, but writing comments which make those problems clear to the student and help him find working solutions. These comments should, ideally, be made in an even more time-consuming individual conference.

Yet I have graduates with student loads of 170 and more. Five classes of thirty students each, or 150 students, is not an unusual load. A national average produced by one survey of good school systems revealed that the normal teacher of English had 130 students. If a teacher with 130 pupils corrects one paper each week per student in the conventional manner, spending just 10 minutes on each paper, he will work from seven to midnight, Monday night, Tuesday night, Wednesday night, and Thursday night. On Friday he will have to correct from seven o'clock to one o'clock Saturday morning if he wants to get the job done and take the weekend off. This schedule does not allow time for classroom preparation or extra duty, such as directing the school play.

Privileged school systems are trying to achieve a maximum goal of 100 students for each English teacher. Even with these "few" students, if the teacher corrects papers in the conventional manner from seven to midnight, Monday through Thursday, he can have Friday night off. When Dr. Conant first published his survey of secondary education, he advocated a hundred students as the standard load for each English teacher. But in the latest edition of his report, he admitted that only one-fourth of the 2000 schools surveyed reported a load of 120 or less. Reluctantly, he has accepted 120 as the norm for the English teacher.[3]

English teachers must fight vigorously for reasonable, workable class loads, but they should not use numbers as an excuse for not teaching composition. As a matter of fact, the higher the load the more important it is that they find ways of dealing with large numbers of papers so that their students can learn to write by writing. I have developed many of the techniques in this book because I found it impossible to do an adequate job of correcting each paper even with a university student load. These techniques allow me to assign nearly 6,000 papers this semester to my 119 students—96 at the University and 23 in a special non-credit course for teachers at Harvard sponsored by the New England School Development Council.

I evaluate every fourth paper in one course, and more than that in the other courses. I do not, however, do my students' job of rewriting. I have discovered that my students learn to write when I do not over-teach and over-correct. I help them diagnose their own programs, one at a time. English teachers must find methods which allow them to function despite their student load.

This book does not argue against the study of language and the study of literature. It does argue for an equivalent status for the teaching of composition. Writing is not taught in our schools because writing is not taught.

[3] James Bryant Conant, *The Comprehensive High School: A Second Report to Interested Citizens* (New York: McGraw-Hill, 1967).

Writing can be taught if English teachers are educated to be teachers of writing, if they do not believe the myths about the teaching of composition, and if they face up to the problems of heavy student loads. Writing can be taught in our schools today without waiting for ideal conditions.

Departments of English ought to develop a curriculum which allows the student to concentrate on one phase of the discipline at a time under the direction of a teacher who is prepared to teach that particular specialty. We must develop English teachers who specialize in teaching language, others who prefer to teach literature and still others who are expert in teaching writing. We should not expect the student to go through a repetitive English course year after year which has a dibble of language study, a dollop of composition and a dabble of literature. Neither should we expect the teacher to be equally prepared to teach the entire curriculum. The discipline of English will not be well taught until we devise new ways of encouraging our students to learn. We cannot continue to blame our students for being bored by English when the courses are repetitive, and we cannot continue to blame teachers for boring their students when the faculty is expected to teach diverse subjects and to teach them all in one rigid manner. Writing will not be taught efficiently until we develop faculty members experienced in the teaching of writing who are given the authority to design a climate in which students can learn to write.

23 The Classroom A Writing Laboratory

If a classroom is designed for a sermon with row upon row of desks facing the pulpit, few teachers will have the courage to resist the temptation to preach. It's safer behind the desk, and, after all, the student congregation can't leave while you talk.

The writing teacher must understand that he does not need a classroom; he needs a laboratory. His students must have a place where they can work, and where the teacher can also do his work, which is to encourage them individually. The ideal writing laboratory should have these characteristics:

> Each student should have his own desk. These desks might face the walls so the students can concentrate on their own work, or the desks might be separated by soundproof partitions, as is often done in the language laboratory to provide small carrels, although I have not found partitions necessary in my writing laboratory at the University of New Hampshire.
>
> The teacher should have an office with a degree of acoustical privacy and a view of the classroom. He should be able to withdraw with a student and go over his paper, giving him individual criticism without the class hearing that personal criticism. It should be a place where both the teacher and the student feel free to be candid.
>
> It is important that the room be soundproofed so that the activity in the room will not disturb other classes, and so that various groups in the room can be working at the same time doing different things without disturbing each other.

There may be an arrangement of tables in a hollow square or circle in the middle of the room so that a class can discuss student papers or mutual writing problems. There should not be a lectern. The teacher should not stand up, but sit around the table with his students.

It should be possible to arrange the tables so that small groups of students can work editing each other's papers. The teacher may also want to use these tables for small group conferences, although he may use the table in his office.

There should be a bulletin board where student and professional writing can be displayed.

There ought to be a library of books on writing which students could read when they are waiting for conferences. Of course, there should be an unabridged dictionary and other basic research writing tools.

There should be provision for an overhead projector, tape recorders, and other audio-visual aids.

There should be adequate lighting for each student to work at his own desk.

The writing laboratory is not expensive, and the normal classroom can be turned into an effective laboratory quite easily. The important elements are: tables arranged so that the student can work individually; a place, perhaps in the corner of the room, where the teacher can hold conferences, an arrangement which encourages the students to discuss writing with the teacher as a fellow writer, not as a remote person lecturing about the subject.

The imaginative teacher can take an ordinary classroom and turn it into a writing laboratory. I've seen this done even in classrooms where the desks are nailed down. I've seen school libraries used for the same purpose. The teacher should remember that he is trying to create a climate, a place where the writer can do the jobs of writing, rewriting and editing which are central to learning how to write. The student should be shown by his surroundings and the way in which the equipment he is to use is arranged that he is discovering how to write on his own, with the aid of his classmates and his teacher.

24 Why a Lesson Plan?

You don't need one—if your teaching each day rises spontaneously out of your students' work, if your supervisors and colleagues understand what you are doing (and permit it), if your students know what they are doing and why.

Most teachers, however, find they need a map of the course to help them teach effectively. A lesson plan gives the teacher control over the course and helps develop a sense of direction and pace. It is also proper for a supervisor to want to have some idea of what is being covered in each course. It is just as important in a coordinated English program for the teacher's colleagues to know what he is doing. It is necessary for this information to exist, in writing, in a team teaching program. Most important, the students should know the lesson plan. Usually, it is not shared with them, but they are the ones who need to know the direction and the pace of the course. In fact, they may even share in the design of the lesson plan themselves, deciding, with the benefit of the teacher's experience, what the course should try to do and how it should try to do it.

There are six fundamental elements in any good writing course lesson plan:

1. *Clear Directions to the Students* The student must understand the deadlines he has to meet. He should know the hour and the place his writing is due. He should be told how it is to be prepared: typed or handwritten, on one side of a piece of paper or both, single- or double-spaced, and so on. He should know all the small details which will make it easier for the student to do the work and the teacher to handle it. For example, each paper should be dated and numbered so that the student or the teacher may refer to his paper efficiently. If possible, the student should have his own copy of each paper so that the teacher may have a continuing record of the student's work and the student will have his own papers to refer to. The student will be expected to do a great deal of writing. If the teacher is to handle thousands of papers during a term, then the course must be organized so that the students will be able to pass their papers in in an efficient routine. The students may even be able to file their own papers each day or to pull the papers out during a workshop session or a conference. Each teacher will discover his own procedures. The important thing is that the directions are clear, that the course is well organized, and that everyone who participates in the course understands the directions.

2. *A Ritual of Work* The productive professional writer develops a ritual of work which keeps him writing regardless of whether or not he is in the mood. School provides an artificial ritual, and the writing course should develop its own pattern within the natural restrictions of the school week. Students should have regular times for lectures or discussions, if those activities are part of the course. There should also be regular periods for conferences, questions, writing, rewriting and editing sessions in class, small group and class discussion, student publication and discussion of it.

3. *A Defined Relationship with Other Courses* The writing course should be coordinated, in writing, with the other English courses as well as other courses in the curriculum. Students should be able to use papers in the writing course which have been written for science, mathematics, social studies and, when possible, language teachers. The student should see that his writing course is not isolated, and that the skills he learns in the course will help him in his other courses. Often the writing course will be just part of an English course and in that case, it is extremely important that the student and the teacher understand the relationship between this portion and the other parts of the English course.

4. *A Code of Ethics* The student should have a clear understanding that what he writes for the teacher's eyes only will be kept in confidence by the teacher. He should know what papers may be published in class, and whether he is to be identified as the author or not. The student should understand what plagiarism is and the importance of doing his own work. The student must understand how he is to be graded—what pieces of work will be evaluated, under what conditions, and according to what standards.

5. *An Order of Topics* It is usually helpful for the student and the teacher to know what topics will be covered in the course and in what order. The student should also know at the beginning of the course what texts (if any) are to be used and how they are to be used.

6. *A Method of Change* The students and their teacher must have a way of adapting the course while it is being taught. Each time the writing course is taught it will change because of the increasing experience of the teacher in dealing with the needs of the individual students in the course. The writing course is created as it is taught. The lesson plan must, first of all, allow single students to be taught individually. Once that is part of the lesson plan, however, the teacher will find that each class has its own character. Some classes will need lectures; others will learn by discussion; some will break up into small groups naturally and efficiently; sometimes most of the students in class will write best out of school and the next term another group will write best in school. The teacher will also learn from his own experience in the teaching of writing. He should evaluate what he is doing to see if it works, and he should constantly try new ways of teaching the basic skills of composition.

Both the teacher and his students should know that any lesson plan is nothing more than a plan; it can be amended, adapted, expanded, contracted or eliminated. The purpose of the lesson plan is to give the course direction. If it is obvious that the direction is wrong, or if a better direction is sighted, then the lesson plan should be put aside and a new one created in its place.

The writing teacher must accept the fact that change is the only constant in the writing course. The writing course should never be repetitious and monotonous, for the writing teacher should always encourage his students to find their own way of teaching themselves writing. If he gives them the chance, his students by their own failures and their own successes will teach him how to teach writing.

25 A Smorgasbord of Lesson Plans

The lesson plan, as we have seen, should come out of the teacher's own background and interest, the conditions of the school, and the student's need. Here are some lesson plans which may give the beginning composition teacher a point of departure. It cannot be emphasized too strongly that the plans given below are tentative and experimental. Only an individual teacher in his particular classroom can make an intelligent plan, and he must be willing to change it when he dsicovers what works and what does not work with his individual students. These are merely suggestions which may give a teacher some ideas for designing his own lesson plan.

The first lesson plan is a year-long, thirty-week course with six five-week units which can be used for both the general and the college prep student.

Assumptions The class size will be twenty students, instructors will teach no more than four sections of the courses.

Students will be in their junior year, but they need not be college bound.

The course will last for a full year, but it could be taught the second half of the junior year and the first half of the senior year.

The course will take the place of the regular English course. It will not be taught in addition to the regular course.

There will be no text, although reading materials will be used with several of the units.

The teacher will have a typist—perhaps a student—who can copy student papers on Thursday and reproduce them for distribution to the class on Friday.

The teacher will write many of the assignments with the students. The students will write more papers than the teacher can correct. The teacher will not be expected to correct each assignment carefully. The students, administration, and the parents will be informed of this policy.

There will be no grades on individual papers. The teacher will review the student's file and assign a letter grade at the end of each marking period. There will be no objective examinations.

The class will meet for lecture and discussion on Monday. The Tuesday, Wednesday, and Thursday meetings will be workshops, during which the teacher can hold a discussion or conduct individual conferences. Friday will be publication day. Students will discuss the papers that they and their teacher have written.

Goals The student will learn to write non-fiction prose with clarity and vigor by following the steps practiced by the professional writer.

Methods The student will write about the subjects he knows and feels strongly about. He will write frequently and rewrite and rewrite and rewrite.

Materials The text in the course will be the student's own papers, published and criticized each Friday. Students will also read some examples of good prose.

Unit One

Objectives To emphasize the primary importance of subject matter, the students in the writing course will *not* be allowed to write papers during the first unit. The student will be shown that the writer should not write until he has something to say.

Assignments	*Materials*
(In every case students will be encouraged to choose their own subject matter and to write from their own experience.) Students will choose an area of the world which interests them and with which they are intimately familiar.	(Papers are to be published each Friday. This will be repeated each week.)

	Assignments	*Materials*
First Week	Teacher will discuss how to see. Students will pass in twenty-five visual specifics about the place they have chosen. Lists will be passed in Tuesday, Wednesday, and Thursday.	Books on seeing, such as *The Family of Man* and *Stop, Look and Write!*
Second Week	Teacher will continue discussion of the importance of concrete detail. Students will pass in fifty visual specifics Tuesday, Wednesday, and Thursday.	
Third Week	Students will pass in twenty-five concrete details using a different sense each day. Monday, hearing; Tuesday, touch; Wednesday, taste; Thursday, smell.	Tony Schwartz record, "Sound of My City," Folkways.
Fourth Week	Students will be given a rather complicated article from which they will extract a dozen facts for a list to be passed in on Wednesday, and a dozen quotations to be passed in on Thursday.	Article from the Sunday *New York Times* Magazine.
Fifth Week	Students will group concrete details from the lists they made during the first three weeks, trying to discover patterns which might produce an article.	

Unit Two

Objectives To learn how to write a simple paragraph effectively, to realize the choices which face the craftsman, to develop a sense of subject and structure.

	Assignments	*Materials*
First Week	Students will pass in each day a descriptive paragraph of the same subject from different points of view.	*E. B. White Reader,* edited by Watt and Bradford, Harper and Row.

	Assignments	*Materials*
Second Week	Students will pass in an argumentative paragraph each day, in which the emphasis is changed.	
Third Week	Students will write the same paragraph five times, changing the tone.	*Mrs. Bridge* by Evan S. Connell, Jr., Viking Press (Compass paperback).
Fourth Week	Students will write a pargraph each day for a different purpose: Monday, to define; Tuesday, to give direction; Wednesday, to inform; Thursday, to persuade; Friday, to amuse.	
Fifth Week	Students will write an opening paragraph on the same subject for five different audiences or publications. Monday, *The New York Times*; Tuesday, *Harper's;* Wednesday, *Mad;* Thursday, *The New Yorker;* Friday, the *Ladies Home Journal.*	Examples of good leads such as the one included in Section 18.

Unit Three

Objectives To learn to use a craftsman's choices to develop an extensive piece of writing, to go through the steps followed by the professional writer, to examine the writer's problems in one genre, such as biography or autobiography.

	Assignments	*Materials*
First Week	Monday, the teacher will discuss the importance of the lead and the outline. Students will choose a subject which can be used in the genre being studied. Thursday, the students will pass in a title, lead and outline of their articles.	Readings from library books on biography listed in the Bibliography. Reading will continue through the unit's five weeks.
Second Week	Monday, the teacher will discuss the first draft. Thursday, the students will pass in a 750-word first draft.	

	Assignments	*Materials*
Third Week	The teacher will discuss the importance of rewriting and rethinking. Each student will pass in a radically rewritten version of his article.	
Fourth Week	The teacher will discuss the importance of rewriting and editing. Students will pass in an edited, polished version of the 750-word article.	
Fifth Week	The class and the teacher will work together to cut each published article from 750 to 250 words.	

Unit Four

Objectives To develop a critical attitude in the student toward his own work. To learn the techniques of researching material, organizing it into a draft, rewriting and editing it.

	Assignments	*Materials*
	The class will choose a subject which they can research and rewrite for five weeks, for example, "A Teen-ager's Week-end." All the articles in this unit will be between 400 and 500 words.	Students will choose an author, such as George Orwell, and begin to read in preparation for the next unit.
First through Fifth Week	The class will divide into two groups of four. One member of the group will serve as a reporter and will pass in a file of specifics on Monday. The next person in the group will write a draft from that file for Tuesday morning. The third person will rewrite that for Wednesday morning. The fourth person will edit it for Thursday morning. On Friday the class will discuss the published reports, and they will shift assignments for the next week. At the end of the unit each student will have served as reporter, writer, rewrite man, and editor. The fifth week the members will choose roles for a final competition.	

Unit Five

Objectives To study a writer as an apprentice watches his master. What are his problems? What are his solutions?

	Assignments	*Materials*
First Week	Students will pass in a paragraph imitating the style of the author each day.	Continued readings in the author chosen.
Second Week	Each member of the class will write a 300- to 500-word essay showing the problems the writer faced in his work.	
Third Week	A practicing writer will visit the class each day. Monday, a lawyer who writes briefs; Tuesday, a businessman who writes sales letters; Wednesday, a newspaperman; Thursday, a policeman who writes up reports of crimes; Friday, an engineer who writes technical reports. (These may be spread out during the year.)	
Fourth Week	Each student will write a paper showing how the writer being studied solves some of the problems defined in the paper written during the second week.	
Fifth Week	Each student will write a 500-word critical evaluation of the writer who has been studied.	

Unit Six

Objectives To reinforce what the student has learned by making him state and demonstrate what he has learned about writing. To evaluate and improve the course.

Assignments	*Materials*
Students will be asked to develop a five-page pamphlet telling next year's students what they ought to know about composition.	In some special cases, copies of this book.

	Assignments	*Materials*
First Week	Each student will develop a list of specific facts which should be included in the final pamphlet.	
Second Week	Each student will turn in at least one proposed lead and outline for the final pamphlet.	
Third Week	Each student will draft the pamphlet.	
Fourth Week	Each student will rewrite a draft written by a classmate.	
Fifth Week	The class will edit the final pamphlet so that the best ones can be reproduced and distributed to next year's class.	

A variation on that 30-week course with six-week units might be constructed in the following manner.

Unit I Students will write daily paragraphs observing the world about them. For the first two weeks they will concentrate on paragraphs of physical description of their world; the following two weeks, paragraphs on the people in their world; and the last week, they will concentrate on the ideas in their world.

Unit II The students will research another culture; for example, by using Oscar Lewis' books, sociological texts, books on foreign lands, or social histories of other times. Again they will repeat the same pattern of two weeks of daily paragraphs on the places in that world, two weeks of paragraphs on the persons in that world, and a final week on the ideas in that world.

Unit III They will write an evaluation of the two worlds which they have described. The evaluation will define the differences between the two worlds and come to a conclusion. The first week the students will write five leads for this particular essay. The second week they will work on a lead and an outline which are acceptable to the teacher. The third week they will turn in a first draft. And the fourth week the draft will be subjected to the class, and each student will write three critical evaluations of five other student drafts. The fifth week they will turn in a final 750-word paper.

Unit IV The students will write a brief biography. During the first week they will present written proposals for a subject, and the second week a written research report. The third week they will write three alternative leads and outlines, the fourth week a draft, and in the fifth week a rewrite of the draft.

Unit V Students will write an article on persuasion. In the first week they will define their thesis; in the second week write research reports; the third week three alternate leads and outlines; the fourth week a draft; the fifth week a rewrite.

Unit VI In the last five weeks of the course they will have absolutely free choice of subject and genre, the only restrictions being that they pass in five pages a week, and that they have a completed piece of work at the end of the five weeks.

It is obvious that such a lesson plan will depend greatly on the background and the skill of the teacher. The lesson plan cannot be a substitute for a good teacher, or for good students, but it is a map of the country to be explored, and as such is valuable.

In creating lesson plans the teacher should keep in mind that the main difference between the advanced student and the slow student, between the twelfth-grader and the seventh-grader, is not in what is to be taught but how it is to be taught. The slower and the more elementary the student, the more important it is that the teacher take time to convince the student he has something to say. In other words, the material should generally be much more autobiographical, and the timing of the course will change. The slower student will need more time to cover the same material; you will have to spend more time on paragraphs, more time on trying to get the student to write vigorously and simply on a subject which interests him. The emphasis on pre-writing will always increase with the number of problems the student has.

It is also important that the material be more lively and varied with the slower student. This student has had an unsuccessful experience with English, does not usually see why he should be writing, or, if he sees why he should be writing, thinks he is not capable of it. The more difficult the teaching task, the more the teacher is called upon to produce a variety of interesting materials which come out of his own reading, studies and experience.

Here are two lesson plans for basic half-year composition courses. I have taught both these courses in college to freshmen and to graduate students. In general, the students are people who have difficulty with writing and need additional training. It is a remedial course at a very advanced level. It would be particularly appropriate for half of a freshman year, for use in a junior or community college, and it could easily be adapted to high school and junior high school. The course is built on the assumption of two meetings a week, and it is supported by a number of materials which the teacher reproduces and distributes to the class. There also is a minimum of one conference a week with each student. If I use a reader or a book on writing, I may give the student a list at the beginning of the course which shows how particular essays relate to the problem that is being dealt with that week. Students are told they may depart from the writing assignment at any time, provided they have checked with me in advance and I have approved their substitute project.

Class Meeting		Assignment	Topic for Discussion
1	Monday		Introduction to the course.
2	Tuesday	A 250-word autobiography.	Discussion of the problems of autobiography.
3	Wednesday	Fifty specifics describing a place.	How to see.
4	Thursday	Fifty specifics describing a person.	
5	Friday	Fifty specifics defining an idea.	Finding a subject.
6	Monday	A paragraph describing a place.	Critical analysis of Kenneth Andler's "Surveyor in the Woods."
7	Tuesday	A paragraph describing a person.	
8	Wednesday	A paragraph describing a person in a place.	
9	Thursday	A paragraph describing a process.	
10	Friday	A paragraph defining an idea.	The specific, the concrete detail; the informed opinion.
11	Monday	Write a paragraph about a subject of your own choosing.	Active verbs, clichés, jargon.
12	Tuesday	Rewrite the same paragraph changing the choice of words.	
13	Wednesday	Rewrite the same paragraph changing the choice of words.	
14	Thursday	Rewrite the same paragraph changing the choice of words.	
15	Friday	Rewrite the same paragraph changing the choice of words.	Examination of what this sort of editing has done to various student paragraphs.
16	Monday	Write a paragraph on a subject of your own choosing.	The paragraph—coherence, unity and emphasis.

Class Meeting		*Assignment*	*Topic for Discussion*
17	Tuesday	Rewrite the same paragraph changing the structure.	
18	Wednesday	Rewrite the same paragraph changing the structure.	
19	Thursday	Rewrite the same paragraph changing the structure.	
20	Friday	Rewrite the same paragraph changing the structure.	
21	Monday	Write a paragraph of your own choosing.	The sentence, the phrase, the word; metaphor.
22	Tuesday	Rewrite the same paragraph changing the emphasis.	
23	Wednesday	Rewrite the same paragraph changing the emphasis.	
24	Thursday	Rewrite the same paragraph changing the emphasis.	
25	Friday	Rewrite the same paragraph changing the emphasis.	Analysis of a student's paper.
26	Monday	Write a paragraph of your own choosing.	Tone; the sound of words; connotation and denotation; parallel construction.
27	Tuesday	Rewrite the paragraph changing the tone.	
28	Wednesday	Rewrite the paragraph changing the tone.	
29	Thursday	Rewrite the paragraph changing the tone.	
30	Friday	Rewrite the paragraph changing the tone.	
31	Monday	Write a lead paragraph and an outline for an article on a subject of your own choice.	Leads, outlines.

Class Meeting		Assignment	Topic for Discussion
32	Tuesday	New lead for same piece.	
33	Wednesday	New lead for same piece.	
34	Thursday	New lead for same piece.	
35	Friday	New lead for same piece.	

(From now on, a paper will be due each week. Class meetings will be held but will rise out of the problems of the students and their writing.)

36	Monday	First draft of 750-word article.	
41	Monday	Second draft of 750-word article.	
46	Monday	Third draft of 750-word article.	
51	Monday	Lead and outline of 1500-word article.	
56	Monday	First draft of 1500-word article.	
61	Monday	Second draft of 1500-word article.	
66	Monday	Final draft of 1500-word article.	

The experienced writing teacher knows that there are few things which he must teach, and he will have a variety of ways of teaching them. The Yale theme-a-day course, which has been successful for generations, has been interestingly described by Richard Sewall and Calvin Trillin.[4] As Mr. Sewall says, "The courses uses no books, no syllabi, no examinations. The heart of the matter is the blank page which the student must face every evening, Sunday through Thursday." He makes the point that many different instructors have approached the course differently within this design, but in general there are a number of slogans which have become traditional:

Individualize by specific detail.

Vivify by range of appeal.

Clarify by point of view.

Use the indirect method.

Characterize by speech and gesture.

Use words for connotation.

Unify by a single impression.

[4] Richard B. Sewall, "The Content of Student Writing," *Essays on the Teaching of English,* eds. Edward J. Gordon and Edward S. Noyes (New York: Appleton-Century-Crofts, 1960); Calvin Trillin, "Onward and Upward with the Arts—No Telling, No Summing Up," *The New Yorker,* June 11, 1966.

My own list of slogans for the effective writer might be as follows:

Focus on your subject.

Seek specifics.

Order disorder.

Plan before you write.

Build a sturdy structure.

Document your case.

Speak in the reader's language.

Develop ideas into thoughts.

Create a dominant impression.

Get black on white.

Speak in your own voice.

Write honestly.

Use active verbs.

Vary sentence structure.

Write in paragraphs.

Sharpen your lead.

Search for the right word.

Show, don't tell.

Control your metaphors.

Cut meaningless words.

Revise until the reader will understand.

Listen to the sound of your words.

Polish line by line.

Here is another variation of the basic half-year course. Students write thirty one-page papers on subjects of their own choice, which are passed in on the first thirty class days. During the time the students are writing daily papers, the following topics are discussed at class meetings.

1 The art of seeing; a sense of the specific.

2 Finding a subject; the difference between an idea and a thought.

3 Informed opinion; point of view.

4 The importance of pre-writing.

5 A critical analysis of biographical, autobiographical, expository and persuasive articles.

6 Discovery by writing; the uncritical first draft.

7 Structure of the paragraph; coherence, unity, emphasis.

8 Sentence variety; parallelism; the passive voice; metaphor.

9 Clichés; jargon.

10 Show, don't tell; implication.

11 Techniques of rewriting.

12 Techniques of editing.

13 Leads and outlines, endings, transitions.

14 Creativity and discipline.

It is pointed out that a revision of a paper counts as a new paper, but a revision means a radical rewriting. During that part of the course students will have individual conferences with the instructor. During the rest of the course students will write a 1500-word essay—an informed opinion on a limited subject. The class will be broken down into small groups of four people. During the first week six alternate leads and an outline of the essay will be due; the next week a first draft; the following week a second draft; the third week a final draft. Each of these drafts will be typed with four carbons. The instructor will meet with tutorial groups and read one student's essay at a time before the other members of the group. This is silent reading and open verbal discussion.

Here is a writing unit which can be completed in a single week. Students should write about a person about whom they feel strongly and with whom they are familiar.

Monday—List twenty-five specific details which reveal the person.

Tuesday—Write a lead sentence which will give both you and the reader control over the piece. It should both inform and entice. Then make an informal outline of the page-long description.

Wednesday—Write a page-long description of the person which makes the reader see him.

Thursday—Write a page-long incident which reveals the person in action.

Friday—Write a page-long essay about the person telling the reader what is significant about this type of person.

Special writing courses will be directed towards the problems that the students will face. A course in journalism should emphasize leads, with the students rewriting leads from newspapers under strict limitations of time and space. A secretarial writing course will emphasize that the secretary is the ghost-writer for the boss, and will convince her she can do the job of rewriting that is going to be one of her chores.

Advanced students in elective or special writing courses can attempt poetry and fiction, but they may learn more if they try longer pieces of nonfiction. One pattern I have found valuable is to have students write two 2500-word articles. Article A is a piece of biography or autobiography;

article B is a piece of exposition or persuasion. The students leapfrog these articles. Revisions of article A, for example, are due on weeks three, five, seven and so on and article B is due on four, six, eight, and so on. This gives the student more of a chance to think about and research and work over an article. And with an advanced class the discussions with the class can be more sophisticated.

A variation is to group all of the lectures and discussions at the beginning of the course, to have very intensive meetings for a week, or two, or three, in which I cover all the problems the students will face, supporting each problem with a dittoed example and model. At the end of that period of the course the students write in a form of independent study. There are no class meetings, just daily workshop sessions and conferences.

The lesson plan is merely a map. It establishes a destination and a means of getting there. It does not limit the student's content, although it may limit his genre. He should try a variety of types of writing, and he should work to different lengths. Every course outline, however, must be modified according to the limitations of the teacher, his students and the writing environment.

26 Writing in the Regular English Course

Each student should, at one time or another, take a specialized writing course and focus all of his efforts on writing under the direction of a teacher who is able to concentrate *his* efforts on teaching writing. Every English course, however, should teach writing.

The teacher who has to teach language, literature, and composition simultaneously may set aside certain days for composition. He may, for example, discuss a particular problem in writing on Monday and assign a series of papers to be completed by Friday, when the class will have a workshop session. The heavier the teacher's load and the more contradictory the demands on his time, the more important it becomes to find ways of helping the student to teach himself to write through frequent writing, self-evaluation and rewriting.

The important thing is that the teacher adapt the essential process of writing as practiced by the professional writer to the other matters he is teaching in the English course. In other words, the writing done in a unit emphasizing the study of language, literature or the humanities should not run counter to what the student has been taught in the writing course. The student must have time to find a subject on which he can become informed; he must also have time to write drafts, then rewrite and edit them.

When the student is studying language he ought to study it as a user of language. The language teacher should use the student's desire to communicate to motivate him to learn to use language more effectively. He should not attack language problems in dull work-book sentences, but identify and solve language problems in his own writing.

The teacher may coordinate the study of literature and the study of writing by taking the student into the process which produced literature. The student should be shown the writer's workshop by viewing drafts of a work which has been judged literature, by reading the writer's journals and letters, by studying the writer's biographies and critical studies. There are books listed in the Bibliography which will help the teacher prepare such units. For example, the student will gain insight into the writing process if, as he studies a poem by Dylan Thomas, he is shown pertinent material from Thomas' notebooks and his letters.

When the student writes about literature he must be given time to do research, digging out specifics from the text to document his critical opinions, and then given time to organize them into a coherent, well-built paper, draft by draft. The student should follow the same process in writing critical studies that he follows in writing an effective paper in any field. He must understand writing is thinking, and that content and form are inevitably intertwined.

The English teacher who teaches a humanities course should be introducing his students to the world of ideas. The students ought to be encouraged to write down their own ideas in a careful, disciplined manner. The humanities course should be an essay-writing course in which the students have the time to develop opinions of their own and to document these ideas with materials discovered in the course.

The English teacher will teach writing in the regular English course if he and his students follow the priorities in writing developed in the following checklist.

The Student Should Remember:	*The Teacher Should Remember:*
Before You Write Do you have a subject you want to communicate? Do you have the specific information your reader needs to know? Do you see a pattern in those details which makes sense?	Do not allow the student to write until he has something to say. But remember some students will have to plunge in and write to discover what they have to say.
When You Write Your First Draft Do you know your audience? Have you written a beginning which will make your reader turn the page? Does one paragraph fit into another paragraph in a logical order? Do you have a consistent point of view? Do you have an appropriate tone? Do you have a subject which fits the limitations of the form you have chosen? Should you change your subject? Should you change your form?	Allow the student to explore and define his subject. The emphasis of your criticisms at this stage should be on what he has to say and the form he is using to say it.

The Student Should Remember:	*The Teacher Should Remember:*
When You Rewrite Do you have a structure that stands up to a critical reader? Does everything belong in the piece? Does each part of the piece fit into the next part? Do the parts add up to the conclusion you want to emphasize? Are you being honest? Is your conclusion different from what you expected? Should you change your subject? Should you change your structure?	Do not criticize details yet. The writer must find a sturdy structure, a form that works before he can pay attention to details.
When You Edit Does each word do its job? Does every sentence advance the meaning of the paragraph? Does every paragraph emphasize the right idea? Does the entire piece communicate what you have to say with clarity and grace?	Now focus on every word, on each comma, on all the details, showing the student who has something to say how he can say it most effectively.
When You Are Through Do you have to start over again? Do you see what you should have seen before you started to write? Should you have chosen a different subject? Should you have picked a more effective form? Should you have edited more carefully so that your writing would be more vigorous and your communication more effective? Do you have to start over again?	Give the student a chance to start over again, to do one job well. He will learn only after he has failed and seen his failures. He should have a chance to develop the only quality shared by all writers—stubbornness.

They were neither citadels nor churches; ~~they~~ ~~were~~ frankly & {admirably / beautifully} office buildings.

BABBITT

~~They rose neither from churches nor citadels; they were office buildings~~

CHAPTER I

Roman small cap. — I

The towers [of Zenith] ~~of a new city~~ aspired above the [early] morning mist; [austere] ~~sheer~~ towers of steel ~~and~~ [and] cement ~~and~~ ~~silvery~~ limestone, sturdy as cliffs, [and] [shafts of silver delicate as silver rods.] ~~and delicate as birch-trees.~~ They were the promise of strange futures in ~~this~~ American city called Zenith.

The mist ~~blessedly~~ ~~obscured~~ ~~the hunched and~~ [took pity on the] fretted [structures] ~~buildings~~ of earlier generations: the Post Office with its shingle-tortured man- ~~sard and arches that supported nothing; houses of minarets and os-~~ ~~tentatiously adorned lightning-rods;~~ [sard, the red brick minarets of hulking old houses,] factories with stingy and sooted windows, ~~dreadful~~ wooden tenements colored like mud. ~~These blotches~~ ~~still made up most of the city, but the good~~ [Most of Zenith was still made up of such grotesqueries, but the] clean towers were ~~[illegible]~~ thrusting them from the business center, and on the farther hills were shining new houses, homes -- they seemed -- for laughter and tranquility.

Over a cement bridge ~~like carven ivory~~ slipped a limousine ~~with of sleek sure lines and soundless engine.~~ [of long sleek hood & noiseless engine.] [These] ~~The~~ four people in evening clothes were returning from an all-night rehearsal of a ~~[illegible]~~ Little Theater play, ~~[illegible]~~ an artistic adventure ~~considerably~~ illuminated by champagne. —

Five The Techniques of Teaching Writing

The skillful teacher of writing will develop his own methods out of his own knowledge, his own personality and his own experience. The experienced skill teacher, who is divorced from content in the usual sense, constantly seeks new ways of identifying and solving writing problems. Few writing teachers will have students who have not heard the basic rules of writing; in fact, they have heard them over and over again to the point of boredom, and beyond. Yet the student is not able to practice these rules. Faced with this problem, the teacher who is trying to make the student discover the principles of good writing for himself will search for techniques, methods, tricks and gimmicks which will make it possible for him to reach a wide range of individual students.

27 How to Teach the Student to Teach Himself

The writing teacher should remember all of the time that he is not his students' ultimate evaluator, editor, critic, or judge; his students will write, according to their own abilities, ambitions and opportunities, for other people. They are the ones who will decide if the student is an effective writer.

It is too easy to evaluate a piece of writing, to say this is good and that is bad. Too many teachers fall into the pattern of a cold civil servant who passes this piece of work and fails to pass that one. We should have standards, and, of course, students must measure up to standards if they are to do their jobs, in school and beyond. The job of the teacher is not to say that the student is writing poorly, but to say why he is writing poorly and to provide an answer which will work for him.

The diagnostician will look at each paper and at the preparation and the background of the student who wrote it, to spot exactly what is wrong and to discover the reason for it, so that the answer may be provided which will attack the root of the problem. One student may have absolutely no knowledge of the rules of grammar; he may not understand the need for the conventions through which we speak to each other. But another student may appear to have the same problem—a fatal case of syntaxcoma, or a total paralysis of the brain—because he is following rigidly all the contradictory grammatical rules he has learned in his years of school. I had a student who wrote miserably until I discovered that she had an English teacher aunt who corrected everything. Once the student wrote for herself her "D's" turned into high "B's." Many times the diagnostician in conference will realize that the student speaks the same way he writes, running words

Sinclair Lewis, **Babbitt.** From the Collection of American Literature, Yale University Library.

together, speaking before he has listened, spewing out syllables before he has decided what he wants to say. This student may be forced to take time with his writing, to write less than other students and spend more time organizing it, deciding in what direction he wants to go.

With experience, the teacher should be able to look at a paper or a series of papers and see beyond the superficial symptom of bad writing. He will spot a pattern which can be treated, and many times he will find that a student has one problem which accounts for almost all of his mistakes. Then that problem can be attacked with a series of treatments. The student may be asked to imitate models, a device that worked well with a similar student last year. It may not take in this case. The diagnostician takes another look, prescribes another treatment for the same problem, and a third, and a fourth, until he finds a way of curing that student's central problem.

When the student is told that twenty or thirty things are wrong with his paper he is overwhelmed. The same thing is true of the teacher. It is easy to be discouraged when you are faced with students who make multiple errors in writing, who have twenty-three separate, identifiable problems in a single page. The case seems hopeless, but the expert diagnostician will reduce most of those problems to one or two central ailments, and then he will treat the most serious one first. By establishing priority he will gain control over his course. He will not have to spend hours on each paper written by the student; he will look quickly at the paper to see if that one central problem is being solved. If it is, then he can identify another problem; if it isn't, he prescribes a new treatment or a repeated treatment. The time he spends on papers and with students will be cut down radically. Most papers do not require more than a quick reading, and most conferences require no more than a quick confrontation once a diagnosis has been made and until the problem is cured.

The teacher who has seen himself as a diagnostician will find he has time to treat many more patients with far less effort and a great deal more effectiveness. It may even be that the average class load of the English teacher will not be impossible if he does not try to treat every symptom as equally serious, but instead uses his intelligence and his experience to identify the key problems of each student and to treat them. The writing teacher's central skill is the ability to diagnose his students' writing problems.

The ultimate test of the skill of the teacher as a diagnostician comes when he has trained his student to be his own diagnostician. Before the teacher gives his own diagnosis, he should ask the student to volunteer a description of his own writing problems and listen to the student's answer. The student may know his own problems better than the teacher ever can, and the teacher should be quite willing to assist the student in solving the problems he sees in his own writing.

One famous advertising executive gave his staff an assignment and when they passed it in he took it home and brought it back the next morning. He called the authors into his office, placed the unmarked presentation before them and said, "Is that the best you can do?"

The people gave excuses and said they didn't have the time, or they didn't have enough information, but of course they could do better. Then he gave the presentation back to them. This pattern was repeated until finally they said, Yes, that was the best they could do. Then he said, "All right, now I will read it."

The writing teacher can learn from this. When the student is well into the writing course he should be presented with his own papers for revision, without any comment by the teacher. He will not have the writing teacher at his side throughout his career to point out the problems which need to be solved on a page. He must be able to read his own writing with a cold, critical eye and to diagnose his own problems, the central problem which has to be solved in a revision. If the paper is poorly organized, he should see it. If he doesn't have the information to support his argument, he should see it. If he has fallen into this writer's bad habit of using "quite" too frequently, he should be able to recognize it himself.

The responsible teacher weans his students. He explains to his students that they cannot continue to be dependent on him as an editor or an audience. The student may have to write for the teacher at first, but soon the student must write for a broader and more varied audience. A natural way to learn how to reach a larger audience is by writing for groups within the classroom.

I had resisted the use of small sections within a writing course because I had suffered through too many windy discussion sessions. I backed into using small groups through a series of accidents, but I am now convinced, by my own experience, of their value.

Small group teaching will be effective, however, only if the students are prepared to accept responsibility for their own education. Before a writing class is divided into small units, the teacher and the students must accept the reasons for this method of instruction. The peer group allows the students to reach an audience other than the English teacher, and the students must know that as writers, in school and outside of school, they have to be able to reach many different people in different disciplines. The students should realize they may be able to help each other better than the teacher can help them, for they are facing comparable problems at a similar stage of development. The students should also be convinced that through working on classmates' papers they will understand the professional writer's problem of choice, because the other class members will demonstrate in their own papers, as well as in their criticisms, that there are many appropriate ways of saying the same thing.

Students should also know that by attempting to help others they will develop the vital ability to edit, to diagnose and solve writing problems. As they develop this ability on other papers they will begin to develop it on their own. Finally, the teacher should recognize that many students who have not been motivated by the teacher will begin to write—and re-write—when they hear their peers developing their own voices.

A class should not be allowed to break into small sections until it understands the reasons for this method of instruction. And the teacher should not proceed until he has created the appropriate environment. The elements in this environment include the students' belief that writing is important—that they need to be able to write to get through school, to succeed in a job, or even to fulfill themselves. Pupils should be convinced by classroom demonstration and through individual conference that criticism and revision are necessary—and constructive—parts of the process of writing. The student writers should also know they have the primary responsibility to teach themselves to write and that they are capable, through re-evaluation and revision of their papers, of solving their own writing problems.

Many students, as well as many teachers, may have had bitter experience with small groups where well-meaning but not well-trained teachers have encouraged them to work in a sort of buzz session anarchy with bull sessions replacing constructive discussion. The students must understand that the writing small group has a clear, achievable task. Each person comes to the writing group with two commitments. One, he exposes his own writing—which he has written as well as he can—to the other individuals in the group so they can help him make it a better piece of writing. Two, he has a responsibility to help the other participants improve their writing. Each group has a common goal—to improve the writing of its members by evaluation time at the end of the course.

The group must always be aware that an important resource is nearby. The teacher may even, at times, sit in with the group. I have found it more valuable to be separate from the groups but clearly available for individual conferences. I am also on hand, willing to joke with a group or join it, if I'm needed. Students should feel free to detach themselves for conferences. The groups, as well, should feel free to consult the teacher as a group on a writing or editing problem.

It is important for the teacher to have alternative activities in mind for students who are not ready to work with others. Students should be encouraged but not driven to work in teams.

I have found that five students is the most efficient size for a writing group. The number is large enough so that it can still function when a member is sick, unprepared, or having an individual conference. And five is small enough so that several pieces of writing can be read and discussed at each session.

Most students can choose their own groups, but I prefer to select the members to break up cliques of students who are too involved with each other outside of class to give or accept criticism openly. I try to put people together who face similar writing problems.

The members of the group should have copies of the papers to read and mark up. There are many methods of providing individual copies but with the five-man group only one extra copy is absolutely necessary. The person who has written the paper does not need a copy, and two other participants can read the original while the other two read the copy. It is important that everyone be able to read the paper together and discuss it as it is before their eyes.

It may be helpful for the writing teacher to have tables around which the students can meet. My classes meet around small tables, and I find it is quite easy to deal with them as a class when a lecture or discussion is in order. I feel free to interrupt the discussions to present a problem or a solution to the class, and I have found that the groups respond well to me when I play this role. They are able to sense the group reaction, and when I ask for questions at the end of a class session I get freer and more pointed questioning because the group is able to sense quickly if it has understood what I have said.

The teacher who is going to use small groups must be prepared for some student resentment at first. Students as well as teachers have been confused into believing that learning is a passive process. Some students (and perhaps some supervisors and parents) will feel that the teacher is not teaching unless he stands before a congregation of students and preaches. The teacher must make an effort to convince everyone involved that the student has responsibility to teach himself.

Most teachers using small group teaching will also have personal problems of guilt, for they have been brought up in the same system and feel worthless if they are not actively doing something—for example, talking—to all the students. Hospitals have nurses who resent the recovery of their patients, and most of us enjoy having our students dependent on us. We resent it when we find they can teach themselves, often more efficiently than we can teach them. We must satisfy our ego, and relieve our guilt, by understanding our proper role as teachers. It is not the job of the teacher to be doing something to the students; it is the job of the teacher to create an environment in which the student can learn.

The teacher's role in small group instruction is to establish a climate of student opinion in which these apprentice writers realize that they have a job which needs doing and that it is a job which they can do together. The teacher's next responsibility is to be available as a resource to help solve writing problems which arise in class discussion, small group participation, and individual conference.

When I sit in the classroom reading or writing, planning or doing paper work while my students teach themselves in small groups, I feel lonely, more than a little bit left out. I have to remind myself that my first responsibility as a teacher is to prepare my students so that they can function when I am not there. Their independence from me should not be cause for guilt, but for pride.

When the teacher can stop teaching, can stand back and see his students teaching themselves, then he has succeeded. His ambition should be to teach as little as possible, and eventually not to teach at all. He is most successful when the students have become their own teachers.

28 How to Create Assignments

The most effective assignment encourages the student to have an informed opinion he can develop and document within reasonable limitations.

The writer first must be armed with information. It may be academic information—the influence of the concept of the great chain of being on English literature—or autobiographical information—how to buy a good second-hand motorcycle. But the writer must have information so that he can have an authoritative opinion of and prove it to the reader. The teacher, out of his knowledge of the student, may, if absolutely necessary, propose an area of investigation, but he should never tell the student what to say.

When a student needs an assignment the teacher should say, "What do you want to say? What are you interested in writing about? What do you care about?" If the student says he has nothing to say, then the teacher may point out that he suffers from an extremely serious case of empty-headedness and that he can't believe that the student really sees nothing, hears nothing, and cares about nothing. If he does, he's a member of the living dead, and although we have a great number of the living dead in society, certainly the student should not want to join that category.

The student must be encouraged to discover his own subjects by exploring the areas in which he is interested, and then to take a position which he can defend by factual, authoritative material.

The student should not be allowed merely to repeat the rhetorical forms which he has successfully exploited in the past. Most students will probably learn best in the beginning through description, but they cannot always write description. It is perfectly appropriate for the student to be forced to write in a form which will help him learn to write better, and the form usually will be interesting to him, or the challenges of form at least will be, if the content is his own. Instead of writing about how to ride a motorcycle, he may write a proposal for a new motorcycle law, a letter to the editor answering an editorial against motorcycle riders, a definition of a good motorcyclist, an argument for a new motorcycle design. He may write a number of rules for motorcycle riders or the opening paragraph of an article on motorcycles in six different publications.

The assignment should force him to write just a bit beyond himself. He should always be reaching for an attainable goal. His writing should have more form, clarity, or grace than that which comes easily to him. He should be stretching his intellectual muscles, moving forward so that he says more and says it more effectively than is normal for him.

We learn to write by writing, and so the student should write frequently; a paper a week in most courses should be an absolute minimum. Several papers a week, or a paper a day, may make it easier for the student to write and may make it possible for him to accumulate the experience in writing which is necessary if he is to solve other writing problems. Of course, every revision is another assignment. He will have to write different ways with different forms to find the way to say what he wants to say most effectively. Most students will enter into the game of craft when they have a subject which interests them and will try to make clear in frequent revisions what they have to say to the reader.

Most assignments in school must be short. It must be possible for the student to finish the assignment within the deadline while doing his other homework. This is one reason he should have writing time in class. A number of his assignments may quite arbitrarily be started and completed within the class period. It is easy to document from the interviews and writings of writers that all writers have had to learn to discipline themselves to write not just when they feel in the mood, but when they have the opportunity, on a regular schedule.

There is another reason that most assignments must be short: the teacher must be able to read them. In fact, most assignments should be read by the teacher with the student during a brief conference. It should be easy for the teacher to scan a page and see if the student has solved the problem which has been diagnosed as that student's problem. Eventually the student may be asked to put together all that he has learned in a lengthy paper. But a novel is merely a series of paragraphs, and the student can learn most of what he has to know about writing in the short paper. The student will learn more by a series of frequent assignments, and the teacher will be able to teach more when he handles a series of short papers.

The good assignment is usually short, offers the writer a chance to solve a writing problem which is bothering him and is on a subject which is important to the writer.

29 How to Not Correct Papers

Not correcting papers may be the hardest thing for a writing teacher to do. The errors are there and so is the virtuous feeling of a job well done as the mistakes are speared on the page. The more mistakes, the more satisfaction. But if the writing teacher follows this pattern he is as corrupt as the mother who keeps her son a child.

The English teacher may have as much trouble not correcting papers as a drunk not taking a drink. It's so easy to slash through a student's paper, so fulfilling, so much fun. It does fine things for the teacher, but little for the student.

Instead of defacing the page, the effective teacher points out the main problem in the paper to the student so he can correct his own paper by re-searching, re-thinking, re-designing, re-writing or re-editing it.

A paper may be effectively corrected in conference when the teacher makes a statement to the student about the paper, or underlines a repeated writing problem in red. Even this problem does not need to be identified each time it appears in the paper. The teacher should say to the student, "These are four vague, generalized statements which mean nothing to the reader. You are giving a blank check to the reader and expecting him to fill it in. Now there are eight or ten other vague statements on this one page. It's not my job to identify them; it's your job to find them and revise this paper so that it does not have one vague, generalized statement in it."

That paper has been corrected. There may have been other problems in the paper—spelling and syntax, logic—but at this time for this student the teacher felt that he must solve the problem of making vague, meaningless statements.

The teacher who is going to cut down the number of marks on the paper will have to stop measuring his own accomplishments by the amount of red on the page. He may also have to educate his colleagues, his supervisors, and the parents. This can be done if he explains that he is trying to deal with one problem at a time. It may be helpful for the teacher to reproduce a written paragraph which explains that the students' papers will have fewer comments on them because they are writing more frequently and are attempting to solve one problem at a time. If he creates, in writing, his own rationale for teaching writing this way, he will find his thinking on the subject is clear, and that the student, the parent, the supervisor, and he, himself, will have a better idea of what he is trying to do in correcting a paper.

There is, however, not just this one way to correct a paper. The time will come when a teacher has to identify a number of problems to show the student that he cannot get away with sloppiness. It may be helpful at times to edit a paper ruthlessly, cutting it and showing how it could be recast. Sometimes the surgery is extensive, but the teacher should want to do the minimum amount of correcting so that he makes efficient use of his students' and his own time. He may correct a paper very carefully or even rewrite it. If he does so, he should reproduce it for the class. They have probably faced the same problem themselves and need the same solution.

For example, he may take the following student paragraph and redo it, posing between the revisions a number of questions, and ask the class to decide which paragraph is better.

I sit in my dormitory room at night near a pool of light at my desk reading a book and wishing someone would drop in for some conversation. To my left is the chest of drawers and on it my perfume, some make-up, a doll from home, pictures from the summer stuck in the mirror, and an ashtray from a night-club. But I have to study. We have, however, fixed up our room and there is a fishnet on the wall between my roommate's bed and mine. The rug, $5.00 secondhand, doesn't quite reach to the opposite walls, and our beds are unmade. I have a term paper in economics, two books to read for English, a geology exam, and our room is right next to the coke machine. I like to be alone but not at night even to study. I like it best when the morning sun makes the room bright. It isn't so much fun to study when people are laughing outside.

Does the paragraph make a dominant impression?
Is there a perspective, a point of view?
Are there specifics?
Are the specifics chosen and used for effect?
Does the paragraph emphasize what it wants to?
Does the first-person narrator help or hinder?
Could the writer show instead of tell?
Is the following paragraph better than the first one? If so, why?
What does the following paragraph need to make it better?

The sound of their laughter suddenly explodes from Room 11, stops at nine, grows louder at eight, jams into six, bursts out in a minute and comes down the corridor, but it passes the closed door. Inside there is one spot of cool white from a tensor light, Samuelson's book on economics, a neat stack of file cards, a ballpoint pen with an extra-fine point, a girl's hand. The rest of the room is filled with dunes of darkness. Outside the coke machine clicks, clunks, growls and ger-lunks as they talk without listening, saying the same things they always say. "He's an animal, but. . ." "Did you see Janie, I certainly. . . " "Here I have this term paper, and what do I. . ." "Last summer I. . ." "Saturday I'm going to. . ." The pen jabs the file card covering the neat script with an angry rash of dots. The pen keeps hitting the card in a frightening, regular rhythm. Suddenly two girls spill into the room, and the girl jumps up from the desk smiling. "Gee, I just leaned against the door, I didn't mean to interrupt." "Sorry, 4.0." The two girls chirp more apologies and dart out to join the laughter, disappearing up the corridor, away from the closed door.

A paper may be publically edited, particularly if it has a problem common to many students in the class, by using an overhead projector. It is important, however, not to ridicule a student. He must be encouraged to write, not discouraged. The best way of doing this, of course, is for the teacher himself to write with the class, and to submit his own paragraph for editing or correction by the class.

The class should correct other students' papers. One way of having them do this is to staple a yellow sheet to each paper, and then to pass the papers around the table in the center of the writing laboratory, having each student identify the central problem of that paper in writing. Each writer gets back his paper with a dozen or more comments by his classmates.

And how do you grade a paper? Unfortunately, that is easy. No experienced teacher has difficulty in slapping an A, B, C, D, or F on a paper which has a meaning within the context of that class. Since he does get to know his students and their problems well and becomes sympathetic to their attempts to solve their writing problems, he probably has to force himself to grade low so that his B's and A's are meaningful. But he should rarely allow himself the comfort of grading.

Most papers in a writing course should not receive a grade. I do see papers in writing courses which are graded with numerical grades—83.5, 82.4; I have seen a 93, which was an A, marked down to a 92, which is a B, because in eight pages there was one erasure. This is idiotic.

When I first began to teach I was a tough grader, and proud of it. When I had students come before me I slashed red all over the page and was smug about the F's and the D's and the C-'s at the top of the page. I proved to them what they already knew, that I knew a great deal about writing in comparison with them and that I was tough and that they were ignorant. For most of the students I needed to reach, the grades were totally meaningless and destructive. They had failed in other writing courses, they knew they could not write, and I had proved it. They tuned me out. They agreed with me, they didn't know how to write. Writing was not for them, it was a gift they had not been given. The student who gets a grade on his paper will look at the grade, he will not look at anything else; and the grade never diagnoses his writing problem, never shows him how to solve it. The grade merely is an arbitrary indication of where he ranks in comparison with other students at a particular time in his educational career.

I am not against grades. We all have to measure up to standards, but to grade each paper is ridiculous. A student should be graded halfway through the course and at the end of the course. He should measure up and should have some record of what he has achieved in that measuring. But we do not grade him in the beginning to show him that he's stupid; we do not necessarily grade on a curve. The student should understand at the beginning of the course that the teacher's ambition is to help him improve. My conceit with my own students is that they will write better at the end of the course than at the beginning. It doesn't mean that I don't give F's and D's. I do. It does mean that my students are given a chance to discover their writing problems and to solve them. It doesn't mean that they're graded for improvement or effort, for that gives the advantage to the bad student. If you start at zero and progress to F, I suppose you have earned an A for effort and improvement. I explain to my students that I am a skill teacher and I will try to improve their skills, and quite often I find the reward comes when I give a rather undistinguished C to a student who begins to get A's on his papers in other courses.

Grades are meaningless during a writing course. You may be demandign a great deal of a good student and praising a very little in a poor student. Each student is working at his own pace and his relationship to the other students in the class is relatively unimportant, for he is not trying to improve his classmates' writing, he is trying to improve his own. Fear of a poor grade is not a good motivation, and undeserved A's in writing presented to students who are articulate in comparison with the boobs they sit with in a given classroom do positive harm to the student who thinks he knows how to write when he doesn't.

The writing paper is not corrected by the teacher. The teacher discovers the student's main problem and shows him a way of solving it. Then the paper is corrected by the student, who revises it in such a way that it solves his problem and becomes an effective piece of writing.

It is helpful at times for the student to put his paper aside and come back to it, but it is rarely helpful to have a paper written in October returned carefully corrected and marked up in January. It is better to have it returned when the writing is fresh in his mind with one perceptive comment—"You didn't know your subject, did you? Now go find it."

When the time comes at the middle of the course and at the end for the grade then the student should be allowed to pick his best papers from his folder and should be graded either on his single best paper, a revision of it which he knows will receive a grade, or on a selection of papers. It may be helpful for him to go through his folder and grade his own work. The teacher may then confirm or change the students' evaluation. The teacher should remember that the student in the writing course must develop the ability to evaluate his own acomplishments, to spot his own problems, and to correct them.

30 How to Edit Papers

The writing teacher will soon recognize the complaints of his students and will soon develop treatments which are prescribed individually according to the background, training, personality and potential of the student.

The more familiar complaints include, "I don't have nothing to say"; "My teacher last year said I wrote beautiful"; "But this is how I feel, inside"; "But I'll lose my spontaneous"; "I guess I know what you mean, sort of, when you express the opinion in your written comments that you believe I seem to have a slight tendency to be, well, wordy"; "I don't dig what you mean a cliché"; "Choppy? Whaddayuh mean? Me? Choppy?" "My secretary will know how to spell"; "My mother went to college and I don't see why I have to worry about things like a what-do-you-call-it, non sequitur?" "I don't know what you want"; "I just ruin it worse when I change things."

There is no simple answer to any of these problems, and many times they will have to be treated repeatedly until they are solved. But it may help to see some of the ways in which specific student papers can be dealt with verbally, by comments on the paper or, preferably, in conference as the teacher marks the paper and comments on it.

"On the Beach"

Pathetic fallacy / sp. / cheesy alliteration

The sun hanges on the pine as natural noises from little natural things pervade the air. ? Now, the lake is bishop-black and

be specific / fancy word / Did it ever? / huh?

tranquil as the night. Once again the lake's lips kiss my feet

are nights tranquil? / over written

and all the objects it embraces. The little, brown water bug

what's this mean?

moves frantically while standing still and a smooth pebble near

awk. dependent clause

him rolls back-and-forth. Lying in the cove, the moored skiff bobs and rolls, takes up the slack and again rides over the stake. Tall pines, gracefully swaying, line the shore; like huge menhirs their shadows converge in the motionless middle of the lake while sun rays dance over them. Periodically, a kingfish follows the curvature of the beach, resembling the bent image of an old man. The inlet is bedecked with rocks from Titanic times, lying where they had fallen one cluster forms the foundation of a little green cottage, barely visible. Pine-incensed air burns the nostrils while little puffs of smoke reel from the mouth. Turning to mount the bank leading to the road, one senses the taste of bark, bitter and rough.

I can't read on—what's this all about? What are you trying to say?

The instructor need not read on.

*

I became a ~~My introduction to~~ muskrat fan by accident. ~~was involuntary.~~ I was assigned ~~had to do~~ a research project on muskrats ~~them~~ for a Forest Resources course at the University of New Hampshire, and ~~But~~ during the project ~~I~~ discovered that they are fascinating animals. to observe. And it is easy, them, too. ~~The first time~~ and you see a muskrat ~~them will bee~~ swimming slowly ~~in open water~~ near the shore. Watch for a small V in the water followed by a brown shape. ~~Bring a pair of binoculars because they are only the size of a small woodchuck.~~ All you have to do is sit quietly by the side of a pond, stream, bog, or marsh in the early morning or evening with a pair of binoculars and the muskrats will ~~do the rest.~~ parade by.

The~~ir~~ dense brown fur of this housecat sized rodent ~~has several qualities which~~ makes it ~~an~~ ideal ~~coat~~ for ~~an aquatic rodent.~~ the water. It serves as both insulated underwear and life jacket because it is waterproof and holds ~~much~~ air ~~with~~in it. This keeps a swimming muskrat warm and floating high in the water. ~~like a cork.~~ And if it spots you, the naked, black tail, flattened on the sides, ~~is used to~~ will slap the water ~~for the same purpose that a beaver slaps its tail,~~ — it is as an alarm signal. A muskrat tucks its naked forefeet up under its chin while swimming so that only the hind feet work to glide him on his way.

~~The habitat of~~ Muskrats ~~varies from~~ live in tropical rivers and coastal marshes as well as ~~to~~ arctic tundras and deltas. In New England, muskrats ~~habitat consists of~~ live in streams, bogs, marshes, lakes, ponds, and even drainage ditches. ~~The only habitat requirements that seem to be universal are water and that the water be~~ They only need reasonably slow flowing water in ~~the case of~~ a stream or ~~calm in the case of~~ a calm pond. ~~Good muskrat habitat is~~ It's easy to spot a muskrat neighborhood because the water is quiet and ~~has~~ there are a wide variety of aquatic plants cluttering the ~~edge of the pond or sides of the stream.~~ bank.

*

All creative writing should steer away from universals. It is important to get a clear picture of the writer from his writing. The amount of uniqueness shown in a poem or description is equal to the uniqueness of the individual. That is why it is more interesting to read a short story or novel rather than a history book.

The history intertwined with the personal plot of Dr. Zhivago made each richer. In the same sense, an autobiography like Cellini's or Sartre's is a better picture of the times they lived in.

*

I saw the approaching figure, ~~but~~ the evening mist. ~~that follows a warm rain clouded my vision.~~ The dark hulk stopped short seemingly paralyzed and scrutinized me like a scared animal. My advance triggered his fright. He rushed at me ~~without warning~~; we collided. His fists beat heavily on my back as his knees francticly snapped to my groin. Weaving rapidly and bewildered by the attack, I began to throw short punches to his body. His trench coat absorbed the impact. Searching intuitively for his head, I punched hard and straight--then I connected; His knees buckled but he didn't go down. I paniced--that was the best I had. His hands locked about ny neck as all his weight clung to me. Seizing his coat, I pulled hurridly tearing the buttons from the front. With the coat open, I slammed his stomach solidly with short snappy punches, then moved to the rib cage. As I worked from fright, his nails dug into the back of my neck. The pain lasted only moments. My head pushed all the harder against his chest enabling only my right hand to be free. Determined, I kept a constant barrage, one handed, on his left side as he twisted painfully seeming to ask me to use the other. Suddenly he released my head and lunged forward with his knee leading. I caught the force in the nuts. Dropping forward, I landed on all four, then rolled to the ground. Fetus-like, I lay on the wet pavement twisting and squirming and gasping for breath. He tottered to a small tree not far from me. I heard his coughing and choking. Turning slightly, I saw him clutch the tree trunk as he puked and slowly slid to the ground.

*

I began to run-
My cares had been undone. ?
I felt <u>so</u> free and happy- meaningless
My life had just begun. ?

These are nice words and the paper is neat but you don't say anything to me

I smelled the fresh wet air,
felt the wind in my hair. trite
Something splashed me - it felt good.
I didn't even care. huh?

My life untill now had been darkness;
All that I saw was a guess.
I knew nothing else but seeing with my hands- ?
It's all so hard to express.

No one appreciates what they see-
No one but someone like me.
I can't get used to using my eyes
to take in all the beauty.

Let's have a conference and talk this through, line by line.

*

I wish someone would tell me what has happened to old-fashioned American spirit! The Spirit of '76, the patriotic spirit of July 4th--firecrackers, cakewalks, community picnics at the lake, even the Spirit of St. Louis is snickered at by today's "young moderns". There was a time when Americans took pride in their nation and its opportunities. Holidays were times to fly the American flag proudly in the front yard; schoolchildren learned the Star-Spangled Banner in the second grade and they didn't forget it; some people even got a little tearful as they saw the flag flapping in the breeze or when they sang the National Anthem. Today the only times we hear America's song is in high school assembly programs and before athletic contests. We have come to a point in our country where we simply do not care! We have become immune to the things in our nation that should give us an overwhelming feeling of pride and spirit. Take a look at this nation --a people derived from all the countries of the world; once they spoke different languages and ate different foods, but now they have invented new dialects--Southern drawl, Boston twang, even Brooklynese. Instead of Italian spaghetti and Irish stew, Americans chomp hot dogs with India relish and get gummed up on fluffernutter sandwiches. We have thousands of miles of the richest land in the world--from the toughness of the New England coast, to the fertility of the Mississippi Delta, to the awe of the Grand Canyon and Sierra Nevadas, to the breezes of Hawaii--greatness is the word to encompass America. So why not be proud? Why not have the same spirit for our country that we have for our college football team? Don't be afraid to show spirit; boast about your country. Maybe you've heard it before but remember: men did fight and die for America and her spirit.

*

Over-written and under-thought. Your generalizations create a wonderful unbelievable time. This exhortation would not persuade anyone. Let's have a conference.

not true

Never a worry, never a doubt. Always cheerful and gay are children when they play. Each day they lead the same life, all fun and games. Then all of a sudden time takes over and steals from their eyes, the beauty of birds, skies, and open meadows. Instead there is now a look of worry and wear. Soon the late years start advancing and those days are gone forever. Then they can't stop glancing at children as they pass. All the youth has been drained from their bodies but not their minds. Now they wonder and wish that they had never grown up.

No

huh?

Wow—too much too soon

superlatives out of control

*

What is there to be gained from mans' existence? This question I ask myself because of the Preacher. I care for the people unborn. The people of the coming generations. But of what use is it to live?

By the time anyone found out, they would already have lived their lives so what worth was it for them to have discovered that it was of no use to have lived?

tendency towards backward sentences

auk.

Whew—slow down ~~don't~~ What do you mean?

*

As a (small) child I had (a choice of) religions. My father was ~~A~~ Catholic and my mother ~~was~~ Episcopalian so to avoid a family argument the decision was mine. ~~I was~~ six ~~or seven so the choice was limited because~~ I knew ~~nothing of the beliefs behind the churches, in fact the idea of various beliefs never entered my mind.~~ ~~I looked at the churches from an outside position on the~~

to choose my own

At

little theology

so I studied religious

[Margin note: Fine possibilities – now go to work on it.]

~~basis of~~ architecture. The Catholic church was the largest in Franklin and looked sinister. ~~to me. I didn't like~~ the way its broad steps rose to three small doors ~~. It~~ reminded me of a cattle ramp. ~~I didn't like~~ the towering slate covered steeple and black cross [was] covered with pigeon dung [and] Inside ~~the church~~ I felt [uncomfortable in] ~~lost with~~ a herd of people who reacted in unison to some unseen ~~and unheard~~ command. I did not become a Catholic. The Baptist and Unitarian churches were also formidable [(show me?)] from the outside so I didn't bother to go in. The Baptist was a huge [(show?)] barn-like [building?] with a white steeple and the Unitarian was a large ocher [?] building with small windows. The Episcopal church, [however,] ~~was different from the others. It~~ was small, ~~and~~ brown [and it had] ~~with~~ a cluster of evergreens by the door. In the middle of the hedge-in lawn there was a black wrought iron sign giving the name of the church as St. Judes (patron saint of hopeless cases). [Know this when a small child? Pt. of view?] I ~~liked the appearance of the church~~ [went in] and felt comfortable in the wicker chairs so I became an Episcopalian.

[Margin note: Show me more of your search – all from pt. of view (physically and intellectually) of a six-year-old.]

. . .

As a child I had to choose my own religion. My father was Catholic and my mother Episcopalian, so to avoid a family argument the decision was mine. At six I knew little theology so I studied religious architecture. The Catholic church was the largest in Franklin and looked sinister. The way its broad steps rose to three small doors reminded me of a cattle ramp. The towering slate covered steeple and black cross was covered with pigeon dung and inside I felt uncomfortable [awk] in a herd of people who reacted in unison to some unseen command. I did not become a Catholic. The Baptist church was a large white building between the Post Office and elementary school. I went there to collect pigeon feathers that drifted down from the bell tower. We had our Cub Scout meetings in the basement, and I didn't like the Cub Scouts.

~~I didn't like the church either.~~ I'd ^also heard from Baptist friends that they had been submerged in water when baptized and this didn't ~~particularly~~ appeal to me. The Unitarian church was two miles across town and too far to walk. It was an ugly yellowish-brown and I didn't know any of ^the people? there. The Episcopal church, however, was small, brown, and it had a cluster of evergreens by the door. In the middle of a neat hedged-in lawn there was a black wrought iron sign giving the name of the church--St. Judes. It was not until much later I learned St. Judge [sp.??] was the patron saint of hopeless cases. Grown-ups were bigger then, but still they smiled ~~and were pleasant to me. They~~ asked me who I was. I went in and felt comfortable in the wicker chairs, so, I became an Episcopalian. this is much better. Do you see the difference?

What do you do when you receive a paper such as the following one, called "The Box," which Mike Greene handed to me during a short-story unit in a regular English course? Instead of writing about the short story he attempted a short story. Should you accept it? And how do you correct it?

I

My friend and I decided one day to build a box. We were in our first year of college then, and renting a cottage from a lady who lived somewhere a few miles away. She was fat but cheery and whenever she talked about us or to us she called us "my boys." She came, through a strange arrangement, once a week--Sundays after she had attended church--to clean house for us, and, although we were not very dirty she always fussed straightening this, dusting, washing, scrubbing that and replacing any of our things that were left around. She loved cleaning the cottage because she loved the cottage and she loved to work. She also loved us. She loved us enough not to charge for her time cleaning.

Reprinted by permission of Mike Greene.

The cottage itself was small, three rooms: a small kitchen with stove, refrigerator, a table and chairs, a larger living room with a fireplace, and a small bedroom which we shared. On the outside the cottage was circumscribed by a wide porch, six feet wide. There, on the back of the cottage, away from the road, we spent many nights studying and drinking and talking. It was there one night that we decided to build the box.

II

We were younger then, 19. And, in our dungarees and white jackets, hair long and scraggly over the ears and on the contours of our necks, he in his white sneakers and I in my brown loafers, we looked like brothers--twins almost. But he was larger than I was, and stronger. I was quieter and spent more time in thought than he.

We set about to build the box with the ardor that one usually expects at the start of such a project, but we soon slowed to a normal steady pace. We wanted to use only the finest materials that we could find and afford. I decided that we could spare one of the coffee tables from the living room--a long, low mahogany thing my mother had given us--so we tore off the top and cut it in half to use for the top and bottom of the box. For the sides and braces we decided to buy some pine, for it was the best we could afford. We took great time and care in the building--measuring, sawing, squaring, planing, sanding, fitting, refitting--until the final construction was under way.

It was then that we decided on the wheels. We thought that since everything else was mobile during those days that the box would be mobile too. So, we bought more pine, stole the wheels from a baby carriage that we found at the dump one day and made a gig on which to place the box.

With the fastening to the gig the box was nearly complete. We had left the top unattached for the christening ceremony. We had decided that, before completing the construction of the box, each of us should place something inside, and so, at a prearranged time one morning as the sun was just beginning to throw its light onto the porch my friend put into the box a sign--made of white cardboard with blue letters--reading, "God is alive and well in Mexico" and I a picture of my "one true love"--a girl I was inextricably in love with and had only talked to once.

III

One evening late in the spring, only a few weeks before final exams, we were feeling especially playful. After a brief wrestling match on the couch, which we had moved onto the porch from inside, we began chasing each other around the porch. We started slowly at first, hiding from each other at each corner, and ended by running at full speed. On my fifth trip by, I grabbed the box and started pushing it ahead of me. When my friend caught up with me he climbed onto it and we pushed each other around and around for several minutes. Finally, laughing hysterically and out of breath we collapsed at the front of the porch, behind the box.

"It's lacking something," he said after a moment when he had caught his breath.

"Exactly," I replied.

We spent several more days working on the box after that. He painted abstract designs and figures on the four sides and, when the paint had dried, I wrote poetry, a few metaphoric images and some of my more prophetic sayings on it. When we had finished it looked as if it might have been used in the Boston Tea Party, but it was complete.

IV

Years sometimes pass like short minutes and it seemed this way to us as we prepared for our last set of final exams late in May. We sat one night remembering the other nights spent there on the porch and then the box. We speculated on what we would do with it when we were ready to leave. We considered one or the other of us taking it, but since it was equally each of ours, we deemed that unfair. After much thought we finally realized that we had no solution except to abandon the box.

When finals were over we packed and left the cottage, each going his separate way, leaving the box there on the back porch. We hoped that maybe the lady who owned the cottage could use it in some way.

Often, though, since then, I have wondered if anyone could have used it except us.

Of course you accept the story, for it is an imaginative and courageous piece of work. The story is a signal that you have a student who is different. That shouldn't be terrifying; it should be challenging. You do not tell a Mike Greene, of course, that since he is different he does not have to face standards. What you do tell him is that you recognize his courage, and that he must face up to the toughest measure of all, his own increasing standards. You try to get out of the way of such a student and create a climate in which he can work hard discovering his own questions and his own answers. You will point out readings to him, and you may discuss his story with him, giving him a chance to reread it, to rewrite it, to find an audience in the class or in a school publication. His story is far from perfect—it would be easy to destroy it with criticism—but it is an unexpected piece of work which should remind you that not every student should respond in the same way to each assignment, and not every assignment should be corrected in the same manner.

It's impossible to recreate what you do in conference on a paper. It would be a lot simpler if you could look at a paragraph or theme and say, "That is wrong, and this is correct." Writing cannot be graded or corrected that easily. Each theme is made up of many interconnecting elements. It is woven out of what the writer has to say and his ability to say it. It will be evaluated by another human being who has a subjective reaction to the piece of work.

The teacher of writing must bring to the paper he is reading what the student has had to put into it—all of his ability and all of his skill. The teacher has to use his experience, his judgment, and his talents to show the student how the paper can be improved, so that he will be able to correct the paper himself in the future when he has left the writing course. Every mark on the paper and every comment should be made to show the student what is wrong and how it can be made right. The difficulty and the delight in teaching writing are that each paper is written by an individual, and that each paper has its own problems which demand an individual response from the teacher.

31 How to Run a Conference

The writing teacher and his student should face each other over the problems the student is facing in his writing. The conference may not be formal for it can take place when the student asks a question at the end of class, in the corridor, during study hall, in the cafeteria or after school. The conference may take just as long as it takes to say, "Jim, you better watch those clichés." The important thing is that the teacher is facing an individual student whose name and whose work he knows.

Each teacher will find his own conference techniques. Generally, the student sits on the teacher's right, not across a desk from him, but beside him so they can both read the student's writing and see what the teacher is doing to it as he marks it, underlining a problem or sketching in a solution by cutting, shaping or revising a sentence. There is usually no reason for a teacher to read a paper before the conference, for he should develop the skill of identifying and solving one writing problem in each conference.

It is important to keep the conference focused on what is on the page. The teacher in conference is not father confessor, social worker, psychiatrist, adopted uncle or pal; he is a teacher of writing who is concerned with how well this student has written on this particular page. The attention should be on what appears in black and white.

In find it helpful to have a clock where I can see it but where the student cannot see me looking at it. Conferences should probably be scheduled for ten minutes each, although most conferences will take only three or four minutes. The teacher who has frequent short conferences with students whose work he knows well does not need hour-long get-acquainted sessions. He should not try to identify every problem on the page. He may say to a student, "You have a lot of problems, but let's get to the most important one," and then focus on that. He is trying to lead the student a step at a time, and he should try to have a conference a week of at least a few minutes' duration.

In general, the conferences should occur at the student's initiative. The student should be able to sign up for them or initiate them in some way during the class period so that he can see the teacher when he has a problem about his work. The teacher should be available, but the teacher should also make it clear that he has friends and doesn't need to chat. When he has something to say to a student he should put on a paper, "See me," or call him to his desk. When the student has something to say to the teacher he should be able to initiate the conference.

Usually the teacher should begin the conference by saying, "What's your problem in this paper?" He is succeeding as a teacher when the student can identify his own problem. Then he should ask the student, "How do you think you can solve it?" If the student has a reasonable solution, he should let him try it; if he doesn't, the teacher should be able to propose a solution or to pass a check list, a demonstration paragraph or some pages from a text to the student, who may then be able to see his own solution.

The teacher makes a mistake when he thinks that his success is measured by the amount of effort he puts into preparation, the amount of talking he does in the classroom, the number of red marks he places on the page, or the number of minutes he spends in conference. A good teacher is lazy, he wants the student to do the work. After all, it is the student who ultimately has to teach himself. But the teacher must be available with all of his skill. An afternoon of conferences is the most exhausting kind of teaching: every three or four or five minutes he has to relate to a new student, scan a new paper, make just the right comment on the paper—and he should do it all in a relaxed manner.

The teacher will find it important to have a place where he can confer with the students comfortably, with a certain degree of privacy, and he must design this conference time so that the students who are not conferring with him are doing their own writing or reading. He should not allow a situation in which a long line of students wait to see him.

The purpose of the conference should be to allow the student to make a tentative diagnosis of his own writing problem of that week and to prescribe a tentative treatment. When he has done that he should have the attention of the teacher—the private attention of the teacher—who will either confirm his diagnosis and treatment, or propose alternatives. The teacher in the conference is an adviser, a coach, a person who is helping the student to teach himself.

32 How to Motivate Students

"If the teacher is interested in the student as a person and the student knows it—no problem," according to Terry Ortwein, head of the English Department of Hanover (New Hampshire) High School.

Of course, it isn't that easy. Or is it? When you talk to those teachers who motivate students you begin to see, although the teachers may be young or old, male or female, strict or permissive, understanding or impatient, they are all interested in the student as an individual. They listen to the student and the student knows it.

These teachers know instinctively that man writes out of personal need. A man's drive to tell another what he knows about life—to relate, to sympathize, to incite, to educate, to entertain, to persuade—starts with a baby's first cry and lasts until an old man's final words. The effective writing teacher mobilizes this force simply by allowing his students to speak.

The teacher does this within the limits of his own personality. He may be a bubbler, a grouch, a moaner, an analyzer, a wit or a martinet. But if he is genuinely interested in his individual students, and if they know it, they will write for him, for almost all students will respond to a listener.

A good listener, however, does not merely nod and say, "Yes, dear," to the nice little student. That is usually what the student has at home—a nodding parental non-listener. The student wants somebody with bite, a person who cares enough to snap back, who is concerned with what the student has to say, who has standards, whose praise means something. To be this sort of a listener the teacher must understand one crucial fact: the content of the writing course comes from the student himself.

Consider this excerpt from a British book, *The Teaching of English*[1]:

"The material of English exists in the mind of the boy who is being taught. The English teacher aims to stimulate the boy to think and clarify his own thoughts. He intends to stimulate the boy to feel and to become conscious of his own feelings. The teacher cannot supply the thought; the teacher cannot supply the feeling. If he attempts to do so, then the boy expresses thoughts not his own, feelings which are conventional or sham."

We must understand that the composition course does not pour information into the student. The skill teacher begins with what the student has in his head. It is the teacher's job to listen to that, to apply critical judgment when appropriate, to encourage the student to develop what he has to say, shape it, form it, document it, clarify it—but the content is in the student.

The Schools Council in Great Britain wrote*:

"Pupils are unlikely to write well unless they have something they really need to communicate in a more lasting form. . . . If children have something to say, and want it to last, they will make very great efforts to write it in the most telling way they can—and that means that handwriting must be legible and punctuation and spelling ought not to pull the reader up. But a pupil wants to communicate only if he feels he is recognized as a unique and valuable individual. How else can he gain confidence? A sound relationship between teacher and taught is the basis of all good writing in school. It is for the teacher to set an example of respect and courtesy in communication, beginning with his own speaking, listening and writing; he must also convince his pupils that he is interested in what they say or write. . . .

"Almost everyone who learns to write well learns to do so by means of 'personal writing.' This means writing which is not concerned with the objective recording of facts, but with recreating the varied impressions and perceptions of individual experience. Its material comes from the senses, the emotions, and the imagination of the writer. The teacher can help boys and girls to see more vividly, to respond more intensely, and to discriminate more keenly in their choice of words to convey the experience, so that the original experience itself becomes more meaningful for the writer. . . .

"Impersonal writing is a fairly late product, a derivation from personal writing; and it needs to be nourished by the continuance of personal writing. At its best, of course (more especially in literature), the impersonal embodies the qualities of personal writing as well; it is both strongly felt and objective, both imaginative and precise."

That is an eloquent statement of how writing ought to be taught, based

[1] The Incorporated Association of Assistant Masters in the Secondary Schools of England, *The Teaching of English* (Cambridge: Cambridge University Press, 1966).

* From *English, A Programme for Research and Development in English Teaching, Working Paper No. 3,* by the Schools Council. Reprinted by permission of H. M. Stationery Office.

on what every writer knows. This does not mean that all writing must be subjective. It does mean that most writers begin to learn by writing subjectively. Scholarship, if it is good, evolves from personal curiosity.

The teacher who motivates his students to write earns honesty from them. All their writing, in a sense, is autobiographical. For example, students may write about an important incident in their life. This starts most subjectively with a listing of the relevant parts, but when they expand the incident, perhaps changing the point of view and the tone, showing the lifelong implications of that incident for their own lives, then for other lives, and perhaps for all lives, they control and use their material. Hopefully, they have read widely enough so that they can combine their own experiences with the insights of others who are more intelligent, more perceptive, or more experienced. But the writer discovers the universal through the personal, and the student must be made to find subjects which interest him and then shown how to make those subjects interesting to other people.

It is important that the student learn the primacy of subject matter. He must have something to say before he can decide how to say it. He must test each word, each sentence, each paragraph, each scene, each chapter against experience, and the best judge of the honesty of his content is his own critical eye. The student can be encouraged to be critical of his own writing by the teacher who continually asks, "Is this true, is this the way it is?"

It is not easy to listen to students. They are young, and that can be a great burden to the middle-aged ear. Each discovers life for himself, but the teacher who watches many discover life year after year finds a monotonous repetitiveness in what they discover. And if they can learn honesty, which does not come naturally to them, then what they have to say may hurt. Our students are not instinctively honest, because it is a frightening thing to be honest. Their parents do not encourage honesty—few people really want an honest person in the home, a person who cuts through the illusions by which we live—and we may not want an honest person in the classroom who asks tough questions we are not able to answer. But good writing, whether it be a political speech, the account of a murder, a production report, or a military order, is honest—precise, accurate, direct.

Finally, if we want to motivate students we must accept students' own motivations. The teacher makes a dangerous decision when he declares that all students ought to want to write or be forced to write literary criticism. The student who wishes to be a great critic may not have a more virtuous motivation than the one who wishes to write brochures which will sell toilet fixtures. The motivations of money or fame or power may each be virtuous or corrupt, depending on the person, the situation, and the effect of the piece of writing. We must help our students to write honestly and well for their own purposes.

Students often believe that only poets, novelists, or perhaps journalists are writers. The student should be motivated by knowing he will have to write if he is an attorney, a detective, a scientist, a businessman, a secretary—all careers where information must be written down and passed on to someone else. The teacher of writing should bring writers into his classes so they can tell the student the importance of writing and reveal their own writing problems and solutions.

Dr. George Snook, an orthopedic surgeon and an instructor in the American Academy of Orthopedic Surgeons, writes articles both on surgery and on military history. He passed on the following advice to my students:

1 Know your subject.

2 Write it down, paying scant attention to grammar, punctuation, style, or form.

3 Rewrite, paring as much as possible. Be ruthless.

4 Rewrite again and again, being more ruthless, if possible, and correcting all errors.

5 Put it away for a while and then start all over again, until you have said as much as you can in the fewest possible words.

We are teaching writers—boys and girls who will write descriptions of automobile accidents and living room suites which are on sale, reports of factory production and laboratory experiments, political speeches and the minutes of League of Women Voters meetings, love letters and business letters.

Although writing may make students better readers, better thinkers, more sensitive seers, more psychologically integrated human beings, the only answer to the question, "Why teach writing?" must be, "To give my students a basic intellectual skill so that they can become themselves."

33 How to Reach the Unreachable

There are few things as frustrating as facing students who dare you to teach them to write. Whether they have something to say or not, when you try to listen to them individually and they turn you off, it is a personal rejection. At least, that's the way we take it.

We cannot afford to brood about those who turn us off, or we will become ineffective for those whom we can turn on. Let us not assume that everyone can write, should write, or may want to write. What we should do is attempt to give everyone freedom of opportunity regardless of his background, his race, his religion, or the limitations with which he came to the classroom. But we are not social workers, psychiatrists, or evangelists. We cannot convert every student. We can attempt to explain to a student why the ability to write will be an advantage to him, but he has to make the decision that he wants this skill. Other students may have something to say out of the agony of their life, but they may not want to deal with it, to reveal it, to explore it. That is their decision and they do have the right of privacy.

The disadvantaged may come from wealthy homes or poor homes; they may be deprived by poverty or by too many riches too soon. We cannot judge them or their background. We must open doors which they may choose to step through. But once we have understood our role can anything be done?

Yes, a very great deal can be done. And it is usually done in the same way that we motivate all students, only it takes more time, a great deal more time. One successful writing teacher I know said, "People think I get results. I just demand less." He is a demanding teacher, but in a sense he was right. He gives his students the chance to deal with one problem at a time and to take weeks to work that problem out. He is interested in making students who cannot write a paragraph write a paragraph, and if it takes half a year he is pleased when that student succeeds in doing something he could not do before.

These paragraphs were written by ninth grade students in Roxbury, Massachusetts.

I am Achilles the mightiest warrior of the country of Greece. I am the son of Peleus and the sea nymph Thetis. I fight hard for my homeland and yet me and my men are cheated out of the spoils of our hardship! Agamemnon. Oh! how I hate the name every time I think of the name I feel a burning in my heart but he is not fit to be king of Mycenae. I will kill him for taking away my maiden Brieseis! Or will I? Yes I will have my revenge of the king of Mycenae. I will go to his tent and cut out his heart and bury it in the graves of our livestock. But Wait! If I go about it underhanded or decieveingly I will lose face. So therefore I will go about it in a way befitting the mightiest warrior of Grecian army. I will face him in open combat. Yes he will pay dearly ha!! Ha! ha!

*

My name is Achilles. I am sitting in my tent sulking because Agamemnon had been unfair. All the spoils that were captured he took and distributed them among himself and the other kinds giving me only a little or none at all. Where I am fighting my head off for them and what do they give me in returned, hardly nothing if something at all. Agamemnon and all the others all they do is sit back and relax while I do the fighting. I should get more than they do, for without me they are nothing. Now they want to take my slave away. They have no right to do it. I wouldn't let them. After all, I am Achilles they can't hurt me nobody knows were my only weakness is at. I might as well relax my mind, I will go to sleep. Good night, you foolish Greeks.

*

What is this I feel. I have live and loved Menelaus for many years. Then why am I going to leave this place, my home and all that goes with it. For a man that is a stranger to my land and me. The love I have for Paris is strange, but it is love so I will question it no more. I will travel with Paris to his home and pray only that the gods protect this love that they have seen fit tojoin.

*

My name is Helen. I have to make the chose of going away with Paris or staying with my husband. I love Paris very much, because he's young and wealthy. But so is my husband but my husband is a bit older than I am. Paris makes me feel free not bound to anything or anyone. I think he could give me anything I wanted and he is very clever. He's kind hearted and loves me very much. My husband wants me by his side so that he can keep an eye on me. I don't want to feel afraid of him, I want to feel like a companion.

Their usage may not be correct, but the vigor of those paragraphs would make many a suburban English teacher envious. And yet those are students who come from the most disadvantaged homes, who are years behind students in the suburbs of the same age and grade. How have they been able to write these paragraphs? Who has motivated them? The teacher's name is Miss Grace Whittaker, an experienced teacher who through the years has learned how to listen and to win her students' respect.

In the beginning her students see a piece of paper as a threat. They will not write. Give them paper and they will throw it on the floor, but they are fascinated by a tape recorder, and the teacher can get them talking and eventually tape what they have to say. It takes days and weeks of patience before they will believe that this teacher will listen to them. They have never had an adult listener. They have to develop trust and respect, and that takes time. Eventually, what they have said may be typed and distributed to them. They may read it to the teacher, facing only one critical question—Does it make sense? Finally, they write papers which are put in a folder, and they have their own papers in their own folder. The completion of every assignment is a major step forward, for these students have rarely ever done their homework, or any work at all in school. There are no grades, no red marks. They may edit their papers in small groups and go over the papers in conference with the teacher. They pick the best one, for they have written far more than can be read or graded.

The papers above have come from a study of myths, Gilgamesh and Robert Graves' *The Siege and Fall of Troy;* they've also studied the Bible—Abraham, Joseph, and Moses—all with the purpose of trying to find out what a hero is. The students use books, movies and discussions: What do heroes have in common? What is the difference between an ancient and a modern hero? They tape-record their discussions and play them back and argue about them. They dramatize the problems of the hero, and they pick any character from *The Siege and Fall of Troy* they'd like to be and put themselves in his shoes.

As Miss Whittaker says, "You don't count the pages or sentences, four lines for one student may be a genuine experience." She has found that the students want to work with moral values; they want to talk about them. Does the hero need to be known and applauded? Can there be an invisible hero? What is right and what is wrong? Once the students are open, and this takes a long time for they have learned how to be guarded and to protect themselves from adults, they will be willing to read and study what seems appropriate to their problems. Classes in hard-core slum areas are not teacher-controlled, they are class-controlled. They are not suburban con-men and teacher-pleasers, because they just don't care, but they are good observers, they can use speech with vigor, and will, and they want to write if given the chance.

The chance means weeks and months of discussing, of opening doors, of pre-writing and planning for a single paper. And the planning needs as much creativity as possible. For example, Miss Whittaker has her class—which has listened to the record of *Julius Caesar,* seen the play, and worked with it as an acting script—crumple paper, spray it with paint and then flatten it out. This leads them to a discussion of the three-dimensional character—what a person looks like on the outside and the inside, what the difference is between illusion and reality. And eventually they are talking about Cassius and Brutus and literature. Miss Whittaker warns teachers that they should not use materials such as Claude Brown's *Manchild and the Promised Land,* because this is what the students live. She finds that they turn to Dickens, to Shakespeare, to the old myths and classics, the pieces of writing which deal with the elementary problems of mankind. These children want to speak, but they have to be convinced that someone is listening, and that takes time.

Herbert R. Kohl has written of his experiences in an East Harlem school[2]:

"I have subsequently discovered other teachers who have explored language and literature with their pupils in this way, with results no less dramatic. The children we have taught ranged from the pre-school years to high school, from lower-class ghetto children to upper-class suburban ones. There are few teaching techniques that we share in common, and no philosophy of education that binds us. Some of these teachers have tight, carefully controlled classrooms; others care less for order and more for invention. There are Deweyites, traditionalists, classicists—a large range of educational philosophies and teaching styles. If there is anything common to our work it is the concern to listen to what the children have to say and the

[2] From *Teaching the "Unteachable"* (New York: *New York Review of Books,* 1967).

ability to respond to it as honestly as possible, no matter how painful it may be to our teacherly prides and preconceptions. We have allowed ourselves to learn from our pupils and to expect the unexpected.

"Children will not write if they are afraid to talk. Initially they suspect teachers and are reluctant to be honest with them. They have had too many school experiences where the loyalty of the staff and the institutional obligations of teachers have taken precedence over honesty. They have seen too much effort to maintain face, and too little respect for justifiable defiance in their school lives. I think children believe that there is a conscious collusion between all of the adults in a school to maintain the impression that the authority is *always* right, and that life is *always* pleasant and orderly."

Being a good, tough, receptive listener, a person who can take it and, more than that, a person who aggressively wants to know what the student has to say—this is what makes the difference. Once you are able to listen, then you can improvise teaching techniques which will work with your students. Photographs or collages may make the students begin to see. Tape recorders can be helpful with students who are afraid of writing. The teacher faced with the hard-core anti-writer should study that marvelous small paperback *Hooked on Books* by Daniel Fader and Morton Shaevitz, which is listed in the Bibliography, to see how reading can lead to writing.

The more difficult the writing problem, the more imaginative the writing teacher may have to be. I had a scientist who had such serious writing problems that they were a major block in his career. When he came to a conference he gripped his arms across his chest and shook with the terror of facing language, and yet in a few weeks he was writing. Why? Because I realized he had never toyed with words. He came from a home where language was rarely used, and, when used, only in the most formal manner. I had him, to his disgust, writing nonsense paragraphs, toying with syllables and the sounds of words. Soon he found it was fun, and in a matter of weeks he was relaxed about writing. He had a fine intelligence, and once he relaxed he wrote well and clearly, for his mind was logical. I would not have a class writing nonsense paragraphs in a university writing course, but I would be willing to try anything with any student which might solve his individual problems.

Miss Josephine Gernsheimer of South Kingstown (Rhode Island) High School, an original member of the New England School Development Council project which led to this book, decided to test our approach to teaching composition by trying it on a class composed of thirteen students who had failed English and were taking it for the second time, and a group of hostile "D" students. She removed the threat of grades, told them that their communications to her were privileged, and worked with them patiently and intensively. They worked, for example, for two weeks on titles and developed more than a dozen devices for writing effective titles. They developed paragraph patterns which would solve their own writing problems. The students began to see that writing was something each of them could do, and before long they began to develop their own voices.

Finally, in a literature unit in the course, Miss Gernsheimer brought the class one of her enthusiasms, Edgar Lee Masters' *Spoon River Anthology*. One of the assignments was to tell the other side of Pauline Barrett's story.

Remember how Masters had Pauline Barrett speak?

Almost the shell of a woman after the surgeon's knife!
And almost a year to creep back into strength,
Till the dawn of our wedding decennial
Found me my seeming self again.
We walked the forest together,
By a path of soundless moss and turf.
But I could not look in your eyes,
And you could not look in my eyes,
For such sorrow was ours—the beginning of gray in your hair,
And I but a shell of myself.
And what did we talk of?—sky and water,
Anything, 'most, to hide our thoughts.
And then your gift of wild roses,
Set on the table to grace our dinner.
Poor heart, how bravely you struggled
To imagine and live a remembered rapture!
Then my spirit drooped as the night came on,
And you left me alone in my room for a while,
As you did when I was a bride, poor heart.
And I looked in the mirror and something said:
"One should be all dead when one is half-dead—
Nor ever mock life, nor never cheat love."
And I did it looking there in the mirror—
Dear, have you ever understood?

Here is what one student wrote to tell the other side of that poem.

It has been three years since my wife died.

I remember that night so well;

I planned every detail of it.

First I took her for a walk in the forest.

I placed some roses on the table.

I think that is what really killed her.

When I left her alone in her room that night,

I didn't even bother to go back in.

The next day I came back with the police.

I mourned for a while for her

Then the next week I married the woman

All the men call Cleopatra.

Remember that that poem and the following one were both written in a class made up of students who were at the very bottom of the barrel. English was not for them. They were considered illiterate, and yet they could write like this.

```
You said that I never understood;
That I didn't love you...
How wrong you were...
Oh, how wrong...
Remember how we would walk in the woods?
I tried to show my love for you...
I even brought you roses...
Oh, how you loved roses.
If only I could have communicated to
You through the beauty of the woods
My love for you...
If only it wasn't so hard to express
Even simple love in such an evil town as this
If only I hadn't left the room for that short time...
If only there hadn't been the knife on the table...
If only... If only... If only...
```

Read those aloud, and remember them the next time you make a quick decision about which students can't write.

This may be the time to mention that I quit high school each year and did not graduate. My parents were told that I did not belong in school. When I see how quickly and how permanently many of our students are evaluated, I cannot forget the years when I was told I was stupid, year after year, and I believed it. The students and their parents usually believe us. If we tell our students, consciously or subconsciously, that English is not for them, they will go away, and most of them will stay away.

No teacher will convert all the hard-core anti-writers. We have equality of opportunity, but, thank God, not a bland equality of accomplishment. Not all people will want to reveal themselves in writing, nor should they. But when we find someone who has not spoken before discovering his own voice, it is the most satisfying thing that can happen to a teacher. It's worth all the disappointments, all the defeats, for that one victory.

34 How to Publish Papers

The act of writing is incomplete and meaningless unless the writer has a reader. The writer's success is measured by his ability to be understood by his readers. At first the teacher may be an adequate reader. But soon the student needs publication, not uncritical publication, not merely praise—not the "These-are-the-best-papers-in-my-class, look-what-I'm-doing" kind of thing that a teacher puts out—but publication which exposes him to the questions of his readers.

In the beginning I've found this is best done in small groups, by having three to five students show their papers to each other. The papers can be passed around in this group for critical comments, or can be reproduced in some form. It is quite simple to have the students reproduce copies of their own papers, either printing them by hand or typing them with a few carbons. I do not find that reading out loud is publication. The good oral reader makes a piece of writing seem something better than it is, and a poor reader can destroy it. This may be my own prejudice. I studied writing in workshop classes where pieces were read aloud for criticism. I could never quite keep track of what was happening. I think it is much better when the reader can face the page, mark it up, criticize it, comment upon it, deal with it as he would deal with it if the writer were not there.

Eventually, publication should expand to the class. There are many copying devices which make this possible. It can be done by an overhead projector, for example, but I think it is best done when the student has an individual piece of paper he can take home, mull over, read, think about, bring back and comment upon.

Critical analysis of good writers is an important part of teaching. But most students feel that it is remote. E. B. White's problem may be their problem, but few students see this. What they want to see is what other students are doing, students in their own class. They should also see what their teacher is capable of doing, for the writing class should work as a unit to improve its own writing.

The school newspaper, literary magazine, and yearbook are motivating forces for the best students. I think they are an integral part of the writing curriculum, but they generally reach only a minority. It is also a rare school system which will, or can, encourage vigorous, honest writing in any publications. It is not the censorship of salacious material which is disturbing in these publications, but the lack of solid, critical material which examines the world around the student honestly and vigorously. Most school systems in most towns will not tolerate this, and so high school publications become bland display places for the work of the goody-goody student. They do not attract, in many cases, the best students, and certainly not those students who have felt that writing is remote from them because it is merely pretty words written by nice girls for prim teachers.

The discipline of good journalistic writing, the opportunity to reach an audience beyond the classroom in the literary magazine, the chance to combine art work and literary creativity in a yearbook that becomes a permanent historical document, are all important, if the school will encourage and support such activities.

This is not a problem of dirty words. If people are afraid of dirty words, then there is no reason to use them and offend them. But the real criticism is of questions, and of honest reports of what students are doing and thinking about.

The teacher can demand and get classroom publication and this publication may be enough. It can be expanded, as John Harris has expanded it at Conard High School in Hartford, Connecticut, by requiring for the writing courses at least one paper a month from other disciplines. The publication can be the paper written for the writing teacher and another teacher. The student of writing who does not publish what he writes can be compared with the athlete who never gets into a game. The act of writing is not complete until a piece of writing is published and read, and the teacher should seek whatever ways he can in his own school to achieve a variety of publications for his students.

35 How to Plan in Time of Panic

One experienced teacher who saw the outline for this book said that this chapter should be titled, "Dear God, Oh God, What Will I Try Tomorrow?" Every teacher has probably experienced this feeling of emptiness before certain classes on certain days. But the problem can be particularly acute for the writing teacher, who is forced to repeat those same simple rules, again and again. It is essential, therefore, for the teacher of writing to continue to find new ways of presenting the old material: new projects, new assignments, new combinations of materials.

The basic preparation of the writing teacher does not come from the subject matter. It comes from the students. Day after day as he reads the students' papers, teaches them in conference, listens to them in discussions about writing, the teacher sees which problems need to be dealt with at that time in that particular course, and he reaches out for materials which will help him do the job. He is on a constant search for teaching ideas, new models, fresh assignments, contemporary insights.

This chapter is one of the last to be dictated, and on the eve of the final day of dictation I happened to pick up *The Many Worlds of Leo Rosten* at a book sale. The book included several of the 1100-word biographical essays which first appeared in *Look* on the "fifty men of the western world who, in my judgment, may be said to have made and shaped our civilization." Mr. Rosten said of writing them: "I don't suppose any discipline ever forced upon me can match that entailed in writing these 1100-word profiles. I am convinced, after all my fumings and ulcerous frustrations, that the best way to teach English composition is through impossible assignments: 'Analyze Thomas Aquinas in 600 words'; 'Describe Constantine the Great in two paragraphs'; 'Summarize Adam Smith's economic principles on one page.' I know of no pedagogical magic that will so swiftly and forcefully teach you how to use language. You will, of course, be learning much more than English: you will be compelled to structure thought, probe to the central and the decisive, drive your mind to a most rigorous purpose."

I'm not sure he was serious, but I decided it would be a good project for the student as I read his pieces about Socrates, Columbus, Machiavelli, and Voltaire. In the same book he includes some profiles of artists in the series, "The Story Behind the Painting," in which each essay is less than 725 words long.

Read the biography of Newton, reprinted below. See how Mr. Rosten makes Newton come alive on the page. But more than that, he puts the reason inside the mind of this man as he saw and solved problems important to the development of civilization.

"Newton"

He is quickly made to come alive on the page

See how this is set up

1665. The bubonic plague raged in England. Cambridge sent all students home—among them one Isaac Newton, a silent, humorless young man who had no friends, was not interested in girls, often dressed freakishly, was hopelessly lost in his thoughts. He returned to his mother's house now, aged twenty-three, with nothing to do except wait for Cambridge to reopen. Nothing to do? In the next eighteen months, he made three of the greatest discoveries in the history of human thought.

Sets scene

Notice how he defines the imaginative step taken by Newton

Should the student try to reduce complex questions to a similar simplicity?

Perhaps such assignments could be done in cooperation with teachers of other subjects

Sitting in the garden one day, he saw an apple fall to the ground . . . Stop. Newton did not "discover" gravitation. Learned men accepted the idea of gravity, but assumed it was limited to a certain small distance above the earth. More important, no one had *proved* that gravitation exists. Newton's great stroke of imagination was to ask: Could it be that the invisible force that had pulled the apple off the branch was the same force that keeps the moon in its orbit? Could it be that the earth not only "attracts" the moon, but reaches out beyond its highest mountains, far, far into space? Do the earth, moon, planets, satellites whirl around the sun, bound by the sun's gravitation? Is gravity found in *matter* itself—any piece of matter? Does the apple attract the earth, too, however infinitesimally? Is gravitation an invisible binding power which holds the entire *universe* together? If gravity is such a force, he speculated, it can be measured. And if it can be measured, the entire solar system could be reduced to one mathematical formula! Newton quickly made some calculations; the results were only "pretty nearly correct." (He learned eighteen years later that his figure for the earth's radius was inaccurate.)

Clarification of complexity

How much study did Rosten have to do before he could write this?

And why, young Newton wondered, did the apple fall *straight* down? Why didn't the apple fall slightly to one side? (The earth, after all, always spins on its axis.) Could it be that objects are drawn not to the earth's surface—but toward the earth's *center?* He had the astounding idea that the gravitational pull of any body (diminished with distance, varying according to size and density) acts *as if all of its mass* is magically compressed, *concentrated in a single point* at the center. The earth, the moon, the sun itself could be treated as *points* in space! The mathematics of the day was too crude to work out the incredibly complex problems. So he improved it—and created the differential and integral calculus, as ingenious a device as ever came from a mortal mind. It is the basis of all modern mathematics.

Newton, believe it or not, now put all his theories, notes, formulas aside and turned to a new problem: light. He made a small hole in the window blind and directed a beam of sunlight so that it hit a small triangular glass,

Could the student do this and compare his observations with Newton's?

passed through this prism and hit a screen, where it appeared not as a spot of white, but in a rectangle of colors: violet at the top, then blue, green, yellow, orange, red. Each color had been bent ("refracted") in the glass prism at a different angle—and the colors differed in their "length," from glass to screen (violet longest, red shortest). Newton called this rectangular band a "spectrum." He then placed a second glass triangle so that the colors emerging from the first prism passed through the second—and, to his astonishment, the colors emerged, reblended, as white! It was a startling discovery, for white light had always been considered "absolute." The paper he published founded the science of optics. (He also made the first reflecting telescope.)

A man and his work might be the theme for a series of student biographies about people in town

For eighteen years, Newton published nothing about universal gravitation or calculus. He worked on the *Philosophiae Naturalis Principia Mathematica* ("The Mathematical Principles of Natural Philosophy") with such ferocious concentration that he suffered a nervous breakdown. He lost his "former consistency of mind," wrote abusive letters to friends. The *Principia*, the greatest single feat of analysis in all science, created a furor. It defined mass, force, inertia. It established the laws of motion. It observed that every action has an equal reaction: "If you press a stone, (your) finger is also pressed by the stone." It calculated the mass of the sun. It explained the moon's "perturbed" orbit. It proved that the earth bulges around the equator; the poles are slightly flattened. It showed that the moon's pull causes the earth's axis to inscribe a circle in space, and explained why the equinoxes take place a little earlier each year. It explained the mystery of the tides, the sea's surging response to the pull of moon and sun. It even explained comets, which astronomers thought moved "lawlessly" and represented God's warnings to men: Newton predicted their movements with beautiful precision. One comet appeared exactly on schedule.

Note how specifically these generalizations are written

Newton pushed theology out of science. He gave men a model of how to understand nature, how to experiment, how to let theories flow from facts—not faith. He created a new cosmology—one that completely replaced the mystical universe of the Middle Ages. He transformed astronomy into a branch of physics. He made mathematics the key to the secrets of the universe.

He was attacked for the outrageous notion that the universe could be reduced to numbers. Newton had removed God from the universe, many said, replaced His glories with a soulless machine, debased creation into "the lifeless story of a planless mind." Newton, a pious man, was horrified. In the *Principia,* he had written: "This most beautiful system . . . could only proceed from the . . . dominion of an intelligent and powerful Being."

Scientists scoffed at the absurd idea that objects "attract" one another from a distance, with no physical contact or intermediary between them. Newton himself had said it seemed bizarre: "It is enough that gravity does really exist, and according to laws we have described, and abundantly serves to account for all the motions of the celestial bodies, and of our sea."

Could a student do a portrait of an athlete, showing his peculiar virtues with equal clarity?

Embittered by the controversy, morbidly fearful of criticism, Newton abandoned science for theology. He made elaborate calculations of the generations from Adam down. He experimented in alchemy and wrote on occult themes—hiding his manuscripts. He twice served in Parliament, was knighted, appointed Warden of the Mint, wasted his time, yet could still astound men by his brilliance. One night after dinner, he solved a problem that had baffled the greatest mathematicians.

Note the vigor and authority of a good quotation

He died in 1727, aged eighty-four. The inscription in Westminster Abbey ends: "Let mortals rejoice that there has existed such and so great an ornament of the human race." But of himself, he once said: "I seem to have been only like a boy, playing on the seashore and diverting myself in now and then finding a smoother pebble or a prettier shell than ordinary, whilst the great ocean of truth lay all undiscovered before me."

It should be obvious to you, and will be obvious to your students, that the big problem is the research, and so they must be given the time to do something much more than look up the encyclopedia article. This assignment must be given far enough ahead so that the student can do some research, pass in a bibliography, perhaps write a short theme defining the "central and the decisive" events in the man's life. Perhaps there should be time to describe in a research report how the student has gone about researching his subject, and finally there should be time to write and rewrite the profile itself.

In the same book Mr. Rosten said, "I am nowhere as skilled in writing as I am in rewriting—a form of masochism in which my compulsiveness flourishes like some damn stinkweed. Some men are addicted to poker, or liquor, or doxies; I am addicted to revising. I have rewritten (not just polished) some stories thirty, forty, fifty times. I know this sounds like the grossest exaggeration, but the secretaries who have fled from me with pitiful bleatings after an umpteenth 'final' draft can testify that I am not boasting. I would long since have been removed to some booby hatch, I suppose, except for one saving trait: I hate to write but I love to rewrite . . . You would think that by now I would have learned to start a new piece of writing with professional ease, even confidence, knowing that the most important first step, for my kind of lunacy, is simply to get something down on paper, however rough and fumbling, so that I can then try to give it shape, point, precision in the strange ebullience of re-creation. Alas, I have learned nothing. Each time I face the seductive and intractable blank pages anew, my heart sinks. I groan, I moan, I delay, I defer. . . ."

The search for material and his own natural curiosity about writing, artists, music, the world about him will lead the teacher of writing to many places. The following quotation might be reproduced for the class as a spark for discussion. Perhaps even a bit of Charles Ives' strange and wonderful music might be played before these words from his "Note to 114 Songs," is read.

"Every normal man—that is, every uncivilised or civilised human being not of defective mentality, moral sense, etc., has, in some degree, creative insight (an unpopular statement). There are many, too many, who think they have none of it, and stop with the thought or before the thought.

There are a few who think (and encourage others to think), but they and they only have this insight, interest, etc. . . . (as a kind of collateral security) they and they only know how to give expression to it, etc. But in every human soul there is a ray of celestial beauty (Plotinus admits that), and a spark of genius (nobody admits that).

"If this is so, and if one of the greatest sources of strength—one of the greatest joys, and deepest pleasures of man, is giving rein to it in some way, why should not everyone instead of a few, be encouraged. And feel justified in encouraging everyone including himself to make this a part of everyone's and his life—a value that will supplant the other values and help round out the substance of the soul?"

Students should be shown bad writing as well as good writing. They may be assigned such sentences as the following and told they are prose doctors whose job is to diagnose the authors' difficulties and to prescribe a treatment for them.

"Among the Anglo-American jurists it is thus habitual to wage a silent war of attrition against the conception of a comprehensive international law on behalf of terms like 'conflict of laws' or 'comity,' which they treat as an arcanum, to be opened only by the exercise of transcendant subtleties legitimized under the recognized legerdemain of principles of jurisdiction, derived from territorial sovereignty, nationality, and other technical concepts."[3]

"Taking all these points together, do we not find good cause to line up, as one strand in the symbolic action in the poem, a sequence from marriage problem, through the murder of the Albatross as a synecdochic representation of Sarah, to the 'blessing' of the snakes that synecdochically represent the drug and the impulsive premarital aesthetic (belonging in a contrary cluster) to an explicit statement of preference for church, prayer, and companionship over marriage (with the Mariner returning to shore under the aegis of the praying Hermit, and the poem itself ending on the prayerful, moralizing note that has annoyed many readers as a change in quality)?"[4] (In case you can't guess, it's about Coleridge and "The Rime of the Ancient Mariner.")

The writing class may be broken up into small groups, in which one member acts as a reporter, collecting the specifics for a given theme. A second class member, following the *Time* pattern, might be a writer who gives shape and form to the first draft. A third would take the finished draft and rewrite it, making it even tighter. A fourth member would edit the entire piece of writing.

The teacher can exploit what is interesting to the students, a local news event, an accident, a controversy, an election, make them reporters who dig out the information about subjects which do arouse their curiosity, and then lead them through the problems of putting that information together into a responsible order.

[3] Myre S. McDougal and Harold D. Lasswell, *The Identification and Appraisal of Systems of Public Order.*

[4] Kenneth Burke, *The Philosophy of Literary Form.*

One of the most common devices for teaching writing is to encourage students to attempt poetry or a short story. The hazards here are enormous. First of all, the teacher is tempted to reward creativity in any bland form. When a teacher is reading hundreds upon hundreds of themes, the slightest spark of imagination is likely to seem creative, and a burst of undeserved praise falls about the writer. As we have said, discipline must play an equal role with the creative urge. In poetry, the student seems to have an open door to getting away with a lack of discipline, and unless the teacher has a true understanding of poetry from the maker's point of view, it is very difficult for him to discipline the student. Fiction written by the adolescent is usually as bad as his poetry. He is not capable of the imaginative feat it takes to develop a character or a situation fully. He writes on a theme which a novelist would be terrified of attempting in 500 pages, in two or three pages. His writing tends to be general, a sort of précis or scenario of what he should be writing about rather than fully developed dramatic writing. Students should not be discouraged from attempting poetry and fiction on occasion, and it may be appropriate in an elective course in writing for the particularly advanced or interested student, but the emphasis of the composition course should be on expository writing, which may include some biographical profiles and descriptions.

The students in the writing course may work on a book of advice on writing for other students; they may try to turn a piece of fiction into a television play; they may write letters to their congressmen or senators; imitate news stories or editorials; write business memoranda; ghost speeches for the President; write an essay on how the school ought to be run. They should constantly be trying new things, and the teacher should exploit this newness. Years ago, efficiency experts at the Western Electric plant in Hawthorne, New Jersey, tried changing the working conditions. They told the workers they were part of an experiment. The workers responded to every change with increased productivity. No matter what the change was or how effective it really was, their production went up. Finally the experts realized they were responding to the attention given to them, and this effect became known as the Hawthorne Effect. Students in the writing course should be told they are participants in an experimental writing course when the course is experimental—and it should be experimental most of the time. The teacher should say and believe that their own suggestions are valuable, and he should be willing to try new things all the time.

John Eastman of Hollis (New Hampshire) High School has rewritten some of the basic paragraphs from *Elements of Style* by Strunk and White as badly as possible, printing them up on transparencies and flashing them on the wall where the students can see, or rather discover, for themselves which version is better. The teacher who wants the class to work on language might bring in the article from *The New York Times Book Review* of June 11, 1967 about Found Poetry, in which the writer takes rather obvious things about him—signs, fragments of writing—and doesn't rewrite any of the lines, but merely arranges the sentences into poetic form. For example, *The New York Times* quotes Ronald Gross, who took an Associated Press bulletin from the *Denver Post* and printed it this way.

Miss Farrow Just Smiled

Singer Frank Sinatra
honeymooned, somewhere,
with his third wife,
Mia Farrow, today
after a Las Vegas
wedding performed
between plane flights.

Exactly where they went
hasn't been determined.

After the ceremony
the couple walked out
on the apartment's patio
and Sinatra beamed:
"How are you, baby?"

Miss Farrow just smiled.

After the ceremony
the couple walked out
on the apartment's patio
and Sinatra beamed:
"How are you, baby?"

Exactly where they went
hasn't been determined.

Singer Frank Sinatra
honeymooned, somewhere,
with his third wife,
Mia Farrow, today
after a Las Vegas
wedding performed
between plane flights.

Exactly where they went
hasn't been determined.

After the ceremony
the couple walked out
on the apartment's patio
and Sinatra beamed:
"How are you, baby?"

Miss Farrow just smiled.

The class which has been working on rewriting and first drafts to the point of boredom should be forced to write in class under deadline. A group which has been working in the classroom a great deal should have out-of-class assignments. Variety, variety, variety. In my journalism classes I find the single most important exercise involves lead writing. Students bring a newspaper to class and, taking no more than five minutes for a lead, rewrite the first few sentences of every news story on page one. This might be an interesting exercise for a week in a composition class, for in five days, with some examination of news style, they can begin to turn out fine variations in a matter of minutes. Sometimes it's helpful to have them do more than one variation on a lead, particularly if you want to make the student realize that writing is plastic, something which can be changed and developed, not a matter of scientific absoluteness.

Sally Byrne at Milford (New Hampshire) High School has her students working on personality collages: they look for visual specifics in pictures from magazines and newspapers and then glue them on a board. This has been particularly helpful with a slow and disturbed seventh-grade class. The seniors help the seventh-graders, and they both learn from this assignment.

One project which is interesting is to have the student list fifty or one hundred specifics about a childhood incident which is most memorable—the first time he was lost in the city, when grandfather died, the August slum riot of ten years before. After he lists the specifics he may try to shape this incident into a few short paragraphs, at first by just reporting it, and finally by using his perspective as an adolescent to begin to give it meaning, to show the implications of what happened to him.

Writing teachers should work with science teachers, history teachers, humanities teachers, people in every other discipline to get ideas for projects and assignments. *A Casebook on the Declaration of Independence* edited by Robert Ginsberg (Crowell) could be very useful in a joint unit with a social studies, humanities or history class. Miss Whittaker's idea of using the myths with the ninth grade Negro children in Boston came from an experimental junior high course in anthropology.

The writing teacher should improvise, adapt, adopt (steal) good ideas wherever he can find them. For example, I discovered that a colleague of mine, Professor Hugh Potter, made his students respond to a lecture at the next meeting by bringing in either a statement or a question about the lecture in writing. He collected these and responded to them. I tried a variation of the same thing. I have had students bring in written questions on writing once a week, then I have collected those questions and either spent a class period or a few minutes at the end of the class period answering these questions by random selection. I have found that the questions which are written out are better, sharper, and more pertinent than many of the questions in class. Some students who will never ask questions in class ask the best written questions, and almost all of the written questions reflect the problems faced by all of the students. The pattern of written questions is a part of my elementary writing courses, and I've used it in high school with a great deal of success.

It's helpful to have students write about writing. For example, students may define, in less than ten lines each, the three greatest problems in writing. When you write about writing you have to focus on how to write as well as what to write, and the combination can be very helpful for the student.

The teacher should be on a continuous search for ideas which will encourage his students to write so that they can face the old problems of writing in new and stimulating situations.

36 How to Teach Writing

"There is no golden key to writing."

That's what Bill Sims tells his English classes. He is right. That is the professional secret shared by the successful writer and the successful teacher of writing.

This does not mean writing cannot be taught. You can teach almost every student the skills of writing, but you cannot teach him that magic which makes him a great writer, and neither can you teach him with one secret formula.

The writer believes in high standards of honesty and skill, but he does not believe in restrictions on writing, on rules that cannot be broken, on principles or methods that must be followed. What counts in writing is what is written, for writing is not an end in itself. What the writer has to say not only determines how he says it, but whether it's worth saying.

When a writer teaches writing he emphasizes that his students first have something to say, that they look at their world and find their subject, and then write about what is important to them. The writer must look around him—in the scholar's library, the scientist's laboratory, or the student's neighborhood—to see the specifics, the facts, the truths which he needs to communicate.

The writer understands that people have a hunger for form, and he feels this need of structure very strongly himself. He wants to discover patterns—meanings, reasons, explanations—in his world.

The writer knows how difficult it is to commit himself to writing and he brings himself to his desk so he will produce a draft he can start to work on, rewriting, rethinking, polishing. Mechanics come last; content comes first.

The writer works at a hard, lonely job. He is never satisfied with what he has written. It is never so good as he wanted it to be, never so good as it could be. He hopes that the student will suffer the same agonies, the same challenges, the same satisfactions, and achieve the same standards.

The teacher of writing must realize that he is a skill teacher. He cannot pattern himself on the academic teacher. He should learn methods from the football coach for the coaching of writing is an individual matter, and all programs in writing should be built on the fact that the student is a doer and the teacher is someone who encourages the student individually and meets him in conference with a paper between them and a pen in hand.

Yes, writing can be taught. There is no golden key, but there is a discipline, a way of doing the job. The student writer can learn the lessons of the writer, and when he has learned them he will find that there is satisfaction and even fun in writing. He will discover he has a voice and that he is able to satisfy one of his basic drives, the hunger to communicate.

I may have wept that any should have died
Or missed their chance, or not have been their best,
Or been their riches, fame, or love denied;
On me as much as any is the jest.
I take my interruption with the rest.
God bless himself can no one else be blessed.

I hold your doctrine of Memento Mori:
And were an epitaph to be my story
I'd have a short one ready for my own.
I would have written of me on my stone:
I had a lover's quarrel with the world.

Robert Frost

Six Resources for the Teacher of Writing

The composition teacher must be flexible in his approaches to the teaching of writing. He is teaching individual students, and he needs different materials to work with different students. The writing teacher must have a documented understanding of the writing process and he should have an inventory of materials he can use to solve new teaching problems.

37 The Writer Writes

The writer is a reader who reads with a special eye for craft. Consciously and subconsciously he looks to see how others have solved the problems he faces. His judgment is often suspect because he may admire or envy too much what he cannot do himself, and he may pass over what he himself finds easy. The teacher of writing should, as much as possible, read with a writer's eye, noting what the author has done and how he has done it. Each writing teacher should develop his own file of models which he can use in his teaching or for his own enjoyment.

The teaching and the enjoyment should not be far apart. I still read with delight, and there are novelists, poets, and historians I turn to for refreshment. There are also some writers who don't fall into those categories, who are less well known, perhaps, in the literature course, but who use the language with glorious skill. A passage from Orwell or White rarely ceases to sustain me. More often than can be expected of any normal man, James Reston clarifies the complications of the day with a sentence or a phrase in his *New York Times* column. Joseph Mitchell is a master, as is James Agee. Robert Wallace and Berton Roueché are not far behind.

How does a writer react to good writing? I repeat, with delight. There is no other word to describe the feeling I have when I pick up, for example, Rebecca West's *The New Meaning of Treason.* Here is a marriage of thought and language. Her book is a careful, probing examination of England's traitors in recent years, and she starts with the trial of William Joyce, who made propaganda broadcasts to England from Germany during World War II. At the beginning of the second page this is the way she describes the Central Criminal Court where he was tried: "Because of the Blitz it stood in a beautiful desert of charred stone. Churches stood blackened but apparently intact; birds, however, flew through the empty sockets of the windows, and long grass grew around their altars."* Do you see why a writer would delight in those trim sentences?

We are introduced to William Joyce. Listen to Dame Rebecca West:

Robert Frost
"A Lesson for Today,"
Harvard Phi Beta Kappa poem read June 20, 1941 by the poet. Manuscript in the hand of Kay Morrison with corrections by Robert Frost. Copyright 1942 by Robert Frost. Reprinted by permission of The Estate of Robert Frost and Holt, Rinehart and Winston, Inc. and by permission of the Harvard College Library.

* This and the following excerpts are reprinted from *The New Meaning of Treason* by Rebecca West. Copyright © 1964 by Rebecca West. All rights reserved. Reprinted by permission of The Viking Press, Inc., and by permission of A. D. Peters & Co.

"The strong light was merciless to William Joyce, whose appearance was a shock to all of us who knew him only over the air. His voice had suggested a large and flashy handsomeness, but he was a tiny little creature and not handsome at all. His hair was mouse-coloured and sparse, particularly above his ears, and his pinched and misshapen nose was joined to his face at an odd angle. His eyes were hard and shiny and above them his thick eyebrows were pale and irregular. His neck was long, his shoulders narrow and sloping, his arms very short and thick. His body looked flimsy and coarse. There was nothing individual about him except the deep scar running across his right cheek from his ear to the corner of his mouth. But this did not create the savage and marred distinction that it might suggest, for it gave a mincing immobility to his small mouth. He was dressed with a dandyish preciosity which gave no impression of well-being, only of nervousness. He was like an ugly version of Scott Fitzgerald, but more nervous. He moved with a jerky formality and, when he bowed to the judge, his bow seemed sincerely respectful but entirely inappropriate to the occasion, and it was difficult to think of any occasion to which it would have been appropriate." (p. 4)

"Write in revealing details," say the teacher of writing. Here is an example of what we mean. We see William Joyce, we know him. Rebecca West writes with keen perception. Here is a short paragraph, and yet it is one that I can't get out of my mind. After the trial she describes Joyce's followers. "The little band of Fascists gathered together in a knot by the door, and after they had wiped their faces, and composed themselves, they went into the street. In the open space in front of the building was a line of parked cars, and behind them stood a crowd of silent people. The Fascists walked away from this crowd, down a street that narrowed and lost itself in a network of alleys. Nobody followed them, but they began to hurry. By the time they got to the shelter of the alleys, they were almost running." (p. 21)

A simple paragraph, but an effective one. No words wasted, every word in place. Introducing another character, she writes, "John Amery was not insane, he was not evil, but his character was like an automobile that will not hold the road." (p. 91) A nice simile. Dame Rebecca West writes perceptively, for example: "His home was in a street of little brick houses down in Wandsworth, the kind of street from which ability keeps pushing up, and occasionally misses its way, if it reads the wrong books and misunderstands what it reads." (p. 255) And her language has bite, because her eye and her mind can cut: ". . . Englishmen are sent to public schools because that is the only place where they can learn good manners, the manners they learn there are recognized as good only by people who have been to the same sort of school, and often appear very bad indeed to everybody else." (p. 257) Later in the same paragraph she refers to "an insolence of diplomats." The writer reads her for what she says, but also for how she says it.

Notice the way these sentences move. "Christine Keeler had suffered a complete collapse. On the tide of her own hysteria she had been swept up and down Fleet Street, out to Spain and back again, in and out of solicitors' offices, on a continual merry-go-round swinging between Marylebone Police Court and the Old Bailey, in and out of the witness box, in and out of expensive flats rented by eccentrics with no visible means of support, into motor crashes, back and forth through booing, jeering, leering crowds. She was a pitiful sight. She remained beautiful, but her beauty was now a thin veil worn by a sick and grubby child. Her one salient characteristic was the desire for respect; she would have enjoyed being the head of a woman's college." (p. 355) And later she turns her eye on the crowd, "The cries and boos of the crowd express the purest envy." (p. 357)

Dame Rebecca is always thinking, always making connections, always probing, for good writing comes directly from good thinking. She says, "Men must be capable of imagining and executing and insisting on social change, if they are to reform or even maintain civilization, and capable too of furnishing the rebellion which is sometimes necessary if society is not to perish of immobility. Therefore all men should have a drop of treason in their veins, if the nations are not to go soft like so many sleepy pears." (p. 361) And so she moves through a very careful examination and conclusion until these nice sentences at the end. "But if we do not keep before us the necessity for uniting care for security with determination to preserve our liberties, we may lose our cause because we have fought too hard. Our task is equivalent to walking on a tightrope over an abyss, but the continued survival of our species through the ages shows that, if we human beings have a talent, it is for tightrope-walking." (p. 370)

Any writer collects his own masters and some non-masters who are good models. In the following pages this writer will look critically, from the writer's point of view, at a number of pieces which have helped him as a writer and as a teacher.

There is something special about the well-made paragraph. The writer delights in a paragraph such as the following one written by Mary McCarthy, one of the most incisive stylists writing today. A close study of this paragraph will reveal how every detail builds up to the dominant impression. There is a clear development from the first to the last sentence as the point of the paragraph is set up, established, and documented.

From Memories of a Catholic Girlhood

Place documented — **Build up to this phrase then documented** — **Eleven specific details which make you see and feel the room** — **Unity**

Whenever we children came to stay at my grandmother's house, we were put to sleep in the sewing room, a bleak, shabby, utilitarian rectangle, more office than bedroom, more attic than office, that played to the Hierarchy of chambers the role of poor relation. It was a room seldom entered by other members of the family, seldom swept by the maid, a room without pride: the old sewing[1] machine, some cast-off chairs[2], a shadeless lamp[3], rolls of wrapping[4] paper, piles of cardboard[5] boxes that might someday come in handy, papers[6] of pins, and remnants of[7] a material united with the iron folding[8] cots put out for our use and the bare[9] floor boards to give an impression of intense and ruthless temporality. Thin white[10] spreads, of the kind used in hospitals and charity institutions, and naked blinds[11] at the windows reminded us of our orphaned condition and of the ephemeral character of our visit; there was nothing here to encourage us to consider this our home.

Reprinted by permission of Harcourt, Brace & World, Inc., and by permission of William Heinemann Ltd. of London.

The student should read a few articles that are so well-built he can appreciate their form as an apprentice craftsman comprehends his master's skill. Kenneth Andler's "Surveyor in the Woods" is a fine example of good form which the student can be helped to see and appreciate.

Each writing teacher should have a file of articles or textbooks or collections of essays, a library resource which can be shown to the student at the time he is able to appreciate what the writer has done. A few classroom demonstrations or analyses of good writing are worthwhile—but very few. It is better to deal with the student individually or to pull a few students together and say, "You're all having a problem with structure. Now look at what Mr. Andler does." It may be helpful to pass out copies of such an essay to the students involved and say, "Read this tonight, and tomorrow bring me a paragraph telling me, as one writer to another, what you see in this. What has this writer done that you could learn?"

The teacher may find it useful to spend several days on at least one piece of writing during the course, analyzing it, digging into it, revealing how it is designed, constructed, and built. The analysis at all times should come from the writer's point of view, not the reader's. How was the writer able to achieve this effect? Why did he organize his article in this way? How does he show instead of tell? Is he using specifics? How would you have done this?

It may be helpful to have the student try to rewrite a paragraph from the article another way, changing the tone or the order of the paragraph. He should have to justify each word in a particularly good paragraph, showing how every single word contributes to the piece. The student should be a critical craftsman, saying in one place, "Yes, I could do a better job of that," and "Boy, he did a good job there."

"Surveyor in the Woods"

Classic topic sentence—each clause relates to a section of the article—but is it dull?

I want to tell you about a woodsman, what he was like, what his work was, and what it meant. His name was Alfred D. Teare and he came originally from Nova Scotia, but all the time I knew him his home was in Berlin, New Hampshire. Probably the best surveyor of old lines in New England, he was —in his way—a genius.

Sets scene

Verbs!

Specifics

I saw him for the first time when I was a boy of twelve; he was visiting my stepfather, a lawyer, who was then engaged in litigation involving boundary lines. Mr. Teare, a wonderful story-teller, held our family entranced with his tales of the woods. He conjured up a marvelous land of mountains, rivers, and lakes, peopled it with lumberjacks, rivermen, timber cruisers, Maine guides, and plenty of bears and moose for good measure. Just the expression, "the Maine woods," as he used it, tingled along my spine. He visited our house several times after that and always brought my stepfather a bundle of pipe-lighters, little sticks about a foot long, taken from the roots of an old-growth pine windfall, for use with an open fire. They smelled good; they had the woods in them as a sea shell has the roar of the sea.

Author establishes his authority

The summer I was fourteen, in 1918, I had a chance to work as a chainer for Mr. Teare, who then was running lines near Reading and Plymouth, Vermont; and I spent several seasons with him thereafter.

Show, don't tell

At that time he was nearing sixty years of age. Over average height in spite of a pronounced stoop to his shoulders and quite heavily set, he appeared to be coming at you aggressively with his head lowered like a buffalo. Although his back was quite bent he had powerful arms and shoulders, and somehow he seemed stronger that way than if he had been erect, particularly when he carried an enormous pack by means of a tumpline.

Details make him come alive

Tricks documented immediately

Tone—logger's exaggeration appropriate

He had a forceful, weatherbeaten, almost leathery face; a dewlap like a bulldog's; a bald pate bounded by a horseshoe of black hair turning gray; blue eyes, and short, strong, even teeth with spaces between them. One of the curious little tricks he delighted in, when occasion required, was biting a fish line in two with hardly more than one snap. His hands, remarkably square with large blunt fingers, were tough and work-hardened with skin like leather. A mosquito never could drill through this hide of his, and often, when one tried, Mr. Teare would watch it with a tolerant amusement until it staggered off bewildered.

Emphasis

Shown in action

Can you imitate this from his description?

"Paw"—is that too much?

He took a peculiar pride in his eyesight; but he must have been far-sighted like many outdoor men, for he had a sturdy pair of glasses which hung from a fish line about his neck and nestled snugly under his shirt in the abundant hair on his chest. To use them, he always hauled them up through his open shirt, and taking them by one end with his blunt fingers, perched them on his nose. He had the characteristic habit of always sitting on his left foot, his left leg bent under him, his right leg out straight. He was nimble enough to do this as long as he lived and it provided him a cushion of sorts on ground no matter how cold or wet. When he made his survey notes he would seat himself thus, affix his glasses with a kind of clumsy ease and write laboriously in a red-covered notebook with a hard smudgeless drawing pencil which seemed lost in his great, rough paw.

Author reminds you of his authority

Summer or winter he always wore heavy woolen socks, and in summer, ankle-height moccasins, half-soled and hobnailed (really the best footgear imaginable), trousers of heavy khaki, a faded blue denim work shirt, and a slouch hat. He never would wear corduroy as he said corduroy gets wet two weeks before a rain.

Generalization followed by documentation

Of Scottish descent and old-fashioned in manner, he used rare and almost obsolete expressions seldom if ever heard nowadays. He used "gran'sir" for "grandfather," spoke of building up a good fire "against the night," and was the only person I ever heard use the archaic "an" for "if." One favorite expression he coined himself, I believe: of an honest man he would say, "He's as square as ninety degrees."

Verb!

Definitions gracefully worked into text

Of course, he reeked with ordinary woods lore. He pointed out to me what a widow-maker was: the dead top of a tree which would come crashing down when an axe-man started to cut at the base. A fool-killer, equally dangerous, was a live tree bent over by a fallen one so that when an unwary chopper drove an axe into it the tremendous tension, suddenly released, sent the tree splitting and charging up to catch him under the chin. A smudge of brakes warded off mosquitoes, of course, but it was news to me that only a bright fire would stop midges or "no-see-ums," for they'd fly right into it. Nothing in the world could stop an onslaught of black flies while we were at work on the line, although the best protection was a smudge pot and smearing our faces and hands with tobacco juice. Mr. Teare advised these things for our sakes; insects didn't irritate him. When we got soaked from a sudden shower, as we often did, and came tramping back to camp through water-laden brush, Mr. Teare said we wouldn't catch cold if we let our clothes dry on us. We always took his advice and slogged around camp like saturated dishrags while we built up a fire, but we never did catch cold from our wettings.

Repetition for emphasis

He was ingenious to a degree and a wizard with an axe. When a tree became lodged, he employed what he called a "Samson Pole" to make it fall in a different direction. This was a strong pole which he held upright, in a notch of which another strong pole was fitted, running as a cross bar to a notch in the recalcitrant tree, and with this device he could exert a tremendous leverage. If an axe handle got cracked he fixed it by binding a fish line tightly about it in a manner few could duplicate. He always had in camp an awl with waxed ends with which he could sew up his moccasins, and if he was far enough back in the woods and the need arose, he would tap them, sometimes using bark for leather.

You see man revealed in action

He was full of lore and ideas of his own concerning the curative properties of herbs. For bronchial trouble he advised the sticky gum which exudes from cherry trees. Balsam blisters were also good. If he had a bad enough cough, he mixed up a mysterious concoction which someone called "spruce gum and blue vitriol," and he downed it with a bearlike roar of distaste. When I cut my fingers deeply near the knuckles with an axe he rushed to my side where I was leaning against a tree, faint from loss of blood in July heat, and mopping up the gash with a handkerchief, he told me to wiggle my fingers. They wiggled; he could see the cords move, and he acted relieved. Then he took his plug of tobacco, chewed up a piece to a soft cud and placed it in the gash. He bound up my fingers with a splint and a handkerchief to keep in the tobacco. No infection set in, thanks to the nicotine, and although some stitches would have been a good idea, none were taken. The cut healed perfectly, though I shall aways bear the scar.

Generalization and documentation

His medicinal theories carried more weight with me when I learned that, many years before, when a doctor had given him six months to live because of his weakened and I gathered, consumptive condition, he had struck out for the woods where he slept on the ground and gulped a prodigious number of raw eggs every day. He came out of it all right and throughout the rest of his years was as rugged as an old gnarled oak.

II

Remember lead sentence: "what he was like"

He was not by any means simply a backwoodsman. He had travelled extensively throughout the United States; his work brought him into contact with the executives of large companies; but most of his life he spent in the woods. They were really home to him although he had a conventional home, a remarkable wife, and five grownup children.

Article is developed, moves forward

While I worked with him we usually camped out in a lean-to tent, open on one side, and before this side we built with huge flat rocks a fireplace in which on chilly nights we kept a fire of four-foot wood. Sometimes we threw into the fire great pieces of punk, a fungus black on the outside, reddish within, which grows in nubs on old birch trees, and then we'd have coals

Abundance of specifics

for the morning. We made our bed on the ground from the tips of fir branches, set upright very close together and then pushed backward at an angle.

At the opening of the tent we had a bench made from saplings, or from a board if we had one, which Mr. Teare called the "deacon seat." Sometimes where a tent would be a nuisance and we weren't going to stay long we built a bark lean-to, and often we revelled luxuriously in deserted and almost ruined farmhouses.

Although the company furnished us a cook one summer in Vermont when we had two timber cruisers with us, almost all the time I was with him, Mr. Teare did the cooking. He was very good at it, too. When we got in from work he would don a white apron (at least it had been white originally), mix up a batch of biscuits on a table of saplings covered with birch bark, put them in his little tin baker which faced the open fire, fry some meat, turn out a rice pudding to which we helpers contributed raspberries or blueberries in season, brew tea, and in no time produce an excellent meal. He delighted in baking beans in the ground, fried excellent doughnuts and a somewhat similar product which he called "doughgods."

Picture repeated

"Good black tea": sentimental glorification of past?

Exaggeration

We always carried our lunch for the noon meal together with a nest of metal cups and a tin tea pail. Invariably we would stop by a spring or brook and build a fire. Mr. Teare would set on his left foot, hunched forward and intent, holding the pail over the fire on a long pole, and he never paid the slightest attention if the smoke engulfed him. When the water boiled, he would swing the pail out for one of us to toss in a handful of good black tea, and then he'd swing it back over the fire for a momentary reboiling in the interest of strength and power. Our pail had seen so much service that merely boiling water in it produced stronger tea than most people would care to drink.

Appropriate tone?

Action shown

After lunch Mr. Teare would get out his long-bladed jackknife, pare off some shavings from his strong plug tobacco, and with the knife still held, blade upright, between thumb and forefinger of his right hand (lest more paring be necessary), he'd work the tobacco with a semicircular motion, between the palms of his hands—grist between millstones—then fill and light his pipe. He never, never used a match for this purpose if a fire were going, principally, I think, because he regarded matches in the woods as precious. He always took a brand from the fire, blew on it prodigiously to bring it to a bright coal, and lighted up with that. Often he would have only embers to choose from and these too he used, holding one somehow in his tough paw. He would press the ignited tobacco down with an impervious thumb and then, when the smoke rolled out, he would settle back to spellbind us with some yarn. The whole business of the noon meal was a never-varied rite.

He worked summer and winter on every passably workable day. In the winter, if camping out, he used a square tent with a stove in it. He wore ordinary snowshoes for fairly level country but bearpaws for rough and hilly terrain. As our lunch always froze we toasted our sandwiches over the fire. When Mr. Teare knocked the icy clods from his snowshoes, stood them up in the snow, and hunched over to start a fire with birch bark and dry sticks, he seemed as integral a part of winter in the woods as the snow upon the ground.

Reverse: specific to general

Sometimes he would stay at farmhouses instead of camping out. During the last forty years of his life, he worked mostly for such large corporations as the International Paper Company, the Mt. Tom Sulphite & Pulp Company, the Draper Corporation, the Brown Company, and others. He travelled extensively through the back country of northern New England and stayed at literally hundreds of isolated farmhouses, using them either to work from directly or as bases from which he could pack his "wangan" into the woods for a camp. Lonely farm families whose homes he had previously visited looked forward eagerly to his coming, for he brought to their routine existence an inexhaustible store of adventure tales and to their drab lives a fresh and lively color.

III

Lead sentence: "what his work was" Immediately begins to prove his topic sentence

The problem of surveying in the timberland of northern New England is one of the most difficult and fascinating things in the world. It's difficult because it consists largely of re-locating the old lines of original lots and ranges run by pioneers with crude compasses as much as one hundred and seventy-five years ago. The early surveyors blazed or spotted the trees along these lines, and for corners set posts, marked trees, or piled up stones. They also blazed trees about the corners for "witnesses." Succeeding surveyors have respotted the lines infrequently, perhaps not oftener than once in twenty years, and in many instances the original lines have not been renewed at all.

Good, clear exposition

When a tree is spotted with an axe the wood grows over the blaze in a few years and leaves nothing on the bark but a scar which only an experienced woodsman can recognize. A novice either notices no spot at all or thinks that every scar he sees is a spot whether it's a hedgehog mark, a windgall, or just a natural blemish.

Andler makes you appreciate importance of Teare's skill—his problems and solutions

Quotation is a specific

The original lots, laid out by the proprietors of each township, classified by number in ranges and divisions, usually contained about one hundred acres each and were described quite accurately and specifically by the early surveyors, who gave points of compass and definite distances in the title deeds; but as these lots were either split up or amalgamated with other lots, people grew very careless when conveying real estate, and fell into the habit of bounding land by the names of the adjoining owners, as in the classic example Mr. Teare used to quote from a Vermont deed: "Bounded on the North by Brother Jim, on the West by Brother Bill, on the South by Sister Sal, and on the East by Mother."

Mood of sadness

Foreshadowing of last paragraph in article

With the migration of farmers to the West, or to the cities, immense areas of rural farm land reverted to the wilderness. Even many New Englanders do not realize how far this went and how extensively the forests have crept in over once-tilled fields. We have seen sites of villages silent in the woods, crumbling cellar holes through which great trees are growing, once proud highways which are now only dim trails, and even a graveyard in Vermont from which three crops of pulp wood have been cut. Gone are the people who owned these farms, their most lasting works faded like old ink, their names nothing but an echo in the land records.

Clear exposition

Consequently, in these abandoned districts, now merely a wilderness, a reference in an old deed such as "bounded on the North by land of Abijah Davis," which may have been perfectly plain to the contracting parties in 1860, means very little now. A surveyor must trace the title deeds in the registry, draw tentative diagrams and fit them together like a jigsaw puzzle, and somehow or other get the chain of title back to the older deeds where references to compass courses and distances provide something definite to work on. By this research one may discover that Abijah Davis owned Lot Number 2 in the 3rd Range and 1st Division and that the line in question was originally "North 85° East 88 Rods and 17 Links."

To his task Mr. Teare brought very peculiar educational equipment. He never went beyond the seventh grade in school as he had to leave and go to work, but in his early years he had followed the sea and had become skipper of a three-masted schooner, and thus he had learned navigation.

Transition

As a surveyor he brought this navigation inland. It was really dead reckoning on land. A college-trained engineer would have thought his methods rule of thumb, but where such an engineer would have seen only woods, Mr. Teare could read them like an open book. For instance, he would go up to some old spruce on which, once he'd pointed it out, you could see a small scar, then taking an axe he'd swing with great true blows; and as large flying chips began to litter the ground he would lay open the white flesh of the tree in a larger and larger gash. After a while he would begin to strike more slowly and carefully, now and then peering into the opening, until finally he had disclosed an old blaze, black and flat with the original axe-marks in it.

Repetition with expansion
His ability is established

Then he would fish up his glasses from his shirt and holding them to his eyes would count the annual rings of growth. More than once I have seen him cut out spots made more than a hundred years before, and he once found spots on the old Masonian curved line, run in 1751 by Joseph Blanchard—the first line surveyed in New Hampshire. Mr. Teare had a spiritual affinity with the pioneer surveyors. He saw at a glance what they'd done, what they meant by their marks. He would sometimes look at a spot which definitely had been made with an axe, glance around and growl: "not a line, just a trapper's trail."

Continuity developed

He could follow not only the original spotted lines but the "lines of occupancy" as well, such as the trail of an old brush fence, all obvious remnants of which had disappeared at least twenty-five years before. This he would do by noting the crooked growth of trees here and there along its course, or a stretch of hazel bushes (which are likely to grow up along the remains of a brush fence), or piles of moss-covered stones in which fence posts had once been set. Whenever Mr. Teare, scattering the leaf mould near one of these stone heaps, uncovered a split ash rail, he would pick it up and fondle it lovingly. "They never rot," he would say with a solid approval of the wood itself and of the pioneer farmer who had taken pains to use it.

Idea of continuity returns

For equipment he used an open-sight compass with about a five-inch needle. There was no telescope on it but sight vanes instead with slits in them, and this compass rested not on a tripod, which would be too awkward in the woods, but rather on a single staff called a "Jacob staff." That was the kind of compass George Washington and Abraham Lincoln used when they were land surveyors, but Mr. Teare's was considerably more accurate. He referred affectionately to his compass as "Mary Jane" and almost always called it an "instrument" instead of a "compass."

When I first went with him he used a Gunter's chain, two rods in length, but in later years a steel tape of the same length. The Gunter's chain is an actual chain with real links and it can be folded up instead of rolled. It is very durable; it can be used to help a man go down over steep ledges, and will perform a hundred and one odd jobs that it would be sacrilege to force on a tape, which couldn't do them anyhow. He never wanted a chain or tape longer than two rods because the ground he had to work on was so hilly and rough. Somehow or other the Gunter's chain seemed to fit him better than a tape.

The idea of the piece is developed by specific details and a deepening tone

This type of surveying, difficult and requiring an analytical mind as well as woodcraft, is a fascinating pursuit—a sort of treasure hunt for old lines and corners. The problem was posed more than a century ago by men who marked those lines and corners in the wilderness and left cryptic directions on how to find them. In deserted areas it is a search through a forest-buried civilization as dead as the bottom layer of an Egyptian city. The fascination of it for Mr. Teare never left him.

You, the reader, can see him

I can see him now hunched over his compass while the needle settles on the proper course, then standing behind it and shouting directions to his axemen, while the two chainers bring up the rear. He is full of anticipation at what he may find at a given distance where he thinks a corner ought to be. He assiduously examines the trees alongside the line to see if he is following the old spotting, and now and then breaks into some rollicking song. His joy in living radiates around him.

Nails down his points

Does Mr. Andler use superlatives a bit too casually?

Mr. Teare's genius, true to the proverb, consisted largely in his capacity for taking infinite pains. He would <u>always</u> make sure of a starting point that could not be questioned. Once he ran twenty-four miles of trial line to locate one corner. Furthermore, he would <u>never</u> let an obstacle or a series of them block him. If a swamp were deep and cold he crossed it nevertheless; if towering cliffs barred his way he scaled them; if blown down trees strewed his path he slashed his way through; if a swollen river cut across a line he felled a tree for a bridge and kept on going. He was <u>absolutely</u> indomitable and he followed an old line as a hound follows a fox.

What about dreadful irony that Teare is agent of people destroying the world he loves?

He hated to see the woods cut by the companies for which he was working, even though he well knew that timber like other crops must be harvested. Often people asked him what he considered the most beautiful thing he had ever seen and he always gave them the same reply—sunset over the Adirondacks and Lake Champlain, from Mt. Mansfield. He worked most of a lifetime in the woods of northern New England and in spite of hardships and privations he never lost his love for these wild and wooded hills, for the silence of the deep forest in winter, the splendor of the mountains in the winey tang of autumn days.

Cliché

Active verb

The <u>infinite variety</u> of his daily scenes of activity pleased him. One day he might stand among tall spruces high up on some mountain, sighting, far below, an isolated farmhouse on which he could take a "triangulation shot," another day he might be following a hardwood ridge of beech and maple, or working in the bearwallow sort of land that often lies atop a mountain, or following the stone walls of abandoned fields. Often he made a traverse survey of the great roaring brooks which come tumbling out of mountain ponds and cut their resounding way down deep ravines; he loved to <u>drive</u> a canoe across a lake or down a river through white water.

Often he would pause at the summit of some hill. Then with his Jacob staff, he would point out to us the mountains and hills as they rolled away into blue distance, calling them by name and referring to certain jobs he had done on each. He knew them all as a father knows his children.

IV

Lead: "and what it meant"

The thing that staggers me when I get to thinking about Mr. Teare is the stupendous amount of work he accomplished in his long career. He surveyed thousands upon thousands of acres in Maine, New Hampshire, and Vermont. And he did not work merely for a monthly pay check; a craftsman, he labored so that his work would endure.

Here's what article is all about

Many if not most surveyors in timberlands leave few marks or monuments. Some of them figure that they'll soon be hired to resurvey the land if the lines become easily lost. Most make a half-hearted attempt to mark their lines and corners, but their work is like snow upon a desert, for the resurgent life in New England woods is almost tropical, as anyone knows who has tried to keep brush out of a field.

Emphasis

Mr. Teare, on the other hand, when he was sure it was right, it *was*—would have the axeman blaze almost every tree along the whole line. One that stood exactly on line he'd spot on both sides, while a tree that stood off a little way to one side or the other he'd blaze with "quarter spots," that is, blazes which were quartered on the bole, not centered, and these faced toward the line.

He continues to show as well as tell what he means

He made his blazes deep enough to take out a shaving of the wood, and they were large man-size spots, not boy's work. Some foresters and engineers complained that every tree would die but Mr. Teare knew better and he was right. He knew one great primary truth: You can't mark a line in New England's fast-growing woods a bit too plain.

Andler, in building his paragraph and designing the entire article, practices the craftsmanship he eulogizes!

Iron rods are impractical to carry in the woods and also a menace to the compass, so for a corner he set a large wooden post, fashioned from a suitable tree near-by, hewn flat on three sides or four as circumstances demanded, sharpened at the bottom and topped at an angle for a "roof." He never pounded it into the ground as that would soften the top and let rain in, but instead forced it in with its own weight. Around it he piled rocks. He stripped the bark off so it would last longer and with a timber scribe—a fascinating little instrument with which he could carve letters almost as fast as one can print on paper—he marked the names of the adjoining owners, the date, and his mark which was two parallel lines with a circle between them. He always said with a twinkle in his eye when he finished a corner and straightened up from piling stones, "There, that'll stand till Gabriel calls all good surveyors home."

About the corner he blazed witness trees in a circle facing the post and inscribed on them the date and his mark. These words, figures, and symbols, being only in the bark, never grow over. One could stand at a corner and, looking back into the woods, see the line stretching straight and true and well brushed out, its blazes shining new and startlingly clear. Few things give one quite the sense of accomplishment that this does—to go forth to a tract of land as nebulous in location as the scene of a fantasy, to find the old lines and corners, and to leave them well marked and definite.

These lines of Mr. Teare's, reaching for hundreds of miles in the aggregate through the deep woods of northern New England, live on today as I can testify, for while working as a land surveyor myself and later while abstracting titles, I have followed many of them. One of the companies had Mr. Teare respot its lines at seven-year intervals and, of course, these are exceptionally plain. But I have followed easily, and without a compass, lines which he had established thirty-five years before and which had never been touched since. The wooden corner posts needed renewing, yes, but that was easily accomplished. One can follow his lines even through areas devastated by the hurricane of September, 1938, where the blazed trees, no longer upright, lie in a tangled snarl upon the ground.

In scores, even hundreds of towns in northern New England, his lines form a reliable basic network from which almost any survey of land in their general neighborhood would be started today. The local people, farmers, timber operators, and investors would no more think of questioning his lines than they would the law of gravitation. More than once when I have told some timberman that several lines of a proposed tract had been run by Mr. Teare I have seen his face light up—he knew that *those* boundaries would be distinct, at any rate. Quite often I have heard one of Mr. Teare's old friends use the expression, "Why, it's as plain as one of Mr. Teare's lines."

Note his appropriate, changed tone

Whenever I happen to come upon one of his corners now that he is gone and, in the solemn hush of the forest, see the post in its cairn standing there, the trees about it alive with dates of those years when we worked together and with his mark and perhaps the initials of the old crew members, I feel an ineffable sadness not only because he is gone but because everything in those woods seems to inquire for him—and he would be enjoying himself so much if he were there.

But he did his work well and it survives him. No more can a mortal really ask. His lines are impressed into the living forest, his corners stand in wooded solitudes silently eloquent of his skill, and his witness trees bear witness not only to them but to him. Wherever he worked he brought order out of confusion and established a lasting thing.

Kenneth Andler has written a beautifully constructed article. When the reader finishes it he says, "Of course." Mr. Andler has convinced the reader through his specifics of the importance of craftsmanship. It is interesting to note that Mr. Andler, who is a practicing attorney in Newport, New Hampshire, is also a writer's writer. Mr. Andler, like Mr. Teare, has worked hard. The author says, "I bet I rewrote it twenty times—and then went over it word by word to get the right words."

E. B. White is the most admired essayist and prose stylist writing in the English language. The following editorials were written a generation ago, but they are still pertinent today, and they are fine examples of the expert, graceful opinion-writer at work.*

* These editorials, first published in *The New Yorker,* are from *The Wild Flag* by E. B. White (Houghton Mifflin, 1946) © E. B. White, 1943–1946.

These are sermons but he avoids an oppressive tone. How?
A White touch
He turns a corner
Sets up comparison

Frost's definition of metaphor—saying one thing and meaning another?

How does this persuade?

He makes his point and gets out of the way quickly

May 15, 1943

Doctor Gallup, the asker, has asked people whether they favor an international police force, and three out of four have said they do. That is very nice. It is also quite misleading. Asking a man whether he wants an international police force is like asking him whether he wants the Rockettes. Of course he does, but the question is not whether he thinks the Rockettes are a good idea but whether he knows what is in back of them, making them effective; in short, whether he is in earnest about the girls and willing to give up time and money to build a stage big enough to hold them, hire an orchestra loud enough to accompany them, buy costumes rich enough to adorn them, and in general sustain an organization orderly enough to give them meaning and make them click. Doctor Gallup should ask his question again, this time adding, "And you people realize, of course, that a police force is no good if simply used as a threat to strengthen agreements between independent powers, that to have meaning it must be the certified agent of the law, that to have law we must first have a constitutional world society, and that to achieve that each nation must say good-bye to its own freedom of action and to its long-established custom of doing as it damn well pleases. *Now* how many of you want an international police force?"

Here's one hand up, Doctor Gallup.

• • •

Convincing clarity by talking about complex issues simply

November 17, 1945

We have begun the task of collecting ideas and documents for the United Nations Organization to go to work on. The first document we wish to submit is a passage from a little girl's notebook, since it is the shortest statement we have read of the terrors of nationalism, or clubism. It follows:

The Club

the members of this club are Susie and Donny, we spy in this club most of the time and also we make pictures of where we want to spy. Sometimes we draw pictures and play games on the blackboard, but still we spy most of the time. We spy mostly when guests come.

Where We Spy And Where We Hide

How easy it would be to overdo this

In the living room we hide under the piano behind the pink chair and also in our club. In the dining room we hide under the table and in the kitchen we hide under the sink in the corner. And sometimes we hide in the hall closet but we dont very much because the guest dont go there very much.

The Things We Do In This Club

when people walk past the club we roll marbles at their feet and when someone sits in the blue chair we hit them on the head. So that is what we do in this club.

Washington, D.C. please note

White's style comes from the way he looks at the world

Nations are less candid than children, and their state departments have a less good prose style, but the essential structure is there; the spy system, the places to hide, the waiting for the false move on the part of the guest, the fateful blue chair, the sudden marble. There will be no peace in the household while those club members are under that piano. . . .

A reading and re-reading of such pieces as Mr. White's and Mr. Bronowski's will give the teacher and the student some appreciation for the fine use of language. They will also reveal the importance of structure. A well-built piece of writing is first of all a well-built piece of thinking. Notice how Mr. Bronowski, who is an outstanding scientist as well as a literary critic, thinks clearly on the page.

From "Science as Foresight"

Likenesses

Clarity—what devices does he use to achieve it?

Man has only one means to discovery, and that is to find *likenesses* between things. To him, two trees are like two shouts and like two parents, and on this likeness he has built all mathematics. A lizard is like a bat and like a man, and on such likenesses he has built the theory of evolution and all biology. A gas behaves like a jostle of billiard balls, and on this and kindred likenesses rests much of our atomic picture of matter.

The writer must seek likenesses

In looking for intelligibility in the world, we look for unity; and we find this (in the arts as well as in science) in its unexpected likenesses. This indeed is man's creative gift, to find or make a likeness where none was seen before—a likeness between mass and energy, a link where none was seen before—a likeness between mass and energy, a link between time and space, an echo of all our fears in the passion of Othello.

How well he makes figures of speech work for him

So, when we say that we can explain a process, we mean that we have mapped it in the likeness of another process which we know to work. We say that a metal crystal stretches because its layers slide over another like cards in a pack, and then that some polyester yarns stretch and harden like a metal crysal. That is, we take from the world round us a few models of structure and process (the particle, the wave, and so on), and when we research into nature, we try to fit her with these models.

The student should perform an autopsy and outline this piece

Yet one powerful procedure in research, we know, is to break down complex events into simpler parts. Are we not looking for the understanding of nature in these? When we probe below the surface of things, are we not trying, step by step, to reach her ultimate and fundamental constituents?

We do indeed find it helpful to work piecemeal. We take a sequence of events or an assembly to pieces: we look for the steps in a chemical reaction, we carve up the study of an animal into organs and cells and smaller units within a cell. This is our atomic approach, which tries always to see in the variety of nature different assemblies from a few basic units. Our search is for simplicity, in that the distinct units shall be few, and all units of one kind identical.

See how clearly and completely this idea has been developed

And what distinguishes one assembly of these units from another? the elephant from the giraffe, or the right-handed molecule of sugar from the left-handed? The difference is in the organization of the units into the whole; the difference is in the structure. And the likenesses for which we look are also likenesses of structure.

This is the true purpose of the analytic method in science: to shift our gaze from the thing or event to its structure. We understand a process, we explain it, when we lay bare in it a structure which is like one we have met elsewhere.

Can a human being be revealed on the page? Robert S. Gerdy was in this anonymous obituary which succeeded in honoring a quiet man, without sentimentality, by revealing the essence of his life. It shows as well as tells, and the tone never falters.

"Robert S. Gerdy"

Robert S. Gerdy was born on January 21, 1919, in New York City, and on the sunny morning of December 23, 1965, walking along lower Fifth Avenue, in this city he loved, he fell to the ground and died. He was only a few steps from his own home and his parents' home, and within strolling distance of his office at *The New Yorker,* where for the last thirteen years of his life he was an associate editor. His work was nearby, and so were friends. He was in the midst of everything he cared about most. He died quietly, just as he had lived. His specific work at *The New Yorker* was to help prepare some of the longer articles for publication—for want of a more satisfactory word, to "edit" them. It is one of the comic burdens of that particular kind of editor not to be able to explain to anyone else exactly what he does. As he works with a writer over a manuscript or a proof, placing his technical and aesthetic judgment at the writer's service, giving counsel when counsel is asked for, lending an objective eye, acting on occasion as a conscience, helping the writer in any way possible to say what he wants to say, only the editor and the writer can know what passes between them. The work of a good editor, like the work of a good teacher, does not reveal itself directly; it is reflected in the accomplishments of others. Bob Gerdy was a consummately good editor. He had the qualities that were needed. He was generous, he was sensitive, he was tactful, he was modest, he was patient, he was imaginative, he was unfailingly tuned in. A physically fragile man, with a strong intelligence, he clearly had no wish to impose his will on anyone, and was content to help each writer attain in each piece of writing whatever it was that the writer himself aspired to. He never suffered from the editor's occupational delusion that he is writing the writer's work. It was enough for him to know that he was doing his own job. In a period in which celebrity is so widely pursued, he chose to practice an anonymous art; in a period dense with publicity, he had no desire to become public; in a period of rampant self-assertion, he was self-effacing; in a violent period, he was extremely gentle; in a noisy period, he spoke softly. He found his own form of joy in helping other people bring their writings to a state of something like perfection. His other joy was to bask in the warmth of his family and his friends. It is a tribute to his extraordinary talents as an editor that many of those friends were the writers he had worked with. All of us,

See the simple directness of this beginning

This short article could be mapped to reveal its design

How does the writer make you see and know Gerdy?

Note this fine definition of the editor's role (and the teacher's role?)

Note surprise use of language at end of the list

He's put in perspective

How could just a few wrong words destroy this whole piece?

the writers and the artists and the editors who were his colleagues, will profoundly miss him.

Thomas A. Williams, who teaches writing at the University of New Hampshire, is one of the best short-story writers and novelists in the country. Read the following article just for enjoyment. Then later go back and examine it to see what he has done and how skillfully he has done it.

What words and constructions make this piece so different from Andler's?

Once, while hunting ruffed grouse on our mountain, I came gradually but certainly to the conclusion that I was not where I really was. I'd crossed Clark Brook, in a steep little valley, and climbed up through great beech and yellow birch into land which was unfamiliar to me. I'd been through it years before, but each depression, or each large boulder, didn't strike me with the kind of maplike solidity it would have on more familiar land. When I came back down to my brook again, it all seemed new and strange, and I had convinced myself that I was a ridge away, on another brook. I wasn't more than a mile from the cabin, standing at a little granite sluiceway and pool I'd fished through not more than a couple of months before, and yet I was absolutely certain that I was, in fact, on Brock Brook, a half-mile away.

He establishes a sense of being lost—of unreality—but he uses concrete details which make the unreality real to the reader

It is the nature of this certainty that fascinates me. Something happens in the wilderness, where there are no straight lines, where the land is owned and stabilized and changed only by the weather and the trees, that is unsettling and at the same time intensely pleasurable. I remember portaging with my father in the Arrowhead Country of Northern Minnesota, when I was nine or ten. I came to the edge of an uninhabited lake and saw a house—windows, roof lines and chimney—made in my selective consciousness out of the random crisscrosses of branches and the trunks of trees. The house was there and yet, as I approached, the branches sorted themselves into wilderness again, and the huge and comforting house vanished. Vanished like smoke, and nothing was left of it—not one sawn board, or shingle, or pane of glass. That hollow feeling, of aloneness, even of abandonment, was the nearest thing to nightmare I'd ever experienced while awake. And yet after that I courted the experience, and looked for more of those houses among the trees, just to see them swirl off into emptiness again, and once again feel that deep pang of loneliness.

This is a subtle subject yet he doesn't write in vague generalizations

The realness of unreality

He reveals himself to the reader. In revealing himself he reaches into us

My experience on the brook reminded me of this compulsive game I've played as a child, because when I climbed up out of the brook's gorge I came to a place on the Clark Trail I knew very well. An hour before I'd sat on that rock and smoked a cigarette. There was the apple tree, bent and blasted, yet still alive somehow, hung with its own dead limbs. I'd eaten one of its wild apples and left the core. There in the damp moss was the butt of the cigarette I (I?) had smoked. But I could believe none of this, because first the world had somehow to jar itself back into place, and my certain knowledge that I could not be there had to fade away into the fragments of hallucination it really was. For a moment I was in a wholly imaginary country—truly lost, nowhere. It wasn't until I had returned to the cabin (was it really there?), and traced my probable route on the geodetic map, that my

Simple language—used with taste, precision, grace

The tiny surprises which are the mark of an interesting style

certainty began to fade out like the memory of a dream. I had to go to the map—wanted to—in order to reassure the civilized part of me that was truly offended by such disorientation. Yet the memory is deep and good.

A graceful transition back in time

I think of those primitive maps made by explorers in galleons, who saw whole shores of terra incognita pass by their landward boards—maps strangely certain in their inaccuracies, in the hard, jagged corners of things. Why did the cartographer's hand carve out that imaginary bay, on that imaginary ocean full of carplike fish bigger than ships? I have the feeling that it was more than inaccuracy, even more than fakery. That is the ocean of absolute certainty, and it has nothing to do with astrolabes, sextants, or lead lines.

A couple of years ago I had the opportunity to examine such a map, this time made in similar wonder and discovery, of our own mountain, and to test its accuracies against the geodetic map I go by. It was made by a nine-year-old boy, and of course to him—against his certainties—the geodetic map was interesting but confused.

Now, halfway through the piece, when the reader is prepared, he comes to the incident he started to write

One August morning, around seven o'clock, someone began tapping rather diffidently on the back door of the cabin. The door is big and heavy, made out of two-inch hemlock planks, but my wife heard, and got up to answer. When she opened the door, there were two boys, aged nine and seven, who politely asked how to get to Canaan. Now by road, Canaan is about twenty miles, and by the Clark Trail, which runs by our cabin, it's about six miles, over the top of Mount Cardigan. My wife at first assumed that an adult was out on the trail, and the boys had been sent to the door to ask directions. But then she began to suspect that they were alone, and had them come inside. Well, yes, they were lost, they guessed. The older one, whose name was Mark, had that wide dreamy face I always associate with Finns, or Lapps. They were both pale and blond. Mark introduced his brother, David, and my wife made them some breakfast, while our two children sat and stared quietly at these travelers.

Necessary exposition gracefully worked in

Neither was scratched, or particularly dirty, and yet they'd spent the night alone on the mountain. Their family had camped on the Canaan side, near the summit (actually within the Township of Orange), and the boys had been given permission to climb to the fire lookout tower if they'd come right back, because supper would be ready soon. When they got to the summit, which is bald granite, the world, somehow when they weren't looking, turned itself around 180 degrees, and they came down the east side instead of the west. We figured this out from what they told us between mouthfuls. David at one point endeared himself to my wife by changing the subject and saying our cabin was nice. I told Mark I'd better take them down to the Appalachian Mountain Club Lodge so we could telephone their parents.

You know the boys because he shows them in action

"Oh, they won't be up this early," he said. "They never get up before nine."

A switch. You want to know about the boys and the suspense carries you over material he wants to work in

I wonder if I'm right in finding here the peculiar aura of hallucination caused by the wilderness. Mark, it turned out, was very observant. When he came by with his family a couple of weeks later they brought presents for our children that were right for their ages and sexes—although no words had passed between them while they ate their breakfasts. And his descriptions to his father of our cabin, and our car, were very accurate. He was a bright and very thoughtful boy. But they had been in the deep woods, not in civilization. I can't imagine him saying such a thing if, for instance, they had stayed out all night in the city. This was different. His father, I found out later, lost fifteen pounds that night, and I suppose Mark later began to realize that this was possible.

He emphasizes and builds up this detail

Nice control, nice understatement

I asked them where they'd slept, and Mark said matter-of-factly that when it grew dark and they couldn't see, they simply lay down and went to sleep. David said, "I slept on my brother's back."—A casual bit of information that still causes emotion in me.

Again, exposition skillfully introduced

The mountain on this side could be extremely dangerous; there are sheer cliffs, clefts in the granite a boy could slide into and never be found, literally impenetrable islands of dwarf spruce, whose dark passages are deceptively welcoming at first, then turn into interlocking and diminishing traps. All around a small forest called "Cathedral Spruce," tall trees have blown down crisscrossed, eight or ten feet deep; they came through that maze, too, by the narrow, cut trail, which weaves and winds between the dark piles of trees. But they lay down and went to sleep.

Verb!

When I got them down to the Appalachian Mountain Club, among the excitements of organized search and rescue—wardens, state police, two-way radios, weary hikers who had been searching all night, even a helicopter fluffing its way across the peak of Firescrew—Mark began to realize that something rather enormous had occurred, and he turned quite thoughtful. When I left the boys with the very weary Art Costin, then the manager of the lodge, and the forest warden who would drive them the twenty miles to Canaan, Mark sat picking at his second breakfast and staring out the window toward a face of Cardigan that was now steep and bright in the morning sunlight.

Are you prepared for this?

It was a couple of weeks later, when the boys came back with their parents, that Mark showed me the elaborate map he had made, which traced in loving detail the landmarks and contours of the strange country that they had traveled through.

Change of pace, mood, sets up ending

"There's where we crossed the second brook," he said, pointing to this document. "And we slept below this cliff, where we heard the bear." There was the bear, its fangs and claws.

"I think that you probably crossed Clark Brook twice," I told him. "Let me show you on the geodetic map."

Nice conflict—sets up next paragraph

He looked at it with polite interest for a moment then turned back to stare dreamily into his own map, at that country of experience whose certainties were deeper than any map of mine.

"I love the woods," he said. "I love to go out in the woods."

To be lost? I wondered. "Weren't you scared up there when it got dark?" I asked him.

Showing, revealing to the reader what he wants him to discover

"I was scared, all right," Mark said. "Everything was black."

"You did the right thing to lie down and try to sleep."

"It was David made me do that," he said. "He just wouldn't move in the dark. He said he wouldn't take one more step."

David was running around, playing with our children, who were, as usual, screaming and yelling with every breath. Mark didn't seem to notice all that racket. He sat at the plank table, quiet, thoughtful, enjoying his fearful memories.

The generality in the end is supported by previously presented specifics

There are few dark places left on our maps, and we need that dark, if only to leave behind us all our rigid, belittling geometries, signs and boundaries—certainties that diminish us, that tell us by the numbers exactly where we are, and that things are merely what they are, not what they seem.

As a reader I was remarkably touched by this article. Its tone captured me and made me think first about the boys, and then about the implications of their experience for them and for all of us. I think it is a significant and profound piece of writing, and I felt its impact personally.

Several months after it was published I taught the article. As a professor of English I was fascinated by the fact that there are ten variations of the word "certain" in the piece, the first one in the first sentence, the second at the end of the first paragraph, the third at the beginning of the second paragraph, and the last in the final paragraph. I also noticed that he first used the word "maplike" in the third sentence, and I charted thirteen variations of the word "map," the last one coming together with "certainties" in the concluding paragraph.

As a teacher of writing I called attention to the fine opening sentence, to the specifics in the article, to the tension which is developed in the idea that some things are both fearful and pleasurable. I discussed with my students how the idea of nightmare or hallucination was developed. I showed how he revealed his world, the boys' world, and how he drew the reader into the situation. I called attention to the nice turn of phrase, the way in which the world had turned itself around, and I talked about unity and coherence and the close relationship of the last paragraph with the first.

These were all valid comments, but they are the remarks of a reader looking at a piece of completed writing. How did the writer look at the same task from the other side when it was a job to do, not a job done? For one thing, he never realized how many times he had used variations of the words "certain" and "map."

The piece had begun for him in experience, and he tells the story of the boys pretty much as it happened and pretty much as he told it to me shortly after it happened. He did not take notes. He is not a journal keeper. In fact, he makes quite a point that the writer "doesn't observe deliberately." Instead of notes there had been experience. He has spent a dozen summers in the woods around the cabin, has hunted, fished and camped in many parts of the world, and was once a boy himself in the woods. The experience of the boys became part of his life, and it could have become part of a novel, short story, poem, or merely an anecdote to tell at a party and be forgotten. Then came the inspiration of the writing desk.

Study the manuscript reproduced beginning on page 193. At the top of the first page there is "Outdoor Column No. 3," a play of words, and the start of an article: " 'My sullen hill is going back to dark,' I wrote once—a line from a bad, but felt poem. Perhaps I was a little closer to the wildness then . . ." Examining the manuscript page you can see the start of a good idea about our need for monsters, animals in the woods and the dark.

There is another page of notes. At the top of the page: "Why do children like to build houses? Because there is wildness outside." And down through the page you can see the idea of wildness and maps develop.

Again he starts. A fragmentary note, "Being lost—maps—wilderness—the two boys, nine and seven, David and Mark." and the article begins. His pages are marked by words crossed out and changed and inserted.

Tom Williams says that in the beginning he had a feeling about composition, about symmetry, not a very formal feeling and not an outline, but a feeling for the size and dimension of the piece. "I wanted to establish my voice, not get right to the kids," he explains, "I wanted to set up the experience, my own experiences, so that my voice would have authority and I'd be able to make a statement later on in the piece."

He feels that the beginning is very important, and that if he can get beyond the first two paragraphs he can get through the piece. He writes carefully. "I am extremely careful about sentences. I never think about paragraphs," he says. "Sentences preoccupy me."

"The beginning makes the rest," he explains. "It forms what comes after it." He wasn't at all sure how the piece would develop, "You don't know it until you put it down." Tom works hard and consciously to achieve a tone, what he calls "his voice, his attitude." He adds, "The tone shows you what your subject is."

When he is writing he believes he is "not thinking"; he is working the material, trying to feel what it is like, looking for the right metaphor, trying to be as concrete and specific as possible.

"You don't know what comes next until you know what comes before," he says, "nobody is intelligent enough to plan it out. . . ."

Most writers feel, as Tom does, when you come to the end "a kind of magic makes it work." There were seven versions of the last paragraph and one might add that work makes the magic.

This article came out of Tom's own experience, out of a trip he took into the woods with his father twenty-eight years earlier, out of all the days in the woods, not observing, not looking for metaphors or symbols, but finding out what life is like.

He found his form under the artificial pressure of an assignment. He accepted the limitations of the piece, a non-fiction article on the outdoors eight pages long, which had to be done within three days.

In fitting this content—an anecdote about two boys lost in the woods, a feeling about wildness, an apprehension and attraction felt during years of hunting and fishing—into the limited form of an outdoor column, Tom Williams discovered something about our world and our illusions about our world.

His experiences in writing and his ritual of writing form a basic approach which can be taught to and perhaps adopted by the student writer. First comes a vast amount of information and a hint of a pattern in it. Next comes the work of fitting it into a form. Then comes the process of rewriting and rethinking, and if it works, discovery—examine five of his manuscript pages and you will see the discovery taking place.

Col # 3
(1.)

~~List of Games~~

Why do children like to build houses? Because there is wilderness outside.

~~The Hornet Post~~ (later)

(Wilderness)

The Parents: "Oh, they won't be up yet."

"I slept on my brother's back."

New York – what somebody said of Byron – "Sitting in a sewer and adding to it."

"Hell, if they like to live in it, let 'em."

The Map made by the 9 yr.-old boy who was lost: the nature of the wilderness, its wildness – Compared to an early map of the Hudson. The same wonder, the same inaccuracy, the rounded corners of things.

{griffins, mermen, carp bigger than ships. Bestiaries}

Yes, it was dangerous (blowdown piled like giant match sticks. Ledges, ravines, running caves.

but → map.

Begin with remarks about the Hudson, the New Jersey marshes, the pollution. (~~Refer~~ Refer to the civilized man's hallucination of houses in the wilderness (Arrowhead country exp. – unnamed lakes)

{Saran wraps + pills. Fr. letters obsolete, etc.}

~~Terra~~ TERRA INCOGNITA: Heart of Darkness (metaphor of the darkness of man's soul.)

This is different: the refreshing indifference of nature, which defines one's power of oneness. If you want that metaphoric darkness, Go to the cities or the towns.

~~Possible~~

– The Canaries – I want ~~to~~ him to see a volcano erupt.

Mark + David 7 and 9

The wide, dreamy face of a Lapp.

The one unknown that doesn't drive us mad. ~~The land~~ – From whose bourne some travelers return (with the look of sheer reality in their eyes).

Col #3 Outdoor Column #3

(2)

Cabin Building

The Refreshing Indifference of Nature

New York City ~~"A piles on the cloaca of New England."~~

Manhattan

summer is ichneumon fly

Summer is icumen in

"My sullen hill is going back to dark," I wrote once — a line from a bad, but felt, poem. Perhaps I was a little closer to the wilderness then, or at least felt that I was, which may be the same thing. Now, I'm not so sure about the word sullen. When the animals turn out of your way, licking their bloody ~~gums~~ teeth, is that personal, or not? They hope you won't find ~~what~~ the fresh corpse they've been eating on, and they're afraid, or cautious, about you (here, too, I've come to a more impersonal word), but sullen? No, probably not. ~~It's~~ Our ~~expectations and~~ desires ~~that~~ define nature as we need it to be defined. ~~Usually~~ We want monsters in it, and then ~~after wanting them~~ we kill them. But we want an unending supply. To me there is something terrible in the new perception, for instance, that we have concerning the Puma, or mountain lion. It's ~~really terrible~~ an almost sickening bit of knowledge — that we must protect ~~one of our dreads~~ this dreadful, beautiful beast. ~~It because it's the last meaningful resource because~~ His dreadfulness is lost; we have won the battle we desired never to end. "I am tired of the harvest I myself desired." This is just the opposite, and no less serious. God, we're going to be elbow to elbow on this planet, if we're careful, and some part of me is sick of mankind. He's not quite a good enough monster because he is ~~a monster~~ such a personal monster, and kills and tortures out of such infantile, understandable urges. How can we fear what must be understood and reformed by

(3) Outdoors #3

Being Lost — maps — Wilderness —
The two boys 9 & 7 David & Mark

#3 GETTING LOST: MAPS.

Once, while hunting ruffed grouse on our mountain, I came gradually but certainly to the conclusion that I was not where I really was. I'd crossed Clark Brook, in a steep little valley, and climbed up through great beech and yellow birch into land which was unfamiliar to me. I'd been through it years before, but each depression, or each large boulder, didn't strike me with the kind of map-like solidity it would have on more familiar land. When I came back down to my brook again, it all seemed new and strange, and I had convinced myself that I was a ridge away, on another brook. I wasn't more than a mile from the cabin, standing at a place little sluice-way and pool I'd fished through not more than a couple of months before, and yet I was absolutely certain that I was, in fact, on

A Brock Brook, a half-mile away. (A) It is the nature of this certainty that fascinates me. Something happens in the wilderness, where there are no straight lines, where the land is owned and stabilized and changed only by the weather and the trees, and it is unsettling and at the same time intensely pleasurable. I remember portaging with my father in the Arrowhead Country of Northern Minnesota, when I was nine or ten. I came to the edge of an uninhabited lake and saw a house — windows, roof-line and chimney — made in my selective consciousness out of the random crisscrosses of

(7) sat picking at his second breakfast and staring out the window toward ~~the~~ a face of Cordigan that was now high and bright in the morning sunlight –

~~But~~ It was ~~several~~ a couple of weeks later, when the boys came back with their parents, that Mark showed me ~~his~~ the ~~map~~ elaborately ~~detailed~~ map he had made ~~showing each side~~ which ~~showed~~ traced in loving detail the ~~traverses and~~ landmarks, ~~and~~ and contours ~~and traverses they had~~ of the strange ~~and wonderful~~ country they had traveled through.

"There's where we crossed the second brook," he said, pointing to this document. "And we slept below that cliff, where we heard the bear." There was the bear, his fangs and claws.

"I think you probably crossed ~~the brook~~ Clark Brook twice," I said. "Let me show you on the geodetic map."

~~"I love the woods," he said. "I love to go out in the woods." But he ~~was~~ still stares dreamily into his own map, at that ~~certain~~ country of experience, whose~~ ~~certainties had left, I know, were dark wonderful memories of fear overcome there in the first in the wilderness, I suppose, the one unknown that doesn't drive us mad. It's the bourne from which a some traveler returns with the look of sheer reality in his eyes~~

~~"I was lost, but that is where I was."~~

... certainties were deeper than ~~any map of mine~~ any map of mine.

~~"I was lost, but that is where I was." It is In the only in the wilderness above where we can be lost and still be sane – the bourne from which a traveler returns. There are too many ways to be lost in this built up world. Only in the wilderness can we be lost and found again ~~really~~ still be sane the bourne from which this traveler ~~had returned~~. With the look of sheer reality in his eyes~~

(8) ... on the geodetic map."

He looked at it for a moment (with polite interest), then turned back to ~~his own~~ stare dreamily into his own map, at that country of experience ~~where things were what they seemed~~ whose certainties ~~are~~ were deeper than any map of mine.

"I love the woods," he said. "I love to go out in the woods."

To be lost? I ~~thought you~~ wondered. But I understood; at least I think I did: to go away from other certainties as dulling as lost the symmetries — geometries ~~and symmetries~~ that tell us by the numbers exactly where we are, and that things are what they are, not what they seem.

NEW Ending:

... at that country of experience whose certainties were deeper than any map of mine.

"I love the woods," he said. "I love to go out in the woods."

To be lost? I wondered. "Weren't you scared up there when it got dark?" I asked him.

"~~Oh~~" I was scared, all right. ~~It was David made me~~ Everything ~~stopped~~ was black."

"You did the right thing to lie down and try to sleep."

"It was David made me do that," he said. "He just wouldn't ~~move~~ take one more step."

David was running around, playing with our children, who were, as usual, screaming and yelling with every breath. Mark didn't seem to notice all that racket. He sat at the plank table, ~~really a kind of island~~ enjoying his ~~memories~~ fearful memories. ~~I think I understood Perhaps it's out there in the dark~~ There are few dark places left on our maps, and we need that dark, if only ~~to get away from certainties~~ to leave behind us all ~~those~~ our rigid, belittling geometries, signs and boundaries — certainties that ~~are~~ diminish us, that tell us by the numbers exactly where we are, and that things are merely what they are, ~~not what they are not as enormous and wonderful as they seem~~ not what ~~mysterious~~ ~~could~~ they can seem.

Every writing teacher should have the novel *Mrs. Bridge* by Evan S. Connell, Jr. in his library. It is, first of all, a magnificent example of clean, clear writing. It is also a fascinating novel, for it reveals a woman through a series of short mosaics.

These mosaics are typical of the ones following. They are fine examples for classroom use and analysis.

From Mrs. Bridge

Every detail in this novel built of mosaics from one woman's life reveals her

1 *Love and Marriage*

Emphasis—how much you know about her from this

Her first name was India—she was never able to get used to it. It seemed to her that her parents must have been thinking of someone else when they named her. Or were they hoping for another sort of daughter? As a child she was often on the point of inquiring, but time passed, and she never did.

You see him

Fine detail

Sets scene

Just the right word

Nice understatement

Now and then while she was growing up the idea came to her that she could get along very nicely without a husband, and, to the distress of her mother and father, this idea prevailed for a number of years after her education had been completed. But there came a summer evening and a young lawyer named Walter Bridge: very tall and dignified, red-haired, with a grimly determined, intelligent face, and rather stoop-shouldered so that even when he stood erect his coat hung lower in the front than in the back. She had known him for several years without finding him remarkable in any way, but on this summer evening, on the front porch of her parents' home, she toyed with a sprig of mint and looked at him attentively while pretending to listen to what he said. He was telling her that he intended to become rich and successful, and that one day he would take his wife—"whenever I finally decide to marry" he said, for he was not yet ready to commit himself—one day he would take his wife on a tour of Europe. He spoke of Ruskin and of Robert Ingersoll, and he read to her that evening on the porch, later, some verses from *The Rubaiyat* while her parents were preparing for bed, and the locusts sang in the elm trees all around.

Wow!—So much in so few words

A few months after her father died she married Walter Bridge and moved with him to Kansas City, where he had decided to establish a practice.

Note

All seemed well. The days passed, and the weeks, and the months, more swiftly than in childhood, and she felt no trepidation, except for certain moments in the depth of the night when, as she and her new husband lay drowsily clutching each other for reassurance, anticipating the dawn, the day, and another night which might prove them both immortal, Mrs. Bridge found herself wide awake. During these moments, resting in her husband's arms, she would stare at the ceiling, or at his face, which sleep robbed of strength, with an uneasy expression, as though she saw or heard some intimation of the great years ahead.

Consider the implications of this deceptively simple statement

She was not certain what she wanted from life, or what to expect from it, for she had seen so little of it, but she was sure that in some way—because she willed it to be so—her wants and her expectations were the same.

For a while after their marriage she was in such demand that it was not unpleasant when he fell asleep. Presently, however, he began sleeping all night, and it was then she awoke more frequently, and looked into the darkness, wondering about the nature of men, doubtful of the future, until at last there came a night when she shook her husband awake and spoke of her own desire. Affably he placed one of his long white arms around her waist; she turned to him then, contentedly, expectantly, and secure. However nothing else occurred, and in a few minutes he had gone back to sleep.

Note how this is set up

Would any other word have been so right? His timing—sense of pace—is flawless

This was the night Mrs. Bridge concluded that while marriage might be an equitable affair, love itself was not.

3 *Preliminary Training*

She brought up her children very much as she herself had been brought up, and she hoped that when they were spoken of it would be in connection with their nice manners, their pleasant dispositions, and their cleanliness, for these were qualities she valued above all others.

His knife is sharp and it makes a clean cut

With Ruth and later with Carolyn, because they were girls, she felt sure of her guidance; but with the boy she was at times obliged to guess and to hope, and as it turned out—not only with Douglas but with his two sisters—what she stressed was not at all what they remembered as they grew older.

What Ruth was to recall most vividly about childhood was an incident which Mrs. Bridge had virtually forgotten an hour after it occurred. One summer afternoon the entire family, with the exception of Mr. Bridge who was working, had gone to the neighborhood swimming pool; Douglas lay on a rubber sheet in the shade of an umbrella, kicking his thin bowed legs and gurgling, and Carolyn was splashing around in the wading pool. The day was exceptionally hot. Ruth took off her bathing suit and began walking across the terrace. This much she could hardly remember, but she was never to forget what happened next. Mrs. Bridge, having suddenly discovered Ruth was naked, snatched up the bathing suit and hurried after her. Ruth began to run, and being wet an slippery she squirmed out of the arms that reached for her from every direction. She thought it was a new game. Then she noticed the expression on her mother's face. Ruth became bewildered and then alarmed, and when she was finally caught she was screaming hysterically.

How much one of Connell's sentences can carry

How has he used words to change their mood and tone?

Note title

13 *Guest Towels*

Boys, as everyone knows, were more trouble than girls, but to Mrs. Bridge it began to seem that Douglas was more trouble than both the girls together. Ruth, silent Ruth, was no trouble at all; Mrs. Bridge sometimes grew uneasy over this very fact, because it was slightly unnatural. Carolyn made up for Ruth, what with temper tantrums and fits of sefishness, but she was nothing compared to Douglas, who, strangely enough, never actually appeared to be attempting to make trouble; it was just that somehow he *was* trouble. Invariably there was something about him that needed to be corrected or attended to, though he himself was totally oblivious to this fact, or, if he was aware of it, was unconcerned. Whenever she encountered him

This can be read aloud to great advantage—it emphasizes his use of the right word, its sound and its connotation

A fine rhythm to this sentence

he was either hungry, or dirty, or late, or needed a haircut, or had outgrown something, or had a nosebleed, or had just cut himself, or had lost something, or was just generally ragged and grimy looking. Mrs. Bridge could not understand it. She could take him down to the Plaza for a new pair of corduroy knickers and a week later he had worn a hole through the knee. He was invariably surprised and a little pained by her dismay; he felt fine—what else mattered?

He was hostile to guest towels. She knew this, but, because guest towels were no concern of his, there had never been any direct conflict over them. She had a supply of Margab, which were the best, at least in the opinion of everyone she knew, and whenever guests were coming to the house she would put the ordinary towels in the laundry and place several of these little pastel towels in each of the bathrooms. They were quite small, not much larger than a handkerchief, and no one ever touched them. After the visitors had gone home she would carefully lift them from the rack and replace them in the box till next time. Nobody touched them because they looked too nice; guests always did as she herself did in their homes—she would dry her hands on a piece of Kleenex.

Read this over to see how a whole way of life is revealed

One afternoon after a luncheon she went around the house collecting the guest towels as usual, and was very much surprised to find that one of the towels in Douglas' bathroom had been used. It was, in fact, filthy. There was no question about who had used this towel. She found Douglas sitting in a tree in the vacant lot. He was not doing anything as far as she could tell; he was just up in the tree. Mrs. Bridge approached the tree and asked him about the towel. She held it up. He gazed down at it with a thoughtful expression. Yes, he had dried his hands on it.

Quiet humor

"These towels are for guests," said Mrs. Bridge, and felt herself unaccountably on the verge of tears.

"Well, why don't they use them then?" asked Douglas. He began to gaze over the rooftops.

"Come down here where I can talk to you. I don't like shouting at the top of my lungs."

"I can hear you okay," said Douglas, climbing a little higher.

Mrs. Bridge found herself getting furious with him, and was annoyed with herself because it was all really so trivial. Besides, she had begun to feel rather foolish standing under a tree waving a towel and addressing someone who was probably invisible to any of the neighbors who might be watching. All she could see of him were his tennis shoes and one leg. Then, too, she knew he was right, partly right in any event; even so, when you had guests you put guest towels in the bathroom. That was what everyone did, it was what she did, and it was most definitely what she intended to continue doing.

Marvelous scene

"They always just use their handkerchief or something," said Douglas moodily from high above.

"Never mind," said Mrs. Bridge. "From now on you leave those towels alone."

There was no answer from the tree.

"Do you hear me?"

"I hear you," said Douglas.

17 *Good-by Alice*

Read this and you know all you need to know about how prejudice is taught Can students show what and how they are taught?

Alice Jones was now appearing every month or so, though her father came to work at the neighbors' each Saturday as usual. On those occasions when she accompanied him she would spend the morning with Carolyn, but then, about noon, she would get on the streetcar and go home by herself. During the morning she and Carolyn would have a confidential talk, usually in Carolyn's room, that is, in the room that Caroyln and Ruth shared. Ruth was seldom at home on Saturday, nobody in the family knew where she went. So Alice Jones and Carolyn would shut the door to the room and converse in low tones or in whispers about school and clothes and friends and boys and how they intended to raise their children.

"How many are you going to have?" asked Carolyn.

Note the beginning lack of communication, the different social attitudes revealed

"Eleven," Alice said firmly.

"Heavens!" said Carolyn. "That's certainly telling."

"What kind of talk is that?" Alice wanted to know. "How many are you going to have?"

"Two, I believe. That makes a nice family."

One Saturday at lunch time, shortly after Alice had started to the streetcar line, Carolyn said that Alice had invited her to come to a party next Saturday afternoon.

Suspense The dainty, phony eating habits of a "nice" person

"Well, that was nice of Alice, wasn't it?" Mrs. Bridge replied, and with a tiny silver fork she ate a slice of banana from her fruit salad, and then a piece of lettuce.

"Where is the party to be?"

"At her house."

"Where does Alice live?"

"Thirteenth and Prospect."

Mrs. Bridge took up a little silver knife ånd began to cut a slice of peach which was rather too large to be eaten in one bite. She knew where Thirteenth and Prospect was, although she had never stopped there. It was a mixed neighborhood.

Once more, just the right words

"Can I go?"

Mrs. Bridge smiled affectionately at Carolyn. "I wouldn't if I were you."

117 *Hello?*

One December morning near the end of the year when snow was falling moist and heavy for miles all around, so that the earth and the sky were indivisible, Mrs. Bridge emerged from her home and spread her umbrella. With small cautious steps she proceeded to the garage, where she pressed the button and waited impatiently for the door to lift. She was in a hurry to drive downtown to buy some Irish lace antimacassars that were advertised in the newspaper, and she was planning to spend the remainder of the day browsing through the stores because it was Harriet's day off and the house was empty—so empty.

How does he set scene for this barren feeling?

She had backed just halfway out of the garage when the engine died. She touched the starter and listened without concern because, despite her difficulties with the Lincoln, she had grown to feel secure in it. The Lincoln was a number of years old and occasionally recalcitrant, but she could not bear the thought of parting with it, and in the past had resisted this suggestion of her husband, who, mildly puzzled by her attachment to the car, had allowed her to keep it.

Thinking she might have flooded the engine, which was often true, Mrs. Bridge decided to wait a minute or so.

Presently she tried again, and again, and then again. Deeply disappointed, she opened the door to get out and discovered she had stopped in such a position that the car doors were prevented from opening more than a few inches on one side by the garage partition, and on the other side by the wall. Having tried all four doors she began to understand that until she could attract someone's attention she was trapped. She pressed the horn, but there was not a sound. Half inside and half outside she remained.

She's trapped—how clear, how simple

For a long time she sat there with her gloved hands folded in her lap, not knowing what to do. Once she looked at herself in the mirror. Finally she took the keys from the ignition and began tapping on the window, and she called to anyone who might be listening, "Hello? Hello out there?"

But no one answered, unless it was the falling snow.

Could the last sentence—the last one of the book—be cut?

Lillian Ross, who is famous for her ability to catch the revealing detail or inflection, has captured one high school class trip in the following fine piece of writing. It should be studied carefully, and it might help the teacher to see how his students could spend some time documenting a school activity, such as a class play, a football week-end, a dance. The whole piece is a classic example of showing, not telling, where the writer has selected information which will bring the reader to his own conclusions.

"The Yellow Bus" by Lillian Ross

A fine report on a high school tradition —the class trip A writing class could play reporter and interview seniors to do a report on a class trip

A few Sundays ago, in the late, still afternoon, a bright-yellow school bus, bearing the white-on-blue license plate of the State of Indiana and with the words "BEAN BLOSSOM TWP MONROE COUNTY" painted in black letters under the windows on each side, emerged into New York City from the Holland Tunnel. Inside the bus were eighteen members of the senior class of the Bean Blossom Township High School, who were coming to the city for their first visit. The windows of the bus, as it rolled out into Canal Street, were open, and a few of the passengers leaned out, deadpan and silent, for a look at Manhattan. The rest sat, deadpan and silent, looking at each other. In all, there were twenty-two people in the bus: eleven girls and seven boys of the senior class; their English teacher and her husband; and the driver (one of the regular bus drivers employed by the township for the school) and his wife. When they arrived, hundreds of thousands of the city's eight million inhabitants were out of town. Those who were here were apparently minding their own business; certainly they were not handing out any big hellos to the visitors. The little Bean Blossom group, soon to be lost in the shuffle of New York's resident and transient summer population, had

How does she establish her tone?

no idea of how to elicit any hellos—or, for that matter, any goodbyes or how-are-yous. Their plan for visiting New York City was divided into three parts: one, arriving; two, staying two days and three nights; three, departing.

What do these specifics add—why are they included?

Six years of planning—will the trip be worth it?

Well, they had arrived. To get here, they had driven eight hundred and forty miles in thirty-nine and a half hours, bringing with them, in addition to spending money of about fifty dollars apiece, a fund of $957.41, which the class had saved up collectively over the past six years. The money represented the profits from such enterprises as candy and ice-cream concessions at school basketball games, amusement booths at the class (junior) carnival, and ticket sales for the class (senior) play, "Mumbo-Jumbo." For six years, the members of the class had talked about how they would spend the money to celebrate their graduation. Early this year, they voted on it. Some of the boys voted for a trip to New Orleans, but they were outvoted by the girls, all of whom wanted the class to visit New York. The class figured that the cost of motels and hotels—three rooms for the boys, three rooms for the girls, one room for each of the couples—would come to about four hundred dollars. The bus driver was to be paid three hundred and fifty dollars for driving and given thirty for road, bridge, and tunnel tolls. Six members of the class, who were unable to participate in the trip, stayed home. If there should be any money left over, it would be divided up among all the class members when the travellers returned to Bean Blossom Township. The names of the eighteen touring class members were: R. Jay Bowman, Shelda Bowman (cousin of R. Jay), Robert Britton, Mary Jane Carter, Lynn Dillon, Ina Hough, Thelma Keller, Wilma Keller (sister of Thelma), Becky Kiser, Jeanne Molnar, Nancy Prather, Mike Richardson, Dennis Smith, Donna Thacker, Albert Warthan, Connie Williams, Larry Williams (not related to Connie), and Lela Young.

What is revealed by the names?

It was also a first visit to New York for the English teacher, a lively young lady of twenty-eight named Polly Watts, and for her husband, Thomas, thirty-two, a graduate student in political science at Indiana University, in Bloomington, which is about twelve miles from the Bean Blossom Township school. The only people on the bus who had been to New York before were the driver, a husky uncommunicative man of forty-nine named Ralph Walls, and his wife, Margaret, thirty-nine and the mother of his seven children, aged twenty-one to two, all of whom were left at home. Walls was the only adviser the others had on what to do in New York. His advice consisted of where to stay (the Hotel Woodstock, on West Forty-third Street, near Times Square) and where to eat (Hector's Cafeteria, around the corner from the hotel).

This is written to amuse a sophisticated New Yorker—this is not very good advice

The Bean Blossom Township school is in the village of Stinesville, which has three hundred and fifty-five inhabitants and a town pump. A couple of the seniors who made the trip live in Stinesville; the others live within a radius of fifteen miles or so, on farms or in isolated houses with vegetable gardens and perhaps a cow or two. At the start of the trip, the travellers gathered in front of their school shortly after midnight, and by one in the morning, with every passenger occupying a double seat in the bus (fifty-four-passenger, 1959 model), and with luggage under the seats, and suits and dresses hung on a homemade clothes rack in the back of the bus, they were on their way.

Watch what she does with this

She has caught him on her pen point

The senior-class president, R. (for Reginald) Jay Bowman, was in charge of all the voting on the trip. A wiry, energetic eighteen-year-old with a crew haircut, he had been president of the class for the past five years, and is one of two members of the class who intend to go to college. He wants to work, eventually, for the United States Civil Service, because a job with the government is a steady job. Or, in a very vague way, he thinks he may go into politics. With the help of a hundred-and-two-dollar-a-year scholarship, he plans to pay all his own expenses at Indiana University. The other student who is going to college has also chosen Indiana University. She is Nancy Prather, an outdoorsy, freckle-faced girl whose father raises dairy and beef cattle on a two-hundred-and-fifty-acre farm and who is the class salutatorian. As for the valedictorian, a heavyset, firm-mouthed girl named Connie Williams, she was planning to get married a week after returning home from New York. The other class members expected, for the most part, to get to work at secretarial or clerical jobs, or in automobile or electronic-parts factories in Bloomington. The New York trip was in the nature of a first and last fling.

Nice phrase

Ralph Walls dropped the passengers and their luggage at the Woodstock and then took the busy to a parking lot on Tenth Avenue, where he was going to leave it for the duration of the visit. His job, he told his passengers, was to drive *to* New York, not *in* it. He had also told them that when he got back to the Woodstock he was going to sleep, but had explained how to get around the corner to Hector's Cafeteria. The boys and girls signed the register and went to their rooms to get cleaned up. They all felt let down. They had asked Walls whether the tall buildings they saw as they came uptown from the Holland Tunnel made up the skyline, and Walls had said he didn't know. Then they had asked him which was the Empire State Building, and he had said they would have to take a tour to find out. Thus put off, they more or less resigned themselves to saving any further questions for a tour. Jay Bowman said that he would see about tours before the following morning.

Foreshadowing

Mrs. Watts and her husband washed up quickly and then, notwithstanding the bus driver's advice, walked around the Times Square area to see if they could find a reasonably priced and attractive place to have supper. They checked Toffenetti's, across the street from the hotel, but they decided that it was too expensive (hamburger dinners at two dollars and ten cents, watermelon at forty cents) and too formidable. When they reconvened with the senior class in the lobby of the Woodstock, they recommended that everybody have his first meal at Hector's. The party set out—for some reason, in Indian file—for Hector's, and the first one inside was Mike Richardson, a husky, red-haired boy with large swollen-looking hands and sunburned forearms. A stern-voiced manager near the door, shouting "Take your check! Take your check!" at all incomers, gave the Indiana group the same sightless once-over he gave everybody else. The Bean Blossom faces, which had been puzzled, fearful, and disheartened since Canal Street, now took on a look of resentment. Mike Richardson led the line to the counter. Under a sign reading "BAKED WHITEFISH," a white-aproned counterman looked at Mike and said, "Come on, fella!" Mike glumly took a plate of fish and then filled the rest of his tray with baked beans, a roll, iced

Just the right word

Good phrase

Switch

tea, and strawberry shortcake (check—$1.58). The others quickly and shakily filled their trays with fish, baked beans, a roll, iced tea, and strawberry shortcake. Sweating, bumping their trays and their elbows against other trays and other elbows, they found seats in twos and threes with strangers, at tables that still had other people's dirty dishes on them. Then, in a nervous clatter of desperate and noisy eating, they stuffed their food down.

Watch this

See how this idea develops

"My ma cooks better than this," said Albert Warthan, who was sitting with Mike Richardson and Larry Williams. Albert, the eldest of seven children of a limestone-quarry worker, plans to join the Army and become a radar technician.

"I took this filet de sole? When I wanted somethin' else, I don't know what?" Mike said.

Has he ever been to a restaurant where "you just set there?"

"I like the kind of place you just set there and decide what you want," said Larry, who is going to work on his grandfather's farm.

"My ma and pa told me to come home when it was time to come home, and not to mess around," Albert said. "I'm ready to chuck it and go home right now."

Is this really the whole idea?

"The whole idea of it is just to see it and get it over with," Mike said.

"You got your money divided up in two places?" Albert asked. "So's you'll have some in one place if it gets stolen in t'other?"

The others nodded.

And they haven't seen it yet

"Man, you can keep this New York," said Larry. "This place is too hustly, with everybody pushin' and no privacy. Man, I'll take the Big Boy any old day."

Frisch's Big Boy is the name of an Indiana drive-in chain, where a hamburger costs thirty cents. The general effect of Hector's Cafeteria was to give the Bean Blossom Class of 1960 a feeling of unhappiness about eating in New York and to strengthen its faith in the superiority of the Big Boys back home.

Nothing to do in this international city

Jay Bowman went from table to table, polling his classmates on what they wanted to do that evening. At first, nobody wanted to do anything special. Then they decided that the only special thing they wanted to do was go to Coney Island, but they wanted to save Coney Island for the wind-up night, their last night in New York. However, nobody could think of anything to do that first night, so Jay took a re-vote, and it turned out that almost all of them wanted to go to Coney Island right away. Everybody but three girls voted to go to Coney Island straight from Hector's. Mrs. Watts was mildly apprehensive about this project, but Mike Richardson assured her it was easy; somebody at the hotel had told him that all they had to do was go to the subway and ask the cashier in the booth which train to take, and that would be that. Mrs. Watts said she was going to walk around a bit with her husband. The three girls who didn't want to go to Coney Island explained that they firmly believed the class should "have fun" on its last night in the city, and not before. The three were Ina Hough, whose father works in an R.C.A.-television manufacturing plant in Indianapolis (about fifty miles from Stinesville); Lela Young, whose foster father works in a Chevrolet-parts warehouse in Indianapolis; and Jeanne Molnar, whose father is a draftsman at the Indiana Limestone Company, in Bloomington.

They knew before they came. She's even caught the tone of voice in this phrase

All three already knew that they disliked New York. People in New York, they said, were all for themselves.

At nine o'clock, while most of their classmates were on the Brighton B.M.T. express bound for Coney Island, the three girls walked to Sixth Avenue and Fiftieth Street with Mr. and Mrs. Watts, who left them at that point to take a walk along Fifth Avenue. The girls stood in a long line of people waiting to get into the Radio City Music Hall. After twenty minutes, they got out of the line and walked over to Rockefeller Plaza, where they admired the fountain, and to St. Patrick's Cathedral, which looked bigger to them than any church they had ever seen. The main church attended by the Bean Blossom group is the Nazarene Church. No one in the senior class had ever talked to a Jew or to more than one Catholic, or—with the exception of Mary Jane Carter, daughter of the Nazarene minister in Stinesville—had ever heard of an Episcopalian. At ten o'clock, the three girls returned to the Music Hall line, which had dwindled, but when they got to the box office they were told that they had missed the stage show, so they decided to skip the Music Hall and take a subway ride. They took an Independent subway train to the West Fourth Street station, which a subway guard told them was where to go for Greenwich Village. They decided against getting out and looking, and in favor of going uptown on the same fare and returning to their hotel. Back at the Woodstock, where they shared a room, they locked themselves in and started putting up their hair, telling each other that everybody in New York was rude and all for himself.

She builds up to this

How much of New York have they seen?

Repetition for emphasis

At Coney Island, the Indiana travellers talked about how they could not get over the experience of riding for forty-five minutes, in a shaking, noisy train, to get there.

"The long ride was a shock to what I expected," said Albert Warthan.

Nancy Prather said she didn't like the looks of the subway or the people on it. "You see so many different people," she said, "Dark-complected ones one minute, light-complected ones the next."

Just the right touch

"I hate New York, actually," Connie Williams said. "I'm satisfied with what we got back home."

"Back home, you can do anything you please in your own backyard any time you feel like it, like hootin' and hollerin' or anything," said Larry Williams. "You don't ever get to feel all cooped up."

Watch out—first defector

"I sort of like it here in Coney Island," said Dennis Smith. "I don't feel cooped up."

Dennis's buddies looked at him without saying anything. His "sort of liking" Coney Island was the first sign of defection from Indiana, and the others did not seem to know what to make of it. Dennis is a broad-shouldered boy with large, beautiful, wistful blue eyes and a gold front tooth.

"I hate it," Connie said.

Jay Bowman organized as many of the group as he could to take a couple of rides on the Cyclone. Most of the boys followed these up with a ride on the parachute jump, and then complained that it wasn't what they had expected at all. Some of the boys and girls went into the Spookerama. They all rode the bobsled, and to top the evening off they rode the bumper cars. "The Spookerama was too imitation to be frightening," Albert said. Before leaving Coney Island, Jay got to work among his classmates, polling

Miss Ross lets them reveal themselves—she gets out of the way them on how much money they were prepared to spend on a tour of the city the next day. They stayed in Coney Island about an hour. Nobody went up to the boardwalk to take a look at the ocean, which none of the class had ever seen. They didn't feel that they had to look at the ocean. "We knew the ocean was there, and anyway we aim to see the ocean on the tour tomorrow," Jay said later.

When Ina, Lela, and Jeanne got in line for the Music Hall, the Wattses took their stroll along Fifth Avenue and then joined a couple of friends, Mike and Ardis Cavin. Mike Cavin plays clarinet with the United States Navy Band, in Washington, D. C., and is studying clarinet—as a commuter—at the Juilliard School of Music. At Madison Avenue and Forty-second Street, the two couples boarded a bus heading downtown, and while talking about where to get off they were taken in hand by an elderly gentleman sitting near them, who got off the bus when they did and walked two blocks with them, escorting them to their destination—the Jazz Gallery, on St. Mark's Place. Mike Cavin wanted to hear the tenor-saxophone player John Coltrane. The Wattses stayed at the Jazz Gallery with the Cavins for three hours, listening, with patient interest, to modern jazz. They decided that they liked modern jazz, and especially Coltrane. Leaving the Jazz Gallery after one o'clock, the two couples took buses to Times Square, walked around for twenty minutes looking for a place where they could get a snack, and finally, because every other place seemed to be closed, went to Toffenetti's. Back at the hotel, the Wattses ran into one of the Coney Island adventurers, who told them that Ina, Lela, and Jeanne were missing, or at least were not answering their telephone or knocks on their door. Mr. Watts got the room clerk, unlocked the girls' door, and found them sitting on their beds, still putting up their hair. Everybody was, more or less unaccountably, angry—the three girls who hadn't gone to Coney Island, the girls who had, the boys who had, the Wattses, and the room clerk. The Wattses got to bed at 3:30 a.m.

They have a different attitude from their students' and it's shown with a specific

?

At 6:30 a.m., Mrs. Watts was called on the telephone. Message: One of the anti-Coney Island trio was lying on the floor of the room weeping and hysterical. Mrs. Watts called the room clerk, who called a doctor practicing in the Times Square area, who rushed over to the hotel, talked with the weeping girl for twenty minutes, and left her with a tranquillizing pill, which she refused to take.

Of course

By the time everybody had settled down enough to eat breakfast in drugstores and get ready to start out, it was after nine in the morning, half an hour behind time for the scheduled (by unanimous vote) all-day tour of the city by chartered sightseeing bus, at six dollars per person. The tour was held up further while Mrs. Watts persuaded the weeper to take a shower, in an effort to encourage her to join the tour. After the shower, the unhappy girl stopped crying and declared that she would go along. By the time the group reached the Bowery, she felt fine, and in Chinatown, like the other boys and girls, she bought a pair of chopsticks, for thirty-five cents. The Cathedral of St. John the Divine was the highlight of the tour for many of the students, who were delighted to hear that some of the limestone used in the cathedral interior had very likely come from quarries near Stinesville. Mrs. Watts, on the other hand, who had studied art, had taught art for five years at Huntington College, in Huntington, Indiana, and had taken an accredited art tour of Europe before her marriage, indignantly considered the cathedral "an imitation of European marvels."

Contrast

Mrs. Watts took the Bean Blossom teaching job, at thirty-six hundred dollars a year, last fall, when her husband decided to abandon a concrete-building-block business in Huntington in order to study for a Ph.D. in political science, a subject he wants to teach. Since he had decided that Indiana University was the place to do this, they moved from Huntington—where Mr. Watts had won the distinction of being the youngest man ever to hold the job of chairman of the Republican Party of Huntington County—to Bloomington. Mrs. Watts drives the twelve miles from Bloomington to Stinesville every day. She teaches English to the tenth, eleventh, and twelfth grades, and, because the school had no Spanish teacher when she signed up for the job, she teaches Spanish, too. She considers the Bean Blossom Township school the most democratic school she has ever seen. "They vote on everything," she says. "We have an average of two votes on something or other every day." Having thus been conditioned to voting as a way of life, Mrs. Watts left the voting on day-to-day plans for the group visit in the capable hands of Jay Bowman. He solved the problem of the tour's late start that morning by taking a vote on whether or not to leave out the Empire State Building. It was promptly voted out of the tour, and voted in for some later time as a separate undertaking.

A little bite here

Is all this voting a good idea—what does democracy do to individualism?

The tour included a boat trip to the Statue of Liberty, where the group fell in with crushing mobs of people walking to the top of the torch. Mrs. Watts found the experience nightmarish, and quit at the base of the torch. Most of the boys and girls made it to the top. "There are a hundred and sixty-eight steps up the torch, and there were forty thousand people ahead of me, but I was determined to climb up it," Jay Bowman reported to Mrs. Watts. "It took me twenty minutes, and it was worthwhile. The thing of it was I had to do it."

For the tour, Jay, like the other boys, had put on dress-up clothes bought specially, at a cost of about twenty-five dollars an outfit, for the trip to New York—white beachcomber pants reaching to below the knee, white cotton-knit shirt with red and blue stripes and a pocket in one sleeve, white socks with red and blue stripes, and white sneakers. The girls wore cotton skirts, various kinds of blouses, white cardigan sweaters, and low-heeled shoes. Mrs. Watts wore high-heeled pumps, even for sightseeing. Everyone else on the tour was astonished at the way New York City people dressed. "They look peculiar," Nancy Prather said. "Girls wearing high heels in the daytime, and the boys here always got a regular suit on, even to go to work in."

See this and wait for Miss Ross to set them up for her poisoned arrow

"I wouldn't trade the girls back home for any of the girls here," Jay Bowman says. "New York girls wear too much makeup. Not that my interests are centered on Nancy Glidden. She's in the junior class. I take her to shows in Bloomington. We eat pizzas, listen to Elvis Presley—things of that nature—and I always get her home by twelve. Even though my interests are centered on the junior class, I'm proud to say my classmates are the finest bunch of people in the world."

And how does he reveal himself

Jay lives with his parents and two brothers in an old nine-room house on thirty acres of land owned by Jay's father, who works in the maintenance department of the Bridgeport Brass Company, in Indianapolis. His mother works in Bloomington, on the R.C.A. color-television-set assembly line. Jay's grandfather, who has worked in limestone quarries all his life, lives across the road, on five acres of his own land, where he has a couple of cows and raises beans and corn for the use of the family. The Bowman family had no plumbing in their house while Jay was a child, and took baths in a tub in the kitchen with water from a well, but a few years ago, with their own hands, they installed a bathroom and a plumbing system, and did other work on the house, including putting in a furnace. Jay's parents get up at four in the morning to go to work. Jay, who hasn't been sick one day since he had the mumps at the age of twelve, never sleeps later than seven. He is not in the least distressed at having to work his way through college. He plans to get to school in his own car. This is a 1950 Chevrolet four-door sedan, which he hopes to trade in, by paying an additional four hundred dollars, for a slightly younger model before the end of the year.

Show, don't tell

"The thing of it is I feel proud of myself," Jay says. "Not to be braggin' or anything. But I saved up better than a thousand dollars to send myself to college. That's the way it is. I scrubbed floors, put up hay, carried groceries, and this last winter I worked Saturdays and Sundays in a country store on the state highway and got paid a dollar an hour for runnin' it."

The Bowman family has, in addition to a kind of basic economic ambition, two main interests—basketball and politics. Jay, like most of the other boys on the trip, played basketball on the school basketball team, which won the first round in its section of the Wabash Valley tournament last season. Jay talks about basketball to his classmates, but never about politics. Talk about the latter he saves for his family. His grandfather is a Democrat. "If it was up to my grandpa, he'd never want a single Republican in the whole country," he says. "And my Dad agrees with him. I agree with my Dad. My Dad thinks if Franklin D. Roosevelt was still President, this country wouldn't be in the trouble it finds itself in."

!!!!

At 5 p.m. of this second day in the City of New York, the members of the Bean Blossom senior class returned to their hotel and stood in the lobby for a while, looking from some distance at a souvenir-and-gift stand across from the registration desk. The stand was stocked with thermometers in the form of the Statue of Liberty, in two sizes, priced at seventy-nine cents and ninety-eight cents; with silver-plated charm bracelets; with pins and compacts carrying representations of the Empire State Building; with scarves showing the R.C.A. Building and the U.N. Building; and with ashtrays showing the New York City skyline. Mike Richardson edged over to the stand and picked up a wooden plaque, costing ninety-eight cents, with the Statue of Liberty shown at the top, American flags at the sides, and, in the middle, a poem, inscribed "Mother" which read:

Who buys this stuff? Bean Blossomers

To one who bears the sweetest name
And adds a luster to the same
Who shares my joys
Who cheers when sad
The greatest friend I ever had
Long life to her, for there's no other
Can take the place of my dear mother.

Glugg—glugg—Miss Ross knows The New Yorker audience. How can you tell the audience for this piece?

After reading the poem, Mike smiled.

"Where you from?" the man behind the stand asked him.

"Indiana," Mike said, looking as though he were warming up. "We've been on this tour? The whole day?"

Wait till he finishes Mike off

"Ya see everything?" the man asked.

"Everything except the Empire State Building," said Mike.

"Yeah," said the man, and looked away.

Mike was still holding the plaque. Carefully, he replaced it on the stand. "I'll come back for this later," he said.

Without looking at Mike, the man nodded.

Mike joined Dennis Smith and Larry Williams, who were standing with a tall, big-boned handsome girl named Becky Kiser. Becky used to be a cheerleader for the Bean Blossom Township basketball team.

How does she create the reality of this scene?

"We was talkin' about the way this place has people layin' in the streets on that Bowery sleepin'," Larry said. "You don't see people layin' in the streets back home."

"I seen that in Chicago," Dennis said. "I seen *women* layin' in the streets in Chicago. That's worse."

The others nodded. No argument.

Mike took a cigarette from his sleeve pocket and lit it with a match from the same pocket. He blew out a stream of smoke with strength and confidence. "I'll be glad when we light out of here," he said. "Nothin' here feels like the farm."

Second defector

Becky Kiser, with an expression of terrible guilt on her attractive, wide-mouthed face, said, "I bet you'd never get bored here in New York. Back home, it's the same thing all the time. You go to the skating rink. You go to the Big Boy. In the winter, there's basketball. And that's all."

"When I was in Chicago, I seen a man who shot a man in a bar," Dennis said. "I stood right across the street while the man who was shot the people drug him out." He looked at Becky Kiser. The other boys were also looking at her, but with condemnation and contempt. Dennis gave Becky support. "In Stinesville, they see you on the streets after eleven, they run you home," he said. "Seems like here the city never closes."

"Man, you're just not lookin' ahead," Mike said to Dennis, ignoring Becky.

"You like it here?" Larry asked, in amazement. "Taxes on candy and on everything?"

The Nazarene minister's daughter, Mary Jane Carter, came over with Ina Hough.

"Dennis, here, likes New York," Mike announced.

"I don't," said Ina. "I like the sights, but I think they're almost ruined by the people."

"The food here is expensive, but I guess that's life," said Mary Jane, in a mood of forbearance.

"Oh, man!" said Mike.

"Oh, man!" said Larry. "Cooped up in New York."

Ina said stiffly, "Like the guide said today, you could always tell a New Yorker from a tourist because a New Yorker never smiles, and I agree with him."

√ "After a while, you'd kinda fit in," Dennis said mildly.

Before dinner that night, Mr. Watts walked through the Times Square area checking prices and menus at likely restaurants. He made tentative arrangements at The Californian for a five-course steak or chicken dinner, to cost $1.95 per person, and asked Jay Bowman to go around taking a vote on the proposition. Half an hour later, Jay reported to Mr. Watts that some of the boys didn't want to go to The Californian, because they thought they'd have to do their own ordering. So Mr. Watts talked to the boys in their rooms and explained that the ordering was taken care of; all they had to say was whether they wanted steak or chicken. On the next ballot, everybody was in favor of The Californian. The class walked over. When the fifth course was finished, it was agreed that the dinner was all right, but several of the boys said they thought the restaurant was too high-class.

The ones who'd wanted to order the first time

It is a tourist trap and New Yorker readers know it

After dinner, it started to rain, and it rained hard. The Wattses and seven of the girls decided that they wanted to see "The Music Man." The four other girls wanted to see "My Fair Lady." None of the boys wanted to see a musical show. In the driving rain, the Wattses and the girls ran to the theatres of their choice, all arriving soaked to the skin. By good luck, each group was able to buy seats. At "The Music Man," the Wattses and the seven girls with them sat in the balcony, in the direct path of an air-conditioning unit blew icy blasts at their legs. The girls liked their shows. The "My Fair Lady" group was transported by the costumes. Ina Hough, who went to "The Music Man," thought that it was just like a movie, except for the way the scenes changed.

How many thousands of details Miss Ross had to collect to be able to select the ones she uses so effectively

The boys split up, some of them taking the subway down to Greenwich Village, the others heading for the Empire State Building, where they paid a dollar-thirty for tickets to the observatory and, once up there, found that the fog and rain blotted out the view completely. "We stood there about an hour and a half messin' around, me and my buddies," Jay later told Mrs. Watts. "Wasn't no sense in leavin' at that price." In Greenwich Village, Mike Richardson, Dennis Smith, and Larry Williams walked along the narrow streets in a drizzling rain. All were still wearing their beachcomber outfits. Nobody talked to them. They didn't see anybody they wanted to talk to. They almost went into a small coffeehouse; they changed their minds because the prices looked too high. They went into one shop, a bookstore, and looked at some abstract paintings, which appealed to them. "Sort of interestin', the way they don't look like nothin'," Mike said. Then they took the subway back to Times Square, where they walked around for a while in the rain. Toward midnight, Mike and Dennis told each other they were lonesome for the smell of grass and trees, and, the rain having stopped, they walked up to Central Park, where they stayed for about an hour and got lost.

Can't you see them

What sort of education have they had when they have no intellectual curiosity?

The next morning, a meeting of the class was held in the hotel lobby to take a vote on when to leave New York. Jay Bowman reported that they had enough money to cover an extra day in the city, plus a side trip to Niagara Falls on the way home. Or, he said, they could leave New York when they had originally planned to and go to Washington, D. C., for a day before heading home. The bus driver had told Jay that it was all one to him which they chose. The class voted for the extra day in New York and Niagara Falls.

The unifying thread of voting

Of course

"I'm glad," Becky Kiser said, with a large, friendly smile, to Dennis Smith. Several of her classmates overheard her and regarded her with a uniformly deadpan look. "I like it here," she went on. "I'd like to live here. There's so much to see. There's so much to do."

Her classmates continued to study her impassively until Dennis took their eyes away from her by saying, "You get a feelin' here of goin' wherever you want to. Seems the city never closes. I'd like to live here, I believe. People from everyplace are here."

"Limousines all over the joint," Albert Warthan said.

Something has happened to them

"Seems like you can walk and walk and walk," Dennis went on dreamily. "I like the way the big buildin's crowd you in. You want to walk and walk and never go to sleep."

"I hate it," Connie Williams said, with passion.

"Oh, man, you're just not lookin' ahead," Mike Richardson said to Dennis. "You got a romantic notion. You're not realistic about it."

"This place couldn't hold me," Larry Williams said. "I like the privacy of the farm."

"I want to go to new places," said Becky, who had started it. "I want to go to Europe."

"Only place I want to go is Texas," Larry said. "I got folks in Texas."

"There's no place like home," Mike said. "Home's good enough for me."

"I believe the reason of this is we've lived all of our lives around Stinesville," Dennis said. "If you took Stinesville out of the country, you wouldn't be hurt. But if you took New York out of the country, you'd be hurt. The way the guide said, all our clothes and everything comes from New York."

Becky said, "In Coney Island, I saw the most handsome man I ever saw in my whole life. I think he was a Puerto Rican or something, too."

That'll be quite a conversation

Albert said, "When we get back, my pa will say, 'Well, how was it!' I'll say, 'It was fine.' "

"I'd like to come back, maybe stay a month," Jay Bowman said diplomatically. "One thing I'd like to do is come here when I can see a major-league baseball game."

How does this piece demonstrate the idea that the author should be invisible, a pane of glass through which the reader sees the subject?

"I'd like to see a major-league baseball game, but I wouldn't come back just to see it," Mike said.

"I hate New York," Connie said.

"Back home, everybody says 'Excuse me,' " Nancy Prather said.

"I like it here," Dennis said stubbornly.

This day was an open one, leaving the boys and girls free to do anything they liked, without prearranged plan or vote. Mike passed close by the souvenir-and-gift stand in the hotel lobby, and the proprietor urged him to take home the Statue of Liberty.

"I'd like to, but it won't fit in my suitcase," Mike said, with a loud laugh.

A group formed to visit the zoo in Central Park, got on the subway, had a loud discussion about where to get off, and were taken in hand by a stranger, who told them the zoo was in the Bronx. Only the boy named Lynn Dillon listened to the stranger. The others went to the zoo in Central Park. Lynn stayed on the subway till it reached the Bronx, and spent the entire day in the Bronx Zoo by himself. The rest of the zoo visitors, walking north after lunch in the cafeteria, ran into the Metropolitan Museum of Art and went in. "It was there, and it was free, so we did it," Nancy Prather said. "There were these suits of armor and stuff. Nothin' I go for myself."

That morning, the Wattses had tried to get some of the boys and girls to accompany them to the Guggenheim Museum or the Museum of Modern Art, but nobody had wanted to pay the price of admission. "Why pay fifty √ cents to see a museum when they got them free?" the class president asked. Mrs. Watts reported afterward that the Guggenheim was the most exciting museum she had ever seen, including all the museums she had seen in Europe on her accredited art tour. "There aren't big crowds in there, for one thing," she said. "And I don't think the building overpowers the paintings at all, as I've heard." From the Guggenheim, the Wattses went to Georg

Contrast Jensen's to look at silver, but didn't buy anything. Then they went to the Museum of Modern Art and had lunch in the garden. "Lovely lunch, fabulous garden, fabulous sculpture, but I'm disappointed in the museum itself," Mrs. Watts said. "Everything jammed into that small space! Impossible to get a good view of Picasso's 'Girl Before a Mirror.' "

By dinnertime, more than half of the Bean Blossomers had, to their relief, discovered the Automat. Jay Bowman had a dinner consisting of a ham sandwich (forty cents), a glass of milk (ten cents), and a dish of fresh strawberries (twenty cents). Then, with a couple of buddies, he bought some peanuts in their shells and some Cokes, and took them up to his room for the three of them to consume while talking about what to do that night. They decided, because they had not yet had a good view of the city from the Empire State observatory, that they would go back there. They were accompanied by most of the girls and the other boys, and this time the group

Good for Dennis! got a cut rate of sixty-five cents apiece. Dennis went off wandering by himself. He walked up Fifth Avenue to Eighty-fifth Street, over to Park Avenue, down Park to Seventy-second Street, across to the West Side, down Central Park West to Sixty-sixth Street, over behind the Tavern-on-the-Green (where he watched people eating outdoors, and on down Seventh Avenue to Times Square, where he stood around on corners looking at the people who bought papers at newsstands.

The Wattses had arranged to meet anybody who was interested under the Washington Arch at around nine-thirty for an evening in Greenwich Village. The boys had decided to take a walk up Broadway after leaving the Empire State Building, but the girls all showed up in Washington Square, along with two soldiers and three sailors they had met in the U.S.O. across the street from the Woodstock. The Wattses led the way to a coffeehouse, where everybody had coffee or lemonade. Then the girls and the service men left the Wattses, saying they were going to take a ride on the ferry to Staten Island. The Wattses went to the Five Spot, which their jazz friend had told them had good music.

After breakfast the following morning, the bus driver, Ralph Walls, showed up in the hotel lobby for the first time since the group's arrival in New York and told Jay Bowman to have everyone assembled at five-forty-five the following morning for departure at six o'clock on the dot. The

He's one of them driver said that he was spending most of his time sleeping, and that before they left he was going to do some more sleeping. He had taken his wife on a boat trip around Manhattan, though, he said, and he had taken a few walks on the streets. After reminding Jay again about the exact time planned for the departure, he went back upstairs to his room.

Note this phrase—an echo of an earlier quotation

Mrs. Watts took nine of the girls (two stayed in the hotel to sleep) for a walk through Saks Fifth Avenue, just looking. Mr. Watts took three of the boys to Abercrombie & Fitch, just looking. Everybody walked every aisle on every floor in each store, looking at everything on the counters and in the showcases. Nobody bought anything. The two groups met at noon under the clock in Grand Central; lunched at an Automat; walked over to the United Nations Building, where they decided not to take the regular tour, and took a crosstown bus to the Hudson River and went aboard the liner S.S. Independence, where they visited every deck and every lounge on the boat, and a good many of the staterooms. Then they took the bus back to Times Square and scattered to do some shopping.

A revealing catalogue

Mike Richardson bought all his gifts—eleven dollars' worth—at the hotel stand, taking not only the plaque for his mother but a set of salt and pepper shakers, with the Statue of Liberty on the salt and the Empire State Building on the pepper, also for his mother; a Statue of Liberty ashtray for his father; a George Washington Bridge teapot for his sister-in-law; a mechanical dog for his niece; a City Hall teapot-cup-and-saucer set for his grandparents; and a cigarette lighter stamped with the Great White Way for himself. At Macy's, Becky Kiser bought a dress, a blouse, and an ankle chain for herself, and a necklace with matching bracelet and earrings for her mother, a cuff-link-and-tie-clasp set for her father, and a bracelet for her younger sister. Albert Wall then bought a miniature camera for himself and a telephone-pad-and-pencil set stamped with the George Washington Bridge and a Statue of Liberty thermometer, large-size, as general family gifts, at the hotel stand. Jay Bowman bought an unset cultured pearl at Macy's for his girl friend in the junior class, as well as silver-looking earrings for his married sister and for his mother, and at a store called King of Slims, around the corner from the hotel, he bought four ties—a red toreador tie (very narrow) for his older brother, a black toreador tie for his younger brother, a conservative silk foulard for his father, and a white toreador tie for himself. Dennis Smith bought a Statue of Liberty ashtray for his mother and a Statue of Liberty cigarette lighter for his father. Connie Williams bought two bracelets and a Statue of Liberty pen for herself. The bus driver and his wife spent sixty dollars on clothes for their children, six of whom are girls. Nancy Prather didn't buy anything. The Wattses spent about a hundred dollars in the course of the visit, most of it on meals and entertainment.

On their last evening in New York, all the boys and girls, accompanied by the Wattses, went to the Radio City Music Hall, making it in time to see the stage show. Then they packed and went to bed. The bus driver, after an early dinner with his wife at Hector's Cafeteria, brought the yellow school bus over from Tenth Avenue and parked it right in front of the hotel, so that it would be there for the early start.

What have you learned about subject? about writing? by reading this piece?

Next morning at five-forty-five, the Bean Blossomers assembled in the lobby; for the first time since the trip had started, nobody was late. The bus pulled out at exactly 6 a.m., and twenty minutes after that, heading west over the George Washington Bridge, it disappeared from the city.

38 The Teacher Teaches

Writing can be taught if we learn from those English teachers who have examined the process of writing and developed ways of allowing students to enter into the process. The following four articles are vigorous personal opinions based on firsthand experience. They should provide the prospective English teacher and the English teacher who wants to improve his ability to teach composition with a number of provocative ideas for thought and discussion.

Lucile Vaughan Payne is a professional writer and editor who has taught in both high school and college. She is the author of a textbook on writing, *The Lively Art of Writing* (Follett Publishing Company, 1965).

"Teaching Students to Write"

Perhaps no greater irony exists in American education than its general failure to produce students capable of expressing themselves even reasonably well in written language—a skill that not only determines to an enormous extent their welfare as students but profoundly influences their entire development as thinking and acting human beings.

Teaching a student to write is, in the final analysis, the same thing as teaching him to think. And this, unless I am grievously misled, is what education is all about. Yet the vast majority of students remain as innocent of writing skills on the day they leave high school or college as they were the day they entered.

Ironic? It is more than ironic. It is an absurdity so monumental that we seem to be dismissing it as a problem and accepting it as a condition of life. In both high school and college, writing is the step-child of the curriculum. In high school it is looked upon as a little something the English teacher can take care of at the end of the week, after she has taken care of grammar and literature. In most universities, it is turned over to green young graduate students who know almost nothing about writing and nothing at all about teaching.

The sorry state of college instruction in composition is not likely to change very soon. Whatever is done to improve student writing will have to be done by high school teachers. Given half a chance, they can do it, but only if the entire concept of the writing program in high school undergoes radical change. As things stand now, the program cannot really be called a program at all. It has no philosophy, no organization, no continuity, no real goal. Every teacher struggles along on his own, guided only by a few pious generalizations about "communication skills" laid down by the state course of study.

One teacher may concentrate grimly on grammar, another on spelling, another on metaphor. Some will ask for no more than reasonably correct answers to questions about the week's literature assignment. Others make their cause the active verb or the subordinate clause or simply the lowly comma. This is not a program; it is a series of individual skirmishes in a losing war.

Reprinted from the *National Education Association Journal,* November 1966, by permission of the *Journal* and the author.

Until very recently the engineers of curriculum seemed to operate on the theory that students would automatically learn to write well if they were (a) adequately instructed in grammar and (b) sufficiently exposed to literature. The fact that things obviously did not work out this way did not deter them from almost religious belief in the theory.

It took decades of frustration in the classroom before the theorists learned what any writer could have told them in five seconds—that nobody ever learned to write by studying grammar.

Generations of students have finally made this point abundantly clear, and grammar as a sustained and serious study in the modern English curriculum has generally been put to rout. Now the theory behind the study of writing would seem to rest on a single proposition: that sufficient exposure to good literature will do the job. Thus more literature has rushed in to fill the gap left by grammar. And the study of writing remains exactly where it was from the beginning: a tiny subdivision of the literature program, the token theme at the end of the week, the Black Friday of the curriculum.

Actually, this arrangement probably does not reflect a theory behind the teaching of writing so much as it indicates the absence of any real theory. But the result is the same—an approach to writing through literature alone. Certainly this is the main approach of the true artist. Certainly it represents a long and honorable tradition, a tradition so firmly established that to question it even slightly is enough to induce shock in most English teachers. But surely, since it is now the only approach in general use in the schools, it is legitimate to ask one small question: Has it worked?

The dismal answer is that it has not. Students are now being exposed to a broader range of literature in high school than ever before. Furthermore, with the techniques of the "new criticism" now in general use all the way down to the ninth grade, certain reading skills have sharply improved. Even average high school students these days can spot a symbol or identify an archetype from a mile off. But they are not learning to write.

I am not suggesting that the literature program be abridged for the sake of the writing program; no student of writing can read too much. Nor do I suggest that the close-reading method of teaching literature is at fault; it strikes me as rather joylessly analytical, but it has considerable appeal for students who lack the capacity to enjoy literature on any other level. I am only pointing out that reading is not writing. And that as a short-term, single-shot approach to writing it simply does not work.

In order to affect writing significantly, reading must be a passionate, life-long pursuit, a kind of love affair with language that begins in childhood. It takes years for even the "born" writer, whose natural element is literature, to assimilate through reading the sense of language that makes his work distinctive and to master the subtle skills that give it form and meaning. To assume that high school students will pick up even a microscopic portion of this kind of learning in three or four years' enforced exposure to literature is to dwell in the land of pure fantasy.

The student who has natural gifts as a writer will profit from the exposure, of course. But for every gifted student there are thousands upon thousands of others whose writing, except for a slight increase in vocabulary, never improves. These students never make genuine, personal contact with language in any meaningful way, never grasp the first principles involved in expressing ideas with clarity much less with grace. These are the students who need help, and these are the ones who are not getting it, will never get it, in a system that makes writing a part of the literature program.

But if writing cannot be taught through grammar or literature, how can it be taught?

I would suggest that we teach it for what it is: writing. Not grammar, not reading, but writing. And that we begin by deciding what we mean when we talk about teaching it. Obviously some things about writing cannot be taught; nobody can "learn how" to be talented. But a number of very important things about writing can be taught, and if we identify them, perhaps it will be possible to arrive at a clear and realistic idea of what a high school writing program should accomplish.

By program I mean a basic program for all students, not a highly specialized course in creative writing for the gifted few. High schools have no obligation to turn out future Faulkners and Hemingways. The idea that they can do so is in any case, it seems to me, a harmless delusion. The schools do have an obligation, however, to instruct all students, to the limit of their intelligence, in the effective use of language. That means teaching them three things: how to organize their thoughts around a central idea, how to test those thoughts for logic, and how to express them in a clear and concise language in a unified piece of prose.

It sounds simple, put thus. It isn't, of course. To organize ideas is simply to think, and thinking is never easy. It is, however, within the range of any student of average intelligence (if it isn't, we are wasting a pile of money on public education), and it is the first step in the writing of any reasoned discourse. How far a student goes beyond this basic goal depends upon the quality of his mind and imagination. But any normally bright student, given proper instruction, can achieve the basic goal.

That's the first essential. The second essential is simply time enough to do the job. It is idiotic to assume that writing, one of the most complex and difficult of human skills, can be taught in the few minutes a week now set aside for it in the typical English curriculum. What is needed is a completely independent, full-scale, required, one-year course in composition. Ideally, such a course would be followed by an optional second year for interested students.

The third and final essential is that the course follow a logical sequence in the development of writing skills. It is not enough to give students sufficient time to practice writing; without guidance they will simply write in circles. Nor is it enough to give them one unrelated exercise after another; that would merely compound the problems already inherent in present slapdash methods of teaching writing.

The course must have a pattern. The pattern that makes the most sense is one that duplicates in slow motion the steps taken swiftly and naturally by competent writers when they address themselves to any prose composition.

That means, first of all, giving students a clear understanding of essay structure. Why the essay? Because the structure of the essay, it seems to me, is identical to the structure of thought, and in ordering his ideas to fit that structure the student finds himself compelled to think, and to think logically. It is a slow, exhausting process for both student and teacher, and most teachers will find the temptation to move on quickly toward the choicer delights of language—metaphor and simile, allusion, style, tone—almost irresistible. But structure must come first.

It is nonsense to believe, as a great many teachers with vaguely artistic notions about writing unfortunately do believe, that structure restricts thought or inhibits the budding imagination. The only thing structure restricts is the area of thought, thus bringing mind and imagination into full play in relation to a single idea. Paradoxically, it frees by restricting.

The discovery of structure, incidentally, has for many students the quality of pure revelation. It is often their first genuine involvement with ordered, logical, truly independent thought, and it is an exhilarating experience for them. Into their glazed and baffled eyes comes a sudden, joyful gleam of understanding. Writing finally makes sense to them.

And suddenly, they want to learn. Having made the miraculous discovery that they have something to say and that a clear-cut method of saying it is within their grasp, they want to say it as well as possible. This they learn by writing. And more writing. And still more writing. Not by studying grammar, but by using language. Not by searching for meaning in what others have written, but by searching for the best way to write what they themselves mean.

Step by step, they move from the structure of the essay as a whole to the structure of its successively smaller parts, writing as they go, moving smoothly and simultaneously with each step toward the marriage of structure and style, constantly writing, examining, rethinking, rewriting — doing, in short, what every writer does instinctively every time he sits down to work.

There is no other way to learn how to write.

It could well be the hardest labor most students will face during their school years. It should also be the most rewarding, for they will learn how to use their most important possession, language. Furthermore, they will automatically become better readers. Although the study of literature does not necessarily make students better writers, the study of writing always makes them better, more appreciative students of literature. Why? Because they come to understand, from experience, what goes on in the writing.

It scarcely matters what subjects they write about during their training —they may never write a single paper on literature—but they will come back to their literature classes with a greater capacity to understand what they read.

If more literature teachers were aware of this, they would themselves agitate for a full-scale composition course independent of their own classes. So would other teachers, for the skills a student learned through an adequate composition course would be immediately apparent in all his written work. Once a student begins to think in writing, he can address himself intelligently to anything in writing—whether his subject is literature or history or economics or double overhead cams.

With standards of organization and clarity once firmly established in all courses, all teachers could be expected to share responsibility for maintaining them. Teachers outside the English department now say, with some justice, that they don't have time to teach their students how to write. Ironically, neither has the English teacher. But guess who gets the blame.

Time. A clearly understood goal. A sequentially structured course in composition. These are the three essentials the high schools must provide if they hope to turn out students who can write well. It needs doing quickly. The schools can't wait the thirty years that it takes, according to some cynics, for any kind of change to take place in education. By then, if things go on as they have been, high school students may not even be able to write their names.

Paul O'Dea, who taught high school for nine years, is a member of the faculty of Mundelein College in Chicago.

"Five Myths in the Teaching of Composition"

There must be others, who as they read advertisements for composition textbooks and articles on the teaching of composition, classify as I. I see five approaches, each honored by time if by little else, each supported by a great number of teachers and perpetuated by textbook publishers, and each grounded on a questionable premise. I choose to call them the five myths, not so much for the force of derogation but because, as in most myths, there is some degree of truth in each.

Myth No. 1: Students Learn to Write Well by Reading Great Literature In the starkest application of this theory, students read and discuss for a number of weeks a given literary masterpiece. During and especially at the end of this unit, students are asked to write an interpretive or critical essay; less frequently, they are, during the course of the unit, invited to write about an insight or problem that they might develop by reference to their personal experience. In either case, the resultant essay is evaluated for its content overwhelmingly. If problems in organization or in development arise, these are treated incidentally if at all, which is probably just as well, since the teacher who uses this theory often has never stopped to instruct the students systematically over a series of related themes as to just what organizations and development are, anyway.

I am here, obviously, describing a course which presumes to teach composition through the study of literature; I am not discussing a unit in literary study which has no pretension to more than the development of the students' understanding and love of literature. Who can ask for more important goals than these?

The appeal of this particular myth is fairly obvious. In the first place, nearly all English teachers are better prepared to teach literature than composition. Also, "teaching composition" this way is much less time-consuming, since there are fewer written exercises to grade.

The defenses for this particular theory are equally apparent. In some cases, teachers will point to the testimony of contemporary novelists and playwrights, who will generally aver that no teacher ever taught them any-

Reprinted from the *English Journal,* April 1965, with the permission of the National Council of Teachers of English and Paul O'Dea.

thing about writing, that they learned to write by writing and writing, and by reading widely. (There is, of course, some distance between these exceptional people and the high school sophomore before us, the one who is half interested in learning to write a competent piece of exposition.) Certainly there is a good deal of truth in the assumption that those who read widely are rewarded in several ways, one of which is increased proficiency in writing, most clearly seen, I suspect, in the areas of diction and sentence structure. Just how this happens, we do not yet know. The point here is that many English teachers, avid readers themselves, are lured into believing that not wide reading only but close reading of masterpieces is the best kind of preparation for writing.

Myth No. 2: Students Learn to Write Essays by Analyzing Professionally Written Essays In many ways this myth is related to the first, but the second myth more clearly rests its case on the assumption that the best way to learn to write is by imitating models. This assumption is most popular at the upper levels of high school and in Freshman English in college, whatever shape that curious beast may take from institution to institution. I think of it as the "Go thou and do likewise" approach.

In this approach the student is given an essay book containing a great number of essays, most of which are expository or argumentative and on widely disparate subjects. The student, with his classmates, is assigned an essay which the class reads and discusses. Then the teacher, after pointing out the salient features of E. B. White's style or Huxley's organization, directs the student to "Suggestions for Writing," furnished by the editor at the end of the essay. The student then proceeds ot write his own essay, presumably in emulation of the professional model. It does not matter that the model is at least ten times longer than the student's essay. It does not matter that the model only vaguely illuminates a particular kind of writing problem relevant to the student's own growth in composition. It does not matter that the professional writer has gone far beyond competency into artistry demonstrated in tone and in rhetorical devices which appear in no textbook. The ordinary student is either just overwhelmed at the distance between himself and the professional writer or slavishly attempts to copy the particular organization and style of Eisely or J. B. Priestley or whomever.

Certainly few can take exception to the general rule that one good way to learn how to write is to imitate those who can write. The fault lies not in the rule but in the stars of our writing world; they are several light years removed from the writing ability of the ordinary student. The latter would better profit by imitating the work of the best writer in his class, a writer who has successfully—according to the teacher's standards—written an essay comparable in every way to the student's own first effort.

Underlying both the first and second myth is the assumption that the student must be given something to write about before he can write. *Given* is the significant word here. To the extent that the student is stimulated or provoked into a revelation of his own emotional or intellectual experience by the study of literature or essays, that study serves a useful purpose for composition. To the extent that he is invited to parrot or to assume an artificial rheorical stance because of what he has read, the study is, insofar as composition is concerned, sterile.

Myth No. 3: Students Learn to Write Well by Grammatical Analysis This is one of the most durable of myths. Siege guns of research have been laid to this citadel, and still it will not go down. Its adherents have lately fled to the refuge of the linguistic revolution, and from the safety of the disagreement among traditional, structural, and transformational grammarians, pray that one fine day there will be a synthesis for grammatical study. I personally doubt that this halcyon day will ever come, but even if it should, we must recall that linguists of every stripe have been notoriously reluctant to suggest that a student's knowledge of English grammar will be a definite contributing factor to his improvement in writing. At any rate, the diagramming and drills go on apace in the fond expectation that he who can spot a misplaced modifier in someone else's sentence on Tuesday will be able to spot one in one of the thirty or forty he will write next Friday. In the "constructive" phase of this myth, students are busy writing out the four (or fourteen) basic sentence patterns that they have had in their heads since the age of three. One defender of this theory offered me the interesting evidence that the students who were best at grammatical analysis were also the best writers. I turned and fled.

*Myth No. 4: Students Learn to Write Better by Reconstructing Other People's Sentence*s This myth seems closely related to the preceding myth, but its perpetrators (usually textbook publishers) are quick to disclaim any connection. Usually, in the foreword to a textbook, they will assure the enlightened teacher that they are including grammar only where it is "functional." What this means generally is that there is less in the way of usage rules and grammatical prescription and more in the way of exercises; often this kind of textbook is a workbook.

There is of course some value in this particular approach, insofar as it seeks to equip the student with the necessary tools for repairing individual sentences in his writing after the fact. Usually, though, the time given over to sentence reconstruction is inordinate, considering what time is left to the study of more important aspects of composition such as purpose, unity, and coherence.

Myth No. 5: Students Learn to Write Better by Taking into Account Extensive Teacher Criticism This last myth is in many ways the most disturbing of all, if only because it prompts conscientious teachers to so much hard work for so little gain. In this approach the teacher relies heavily on a criticism of the student's theme, a criticism so detailed that it sometimes exceeds the length of the theme itself. In most cases, the marginal and final comments are overwhelmingly negative and thus complement the many red-pencilled spelling, diction, and punctuation errors in the body of the paper. It is only apparently strange that the student is often supposed to do very little about all this carefully written criticism, except possibly to correct the mechanical errors. The reason for this is obvious, since the correction of the larger and more important aspects would require nothing less than the rewriting of the whole theme—a matter usually precluded by the lack of time, if not by the teacher's reluctance to read basically the same themes again. The negative emphasis underlying this fifth myth is best illustrated for me by the anecdote about a teacher's remarking to a class, "I'll have all your themes corrected by Friday."

The advice about teaching composition which has been so frequently advanced in the pages of this *Journal* is, so far as I can see, outside the scope of the five myths. The things I remember most follow. Try to establish a writing situation where there can be *real* communication, where the student is given a genuine opportunity to inform the teacher *and* the class about his specialized knowledge of bird-watching or whatever, or is encouraged to think that his opinion about the function of the witches in *Macbeth* might be interesting to the whole class. Let the theme topics come out of any heated discussion, intellectual fights which the teacher carefully starts and guides. Arrange the year's writing in a sequential series of themes which seek to promote specific writing skills one at a time. Do not try to teach everything at once on one theme. Remember that encouragement is a more effective teaching device than negative criticism. Stress rewriting and allow time for it instead of mechanically assigning a different theme each week. Allow for time for conferences with individual writers, even if that means a class period of reading time for the majority of the class. And let myth be properly an aspect of literature, not of instruction in composition.

Matthew F. Doherty taught English in North Babylon (New York) Senior High School before becoming an editor for the New York State Teachers Association.

"The Missing Link: Rewriting"

The teaching of writing continues to be the subject of a whirlwind of contradictory articles, studies, proposals, ad infinitum. Small wonder that frustrated and confused English teachers are often drawn to the vacuous middle, uncommitted to any single, effective approach to writing.

Yet rarely in this storm about the teaching of writing are we offered glimpses of the simple truth—that writing is basically a self-taught skill produced mainly by *rewriting,* and that the teacher's primary role must be to guide the youngster through this difficult act of self-teaching. All *good* writing, as we know, is more perspiration than inspiration, and it is the culmination of *rewriting,* in the process of which the writer sweats, learns, and produces. Nevertheless, most of our existing methods and the bulk of our proposed methods seem strangely designed to circumvent this basic truth. We try many kinds of complex procedures, few of which demand hard, down-to-earth, laborious editing and revision.

We are all familiar with Flaubert's agonizing reappraisal of each word and sentence as he produced *Madame Bovary,* with Hemingway's painstaking editing of *The Old Man and the Sea,* with Benjamin Franklin's rewriting of the classics to discover by comparison his own flaws, and with

Reprinted from the *English Journal,* December 1965, with the permission of the National Council of Teachers of English and Matthew F. Doherty.

Maugham's similar technique to explore style. And Saul Bellow admitted to between 15 and 25 drafts of *Herzog* before he achieved a final copy. These men and most other lovers of the written word regard rewriting as a routine modus operandi. This regard seems to increase proportionately with greater degrees of writing eloquence and mastery.

In the world of action around us, rewriting is as essential to writing as is pen, paper, and typewriter. Newspapers depend on editors, rewrite men, and proofreaders, and competent executives carefully revise important letters. Without doubt, teachers scrupulously edit their own letters of application and reports to higher authority. Examples such as these are endless.

Despite this overwhelming evidence of the need for and the existence of rewriting in the process of writing, many teaching methods blatantly avoid the fact. It is quite common for English teachers to accept what is, in effect, a first draft, place their comment and grade thereon, and regard it as a finished assignment. Other teachers make weak gestures toward rewriting by compelling students to correct minor mechanical errors. If students are not forced to involve themselves in actual, painful, total rewriting, then they are *not* writing; they may simply be playacting and conforming, and thus learning relatively little. In fact, they are learning the wrong lesson.

These are harsh words, perhaps, but we would be unmercifully ridiculed if we attempted to teach reading without books or speech without speaking. Writing *is* rewriting, and there exists no really valid shortcut or panacea.

Why, then, do many English teachers continue to try all kinds of methods, but evade this utterly essential technique? Teachers generally reply that there is simply not enough time to implement proper rewriting procedures. The pressures of teaching grammar, literature, drama, spelling, vocabulary, and speech, as well as writing, preclude the enormous amount of time needed by teachers to read and edit first drafts, to return these to the students for revision, and then to read and evaluate the resultant final drafts.

We are professionally obliged, however, to fix our gaze on reality, validity, and truth.

We know, for example, that most of us mix praise with criticism in our comments on student papers, because it is psychologically sound to encourage the budding writer. But when the final paper is a hastily-written first draft, however good it might be, is not this praise a form of educational negligence? We are, in fact, encouraging a shoddy and mistaken approach to the most demanding of the language arts.

Furthermore, teacher comments and corrections are utterly meaningless, unless the student is *required* to execute the revisions in a rewritten draft. We are all too familiar, from our own experiences, with the human inclination to accept praise and ignore criticism, particularly on a piece of writing. We know that students make the same errors in mechanics and style over and over again, ignoring our most astute comments on previous compositions. Obviously, they must learn by doing. In writing, the "doing" is in the rewriting.

A notion is current, too, that if writing is made excessively laborious for the student, he will lose his already battered motivation and appreciation. But writing *is* a sweaty occupation, and progress and satisfaction multiply with the healthy expenditure of *meaningful* effort. We spare the youngster no amount of arduous physical calisthenics so that he may achieve touchdowns on the football field, yet we often try to make training in writing as pleasant and as easy as possible. We do this despite the reality that in a flash of time the body is too soft for football while the trained intellect remains fit for *many* years.

Another aspect of reality that we tend to ignore is that most good writing stems from acquired habits and skills rather than from innate talents. The creative writer, the artist, finds his own way *despite* teachers. But the vast majority of persons, those who are or who will be involved in reports, business letters, college essays, etc., are in need of learning the *skills* of writing, the essential element of which is rewriting. Whether the youngster is an honors candidate or a so-called slow student is irrelevant. The basic step of self-editing can and should be taught to *all* students. Since writing is primarily an intellectual skill, the degree of competence will, of course, vary, but training in self-editing is invaluable to *all* who pick up pen and paper.

Teachers who believe that rewriting is an essential element in writing are faced with complex problems in the classroom, as it now exists. But these are not insurmountable problems, and there are solutions, although any solution under present conditions must be, by necessity, a compromise of sorts. We could, for example, cut the number of assigned essays in half. As far as numbers of words are concerned, the student would be writing as many per semester, since he would be writing each paper at least twice. But to measure numbers of words is sheer nonsense, just as it is sheer nonsense to be satisfied with a number of essays without regard for their validity and quality. The value derived from the revision and rewriting of one essay far exceeds whatever value lies in the writing of several unedited compositions.

Even in this type of compromise situation, however, the teacher's burdens are magnified. It is far more difficult to make extensive corrections and suggestions on a first draft, consult with the student, and then evaluate a final draft, than it is to read two separate essays, placing thereon subjective grades and essentially useless comments.

A method designed to relieve burdens on the teacher is that of creating a framework in which students edit one another's work. This can be done through committee or buzz-session techniques, but the disadvantages are obvious. Students are usually qualified to proofread for mechanical errors. But they are not virtuosos in form and content, and they should not be placed in that position of authority over others.

The simplest method is to place full responsibility for editing and rewriting on the individual student, requiring two copies of each assignment with substantial evidence that the youngster's first draft is a first draft, a paper that contains the obvious scars of self-editing. Two dangers exist here. No one, and especially the tyro writer, likes to change what seems like a golden thought culled from his very soul. The ability to apply the knife and to cut unmercifully comes with maturity and self-discipline. But at least the process is there and maturity will inevitably follow. The second danger stems from indolence and from the sheer genius of many students to pretend compliance. This writer has found that some youngsters will write their final copy first, neatly and meticulously, and then create a second copy which is jumbled and lined-out and rumpled, brilliantly devising what appears to be an agonizingly-written first draft.

The ultimate burden, obviously, is upon the teacher. Without doubt, imaginative teachers are exercising unique ways of implementing rewriting in the classroom. But we are hearing far too often from those who evade the basic issue. The most sincere and thoughtful proposals are unfortunately invalid if they ignore or circumvent the process of rewriting.

Our obligation, then, is to seek first things first. Before we advocate new methods which ignore reality and which thus compound confusion and apathy among teachers, we must fight for the proper emphasis on *rewriting* as a first principle. Then we must struggle to gain the time and the means needed to implement this principle.

Once the youngster recognizes that he contains within himself the mental muscles needed to reshape words and remold thoughts, he will be far along on the road to self-teaching and self-discovery, prime steps on the way to good writing.

John Sweet is a member of the English Department of Horace Greeley High School in Chappaqua, New York.

"Some Notes for Student Writers"

Being clear about what happens in writing is something like trying to be clear about what happens when a race horse runs. The horse trainer, Sunny Jim Fitzsimmons, knew how to watch a horse. He could see each part, and he knew how the parts fitted together in the process of running.

What is writing anyway? Perhaps I look at a spoon. With my mind I connect with its surfaces and with its parts. (It does have parts.) And here is the miracle. I put what I see on paper in such a way that a reader can "see" what I saw. Further, a sensitive reader can take my description of the spoon and what I saw about it, and he can know something about the kind of person I am and what my feelings were at the moment of writing. Was I bored? Interested? Do I have a sense of humor? The reader gets my description of the spoon and my way of seeing at the same time. That is what writing is: seeing, placing what I saw in words so that the reader sees, and doing both these things in such a way that the reader knows something about me as well as the spoon.

Notice that the word *see* appears over and over again in the above description. This is no accident. Seeing, really seeing, is vital to writing. (In a way, we "see" with our fingers, our ears, and our noses too.) When we were children, we saw thousands of things freshly and clearly. Now we have to force ourselves to learn to see again. This is the First Commandment if you would learn how to write: *make yourself see.*

When we see a poor piece of writing, we don't find it "bad" because of wrong commas and misspellings. It's bad because we grow uncomfortable

Reprinted from the *English Journal,* February 1967, with the permission of the National Council of Teachers of English and John Sweet.

for the writer. He pokes his limitations at us. We say to ourselves. "Poor fellow. Why can't he present himself and his world clearly on paper?" Learning how to write is learning how to master our limitations so that these limitations don't get in the way of the reader.

The following suggestions are directed to young writers. I hope they will be useful as reminders to teachers and genuinely helpful to their students.

Seek These Like Oxygen

The particular detail: Most of us can generalize. ("Tyranny is bad." "*Hawaii* is a good novel." "He was a proud boy.") In not one of those statements is there anything a reader can see. Suppose your assignment is to describe a person. For 20 minutes you might observe a boy who works in a filling station. With careful work, you might notice 20 or 30 things about him. Now what are the *significant* details which you saw? He wears shabby shoes. He carries a comb in his pocket to keep his perfectly combed hair in place. Perhaps these two details will be your real key to him: poverty (the shoes) and price (the combed hair). These details will become the heart of your paper. The other items you noticed will become the minor facts leading up to your major impression: pride and poverty working against each other in the same person.

As you watch the boy, seek the one gesture which seems to be most characteristic of him. Try to reproduce the way he speaks. One sharp phrase might give us the feel of his whole way of talking. Two significant details, one sharp phrase of speech, and one revealing gesture—these will *show* us this boy. Try to find those particular details which will make him real to us. Anyone can generalize; with telling detail you can show us what you saw in that boy.

Release your feelings: Make the reader feel by doing some feeling yourself as you write. We write at our best when we are emotionally involved with what we write about. Of course it's true that some of the things we write about in school deal with objective information. We must hold our feelings down in some papers. Nevertheless, when you can, get those feelings of yours on paper. Many young people tend to hide their true feelings. In exposing them, they might be laughed at. But, remember, there is no such thing as eloquence if there is no feeling in the writer. If you want the reader to feel, you have to feel too. If you are reluctant to have your feelings exposed to the class, mark your paper "confidential." The teacher will respect your request.

Use your senses as a bridge to the reader: Make the reader see and feel and hear by employing your own senses in the words you write (the *gritty* sand on the shower floor, the *tingly* sting of iodine, the *fish-white* skin under my bathing suit). You have eyes, ears, a nose, a sense of touch. Make those senses work for you. Get back to the world of your senses and you will find you have made contact with your reader. Why? Because we have those same senses too. They go to work in us as we read what you wrote.

Ignore These Like The Plague

Apologies: Don't impose your own misgivings on your reader. Why burden your message with freight it doesn't need? The Bible makes an amusing comment, "The guilty flee when no man pursueth." So don't you flee with apologies. More importantly, students tend to be too stern judges of themselves. Perhaps you are better than you think. Don't apologize, because you rob your reader of any hope for pleasure in your theme. Don't apologize, because it's cheeky to assume that he can't decide for himself what is good and what is not.

"I must please the teacher": Nonsense! It would be more sensible to try to please yourself. Since teachers are of different ages and temperaments, you cannot possibly know us well enough to please us. Actually, we don't even want "to be pleased." Rather we want you to grow to that point in security where you can be yourself on paper. Many of you tend to be too modest. We know that you understand much more than you succeed in getting on paper. This is true for writers of any age. Nobody ever got a whole experience completely on paper—not even Shakespeare. Do what you can with what you've got. Don't write to impress; write to *express*. The last is your door to good writing.

Before You Start To Work

Jot down some quick notes: Before you start to write, write down a list of all the ideas and particulars which come to you. Don't try for any special order at first. Now scratch out what doesn't seem to fit. In sequence, number the remaining items in the order in which you think you'll write them into your rough draft.

A few quick scratch notes at the top of your essay examination on "The Causes of the Civil War" will show your history teacher that you are a student who understands the help of order in writing clearly. More importantly, you will write a better answer to that exam question. You will get a better grade.

How many parts will you have in your theme? By parts I mean paragraphs. This is a vital question. The average student theme of 300 words rarely has more than two or three "main body" paragraphs. What are the topics of those paragraphs? Once you know those topics, you can begin to write with comfort.

Limit your topic: You may have heard that 50 times, but the fact remains that a major fault in student writing is the failure to limit. You just can't hope to cover a large topic in the average four-paragraph student theme. Which of these is the best topic for a 300-word theme? *Viet Nam, LBJ and Viet Nam, This Year in Viet Nam, Last Month in Viet Nam, My Brother in Viet Nam.* Perhaps the last named would be suitable for a short theme. A composition on *A Penny* is often used by English teachers as a device to remind students of the force which can come with limitation of topic.

Don't ignore the commonplace: Students sometimes exaggerate the value of being exciting. If the topic is not a hold-up or a fire, they feel it is too commonplace. The truth is that the commonplace is interesting precisely because it is common. We all use thumbtacks, match-books, and ballpoint pens, but we stop seeing them after a time. When a student sees them freshly, we will read him with genuine interest because that commonplace object is a part of our experience. A commonplace topic can result in a most uncommon theme, if you will make us see again.

Write to a clear target: A student will write much more effectively if he has a clear sense of his reader. For example, a student's letter to his friend is often better than his themes, because he has a clear sense of his friend as he writes. Don't write to your teacher, because it is discouraging to try to say something to a person who seems to know more than you do. Your best target is your class right there in the same room with you. Why? Because you know them, and you are not afraid of them. Make your teacher into a kind of editor who looks over your shoulder at an interclass communication.

Take sides: The next time your social studies teacher says, "Let's talk about automation," look around you. You will see many a blank face. But if he says, "Are you for or against automation?" the class will come to life. Sides are taken. Side-taking increases reader interest, and it gives you a focus as you search for what you want to say. Suppose you have a book report due and you don't know what to say about the book. Ask yourself, "Am I for it or against it?" If you didn't like the book, choose three things which irritated you. Each can be developed into a paragraph. The three paragraphs are your book report. Perhaps you don't like to take sides because you are afraid of the red pencil. However, if you would look over the teacher's shoulder as he reads the class themes, you would be surprised at how few students have discovered the salt of interest which comes with side-taking. If the teacher once marked you down for disapproving of a "classic," perhaps you failed to support your case well. Experiment a little. You may find your teacher to be much more open-minded than you think.

As You Do The Actual Writing

Don't tell, show! You may tell us, "It was hot." Or you may show us by writing, "My shirt stuck to my back. Sweat ran into my glasses." In the first sentence, we had to take your word for the heat. In the other two sentences, *we were there.* We too have had these same stickings and sweatings. Showing makes it possible for the reader to identify with the writer. When you show, you get out of the reader's way and let him come right at the experience itself.

Get yourself into your papers: Do you know the most interesting thing you have to write about? Yourself and your own way of seeing things. We are most interesting to read when we reveal the work as it looks from our particular windows. Thousands of English teachers have read thousands of themes and said, "It's OK, but it's dull. There's nothing of you in it." Do you want to be "original"? Remember that you are most original when you are most yourself. Learning to write is learning how to get that same self on paper. Try to be yourself, and then add that seeing and showing will make the reader see, too.

"Write what you know," is an ancient piece of advice to writers. It is not always easy to follow. For example, if you have not understood *Lord Jim,* it is hard to write down what you know about that novel. If you have not understood the book, that might be precisely what you should write about, because your own direct experience has been one of puzzlement. Or, suppose the assigned theme topic was "Foreign Aid." Rightly you might feel you knew very little about it. But you can still treat the topic by writing on your own attitudes toward aid to others in your school and in your neighborhood. You would then have brought your own experience to the topic no matter how remote it might have seemed to you at first.

Identify! Identify! Identify! One element present in all good writing is the identification of the writer with the thing written about. For example, when you throw a bowling ball, your body will move with it in an effort to make it hit the right pin. Or a boy will build a table in shop class. Perhaps he knows and loves every inch of it. He identifies with that table so much that it is a part of him. In the same way, the writer loses his imagination and gets to his reader forcefully when he is able to identify with his topic. He feels. He IS the thing or person written about. Try to choose topics with which you have a strong sense of identification.

Get close to it: If you write from memory, you will find yourself using fuzzy clichés and stereotyped ways of thinking and feeling. Your writing will be dead, because the experience is dead. Students tend to think that only "big things" are worth writing about but remember that the exciting adventure in the car last year may now be cold to your senses. You won't be able to make it fresh again for your reader. On the other hand, an amusing incident at the breakfast table this morning might give you a far better paper, because it was real and immediate in your memory. You can recall it more vividly. You have a better chance at making the reader see. Take these two topics: "The Cold War" and "This English Classroom." The latter will probably produce a better paper, because you are in immediate sensory contact with your topic.

Learn the power of endings: The ending is a strong place in sentences, in paragraphs, and in the whole theme. Examine these two examples, "For God, for country, and for YALE." "Blood, sweat, and TEARS." Those two final words hit us with a special force, and much of that force comes from the fact that they are end words. Your theme closing sentences are often weak at the very moment when you want a forceful nail. Remember that this important last sentence is the last thing the teacher reads before he puts the grade on your paper. Make them strong, those endings. What you want is a special kind of emphasis. Here are three kinds of emphatic endings to themes: use a quotation, a sharp point of humor, or a very short sentence. If well done, any one of these can give you emphasis. Find that nail!

The Final Touches

Cut it down: It is a rare theme which cannot be greatly improved by cutting. So much student writing shouts at the reader, "I didn't have anything to say, but I had to say something." You can train yourself to cut your themes by always writing a little more than the assignment requires. In each theme, you are after a single effect. Mercilessly cut every word and sentence which does not contribute to that effect. Padding always hurts writing; cutting always helps it.

All good writing is re-writing: You should write your rough draft with little thought to spelling and punctuation. The rough draft is like a foundation on which a house can be built. You can sit on the front porch and think about your theme, but you can't really get to work on it until you have staked out the rough lines of it in a rough draft. Even if they prove to be the wrong staked-out lines, this rough draft will lay out some foundation for you to tinker with. As a matter of fact, this very article had five different rough drafts. Edit what you have written. Look up the hard word to spell that you are not sure of. Rearrange the sentence order so that you have strong sentences at the end of each paragraph and of the theme. Do all these things after you have let the flow come naturally. The rough draft may have been a fumbled thinking on paper. Re-writing takes that shapeless rough draft and aims it at a reader. Re-writing helps you say what you mean. As you re-write, and *only* as you re-write, do you begin to become a writer.

Read your rough draft aloud: In your effort to write with force, you have a gifted assistant on your side. You too rarely use him. He is your own ear. You may improve your own writing by as much as 20 per cent if you will read your rough draft aloud, shaping and cutting as you go. Your ear will find poor rhythm. Your ear will find the sentence that is not clear. Hear it; then make it better.

This is a list for your use. Perhaps some of these suggestions will point the way to more effective writing.

Writing is hard work. It's hard work for the first-grader and for John Steinbeck and for all of us in between. No list of tips will make you a writer. There's just you and the blank page and all that life out there to get a hold on.

Learn to love this hard thing—writing. You'll never know what you can do with it until you push and push and push some more. Perhaps there is no such thing as talent—there is only pressure. You will have to supply that pressure. Nobody else can do it for you, not really.

If you want to write, write! It may break your heart, but it will make you more of a person in the process. Richard Sewall wrote, "No one knows who he is until he has tried to put himself on paper. And no one knows what his world is until he has tried to describe it."

Find out who you are. Find out what your world is. It's worth it.

39 What the Masters Know

There is a danger in aphorisms which are taken out of context and make complex matters seem too simple, but they can be helpful to the teacher and the student if not taken too seriously. The following quotations are the result of the author's years of collecting thousands of interviews, essays and books about writing by writers. This is the distillate of that collection.

If the teacher of writing reads these statements through he will discover a coherent tone, an attitude, about writing. He may catch the spirit and the approach of the professional and in turn be able to pass it on to his students.

The quotations are an indication of what stands behind this book—thousands of writers who have, in their own lonely way, faced the problems of writing. These quotations can be used by the teacher of writing to support his classroom presentation. They may be essay topics, or points for class discussions. They may also help to illuminate a piece of writing, or an author, or the whole process of literature. They will be valuable in the literature class as well as in the writing class.

The teacher of writing should begin to delight in their contradictions. No one can catch just what writing is, but whatever that magic may be it lies somewhere between or around these quotations, and the student writer who becomes familiar with them will approach the writer's workroom.

These are not rules, they are statements of art and craft by writers and others who can bring an insight to the craft of writing—simply that. They are generally by literary writers, for those are the men and women who have dedicated their lives to writing. In one sense they are no more writers than the person who produces a business letter, a scholarly article, a legal brief or an engineering report, but these are the people who can do all kinds of writing. If you can write a sonnet you can write an advertisement; if you can produce a novel you can produce a company report.

Each student of writing and the teacher of writing should have his own collection of similar illuminating statements for student examination and class discussion:

Edward Albee: Fiction is fact distorted into truth.

Henri Frederic Amiel: The great artist is the simplifier.

Sherwood Anderson: The life of reality is confused, disorderly, almost always without purpose, whereas in the artist's imaginative life there is a purpose. There is determination to give the tale, the song, the painting form—to make it true and real to the theme, not to life. . . .

Ivo Andric: In a thousand different tongues, under most different conditions, from age to age, from the ancient patriarchal storytelling in huts around the fire to the works of modern story-tellers which are just being published in great world centers, the tale of man's fate is being told, a tale that men endlessly tell each other. The way and forms of that telling change with times and conditions, but the need for tales and story-telling remain so that the tale goes on and on and there is no end to the telling. . . .
It is perhaps in these stories, oral and written, that the true history of mankind can be found. . . .

Matthew Arnold: Have something to say, and say it as clearly as you can. That is the only secret of life.

Francis Bacon: The contemplation of things as they are without error or confusion, without substitution or imposture, is in itself a nobler thing than a whole harvest of invention.

Saul Bellow: I feel that art has something to do with the achievement of stillness in the midst of chaos. A stillness which characterizes prayer, too, and the eye of the storm. I think that art has something to do with an arrest of attention in the midst of distraction.

John Berryman: Writing is just a man alone in the room with the English language, trying to make it come out right. The important thing is that your work be something no one else could do.

Robert Bolt: It is not easy to know what a play is "about" until it is finished, and by then what it is "about" is incorporated in it irreversibly and it is no more to be separated from it than the shape of the statue is to be separated from the marble. Writing a play is thinking, not thinking about thinking. . . .

Catherine Drinker Bowen: One of the marks of true genius is a quality of abundance. A rich, rolicking abundance, enough to give indigestion to ordinary people.

• • •

Writing is not apart from living. Writing is a kind of double living. The writer experiences everything twice. Once in reality and once more in that mirror which waits always before or behind him.

Elizabeth Bowen: I am dead against art's being self-expression. I see an inherent failure in any story which fails to detach itself from the author.

• • •

"How am I to know," the despairing writer asks, "which the right word is?" The reply must be, . . . "The wanted word is the one most nearly true. True to what? Your vision and your purpose."

• • •

Style is a matter of coming to terms with language . . . in our individual writings we have the same aims—clearness, truth, evocation, some touch of grace.

Ray Bradbury: Creativity is continual surprise.

Sir Arthur Bryant: Biography, like all other art, is the art of selection.

Buffon: Writing well is at the same time perceiving well, thinking well, and saying well.

Anthony Burgess: We go to art for the *illusion* of order, and this gives us a euphoria with no morning-after of shame or hangover. Art is close to drink or drugs or sex in providing a temporary conviction that the universe has a meaning, but we have no grounds for supposing that this conviction has a real or true referent. Illusions living in illusion, we must find some illusions better than other illusions.

Ben Lucien Burman: My goal in everything I write is simplicity. I'm a demon on the subject of revision. I revise, revise, revise, until every word is the one I want.

Samuel Butler: A man's style in any art should be like his dress—it should attract as little attention as possible.

Albert Camus: What, in fact, is a novel but a universe in which action is endowed with form, where final words are pronounced, where people possess one another completely, and where life assumes the aspect of destiny.

Truman Capote: Even Joyce, our most extreme disregarder, was a superb craftsman; he could write *Ulysses* because he could write *Dubliners.*

Lewis Carroll: "When I use a word," Humpty Dumpty said, in rather a scornful tone, "it means just what I choose it to mean—neither more nor less."

"The question is," said Alice, "whether you *can* make the words mean so many different things."

"The question is," said Humpty Dumpty, "which is to be the master—that's all."

Joyce Cary: Your form is your meaning, and your meaning dictates the form.

• • •

Inspiration is another name for knowing your job and getting down to it.

Bruce Catton: . . . What do we mean when we talk about literary skill? In a vague sort of way, we mean the ability to write well; and the first and foremost of all the skills that go to make up good writing is the ability to write clearly. Clarity of expression is what you must have to start with. Put on top of that any flourishes you like, you must begin with the ability to say what you mean in a way that other people can understand.

Now, clarity of expression, which is at the basis of all literary achievement, depends on clarity of thinking. If you think clearly you may be able to write clearly; otherwise, not. And this is precisely the point that anyone who undertakes to write anything in the field of history needs to understand first of all. He is producing literature: which is to say that whatever he is dealing with he is first of all using words, and the words have to make sense. Whatever he says, he is obliged to say it so that someone else will know exactly what he is talking about; he needs to say it clearly, and in order to do that he needs to think it clearly.

René Char: A poem is born of the urge to become and the urge to remain.

Chateaubriand: Talent is nothing but long impatience.

Winston Churchill: Writing a book was an adventure. To begin with it was a toy, an amusement; then it became a mistress, and then a master, and then a tyrant.

• • •

. . . the short words are best and the old words are best of all.

B. J. Chute: Grammar is to a writer what anatomy is to a sculptor, or the scales to a musician. You may loathe it, it may bore you, but nothing will replace it, and once mastered it will support you like a rock.

John Ciardi: He writes for those glimpses of order that form can make momentarily visible.

• • •

. . . the last act of . . . writing must be to become one's own reader. It is, I suppose, a schizophrenic process. To begin passionately and to end critically, to begin hot and to end cold; and, more important, to try to be passion-hot and critic-cold at the same time. For the act of writing a poem is not the act of having an emotion but the act of communicating it.

• • •

The artist writes compulsively, as a way of knowing himself. . . . The drunkard hopes to lose himself in his bottle, whereas the writer hopes to find himself on his page.

Walter Van Tilburg Clark: Fundamentally a writer uses his ears and eyes better than the average person. As a result his memory is keener and he remains more concerned about life, continually making associations between his past and his present.

Jean Cocteau: Take a commonplace, clean it and polish it, light it so that it produces the same effect of youth and freshness and spontaneity as it did originally, and you have done a poet's job.

Joseph Conrad: My task . . . is, by the power of the written word, to make you hear, to make you feel—it is, before all, to make you see.

• • •

Every novelist must begin by creating for himself a world, great or little, which he can honestly believe.

e.e. cummings: To be nobody—but yourself—in a world which is doing its best, night and day, to make you everybody else—means to fight the hardest battle any human being can fight; and never stop fighting.

Charles Darwin: I never study style; all that I do is try to get the subject as clear as I can in my head, and express it in the commonest language which occurs to me. But I generally have to think a good deal before the simplest arrangement occurs to me.

Degas: The artist does not draw what he sees but what he must make others see.

Laurence Durrell: Poetry turned out to be an invaluable mistress. Because poetry is form, and the wooing and seduction of form is the whole game.

Ralph Waldo Emerson: Cut these words and they would bleed.

Paul Engle: There is no such thing as material by itself, apart from the way in which a person sees it, feels toward it, and is able to give it organized form and expression in words. For a writer, form is a part of content, affecting it, realizing it. A man may go through the most dramatic and horrible experiences in war, but actually draw out of them less "material" for writing than shy Emily Dickinson in the second floor of an Amherst house, lowering notes out of the window and thinking gently of death.

William Faulkner: It begins with a character, usually, and once he stands up on his feet and begins to move, all I do is trot along behind him with a paper and pencil trying to keep up long enough to put down what he says and does.

• • •

Get it down. Take chances. It may be bad, but it's the only way you can do anything really good.

• • •

I don't think any author can be satisfied with his work. If he were, there'd be nothing left for him to do but cut his throat. Being a writer is having the worst vocation. You're demon-run, under compulsion, always being driven. It's a lonely, frustrating work which is never as good as you want it to be. You have to keep on trying, but still it's not good enough. It's never good enough.

• • •

I always write out of my personal experience, out of events I've been present at, out of stories I've heard from people. I think people try to find more in my work than I've put there. I like to tell stories, to create people and situations. But that's all. I doubt if any author knows what he puts into a story. All he is trying to do is to tell what he knows about his environment and the people around him in the most moving way possible. He writes like a carpenter uses his tools.

• • •

. . . there is nothing that can match the pleasure of creation—of creating some form of art, because only that way can you affirm your immortality. That is all any artist is trying to do; he knows that after a few years he will pass through the final gate into oblivion. He is simply going to leave on that wall "Kilroy was here." Not for power, not for money, but simply to say "I was here for a little while, I left this mark."

Gabriel Fielding: The . . . enormous satisfaction . . . is the conviction that when one is writing one is about to discover something which has existed for a long, long time, but which has been hidden from knowledge. Writing to me is a voyage, an odyssey, a discovery, because I'm never certain of precisely what I will find.

Dorothy Canfield Fisher: Very young writers often do not revise at all. Like a hen looking at a chalk line, they are hypnotized by what they have written. "How can it be altered?" they think. "That's the way it was written." Well, it has to be altered. You have to learn how. That is chiefly what English classes can teach you. They can't give you thoughts and materials to write about. Only your inherited brain cells and the enriching experience of life as you live it can do that. But you can learn to put what material you have into form. In manual training you wouldn't hand in a lot of sticks and boards bunched together with string and call it a table. It's no better to hand in a detached bundle of statements, starting nowhere in particular, training along a while and then fading out—and call it a theme.

F. Scott Fitzgerald: To have something to say is a question of sleepless nights and worry and endless ratiocination of a subject—of endless trying to dig out the essential truth, the essential justice. As a first premise you have to develop a conscience. And if on top of that you have talent so much the better.

• • •

All good writing is swimming under water and holding your breath.

Gustave Flaubert: Whatever the thing you wish to say, there is but one word to express it, but one verb to give it movement, but one adjective to qualify it; you must seek until you find this noun, this verb, this adjective.

• • •

Has a drinking song ever been written by a drunken man? It is wrong to think that feeling is everything. In the arts, it is nothing without form.

Ford Maddox Ford: A good style in literature, if closely examined, will be seen to consist in a constant succession of tiny surprises.

E. M. Forster: How do I know what I think until I see what I say?

Felix Frankfurter: All our work, our whole life is a matter of semantics, because words are the tools with which we work, the material out of which laws are made, out of which the Constitution was written. Everything depends on our understanding of them.

Robert Frost: The figure a poem makes. It begins in delight and ends in wisdom . . . For me the initial delight is in the surprise of remembering something I didn't know I knew.

• • •

A real poem is sort of an idea caught in dawning—you catch it just before it comes. Think it out beforehand and you won't write it.

• • •

A poem is never a put-up job, so to speak. It begins as a lump in the throat, a sense of wrong, a homesickness, a lovesickness. It is never a thought to begin with . . . It finds its thought and succeeds, or doesn't find it and comes to nothing.

• • •

There is at least so much good in the world that it admits of form and making of form. And not only admits of it, but calls for it . . . In us nature reaches its height of form and through us exceeds itself. When in doubt there is always form for us to go on with. Anyone who has achieved the least form to be sure of it, is lost to the larger excruciations. I think it must stroke faith the right way. The artist, the poet, might be expected to be the most aware of such assurance, but it is really everybody's sanity to feel it and live by it. Fortunately, too, no forms are more engrossing, gratifying, comforting, staying, than those lesser ones we throw off like the vortex rings of smoke, all our individual enterprise and needing nobody's cooperation: a basket, a letter, a garden, a room, an idea, a picture, a poem . . .

The background is hugeness and confusion shading away from where we stand into black and utter chaos; and against the background any small man-made figure of order and concentration . . . To me any little form I assert upon it is . . . to be considered for how much more it is than nothing.

• • •

John Ciardi reported that when a lady questioned Robert Frost after a reading: " 'But, Mr. Frost,' she cried, 'surely when you are writing one of your beautiful poems, surely you can't be thinking about . . . technical tricks.'

"Mr. Frost put his hands together, the spread fingers touching tip to tip, looked owlish for a moment, and leaned forward into the microphone and said in a playfully, gravelly bass: 'I revel in 'em!' "

Theodor Seuss Geisel (Dr. Seuss): No dependent clauses, no dangling things, no flashbacks, and keeping the subject near the predicate. We throw in as many fresh words as we can get away with. Simple, short sentences don't always work. You have to do tricks with pacing, alternate long sentences with short, to keep it vital and alive. Virtually every page is a cliff-hanger—you've got to force them to turn it.

Jean Genêt: When I was in the Sante Prison, I began to write, it was never because I wanted to relieve my emotions or to communicate them, but rather because I hoped, by expressing them in a form that they themselves imposed, to construct an order (a moral order) that was unknown (above all to me too).

Goethe: There are no crimes, however great, that on certain days I have not felt capable of committing.

Graham Greene: The novel is an unknown man and I have to find him.

• • •

Isn't disloyalty as much the writer's virtue as loyalty is the soldier's?

Nancy Hale: Form and technique are the salvation of those who, like the writer, feel threatened with inundation by the forces released by experience. They constitute the artist's kind of thinking . . . The writer, unable to find satisfaction in any order he can discover in or impose upon life, creates his own forms: something to put experience in.

• • •

[The writer] should be critical of everything that seems to him most delightful in his style. He should excise what he most admires, because he wouldn't thus admire it if he weren't by so doing, in a sense protecting it from criticism.

• • •

Many an author will speak of writing, in his best work, more than he actually knows.

Thomas Hardy: The business of the poet and novelist is to show the sorriness underlying the grandest things and the grandeur underlying the sorriest things.

William Hazlitt: The more a man writes, the more he can write.

Piet Hein: Art is the solution of a problem which cannot be expressed explicitly until it is solved.

Ernest Hemingway: First, there must be talent . . . Then there must be discipline . . . Then there must be . . . an absolute conscience . . . to prevent faking.

• • •

I was trying to learn to write commencing with the simplest things.

• • •

I was trying to write then and I found the greatest difficulty, aside from knowing truly what you really felt, rather than what you were supposed to feel, and had been taught to feel, was to put down what really happened in action; what the actual things were which produced the emotion that you experienced.

• • •

My working habits are simple: long periods of thinking, short periods of writing.

• • •

H: I rewrote the ending to *Farewell to Arms,* the last page of it, 39 times before I was satisfied.

Interviewer: Was there some technical problem there? What was it that had you stumped?

H: Getting the words right.

• • •

Q: How do you write a novel? Do you make it up?

A: Yes, you make it up, out of everything you've ever known, out of everything you've ever seen, everything you've ever felt.

John Hersey: The reward of writing is in the writing itself. It comes with finding the right word. The quest for a superb sentence is a groping for honesty, a search for the innermost self, a self-discipline, a generous giving out of one's most intimate rhythms and meanings. To be a writer is to sit down at one's desk in the chill portion of every day, and to write; not waiting for the little jet of the blue flame of genius to start from the breastbone —just plain going at it, in pain and delight. To be a writer is to throw away a great deal, not to be satisfied, to type again, and then again, and once more, and over and over. . . .

Aldous Huxley: [The writer] has the urge, first of all, to order the facts one observes and to give meaning to life.

Christopher Isherwood: I am a camera with its shutter open, quite passive, recording not thinking. Recording the man shaving at the window opposite and the woman in the kimona washing her hair. Someday, all this will have to be developed, carefully fixed, printed.

Henry James: The power to guess the unseen from the seen, to trace the implications of things, to judge the whole piece by the pattern . . .

Samuel Johnson: Read over your compositions, and when you meet with a passage you think is particularly fine, strike it out.

Joubert: To write well, one needs a natural facility and an acquired difficulty.

Alfred Kazin: The vital difference between a writer and someone who merely is published is that the writer seems always to be saying to himself, as Stendhal actually did, "if I am not clear, the world around me collapses." In a very real sense, the writer writes in order to teach himself, to understand himself, to satisfy himself; the publishing of his ideas . . . is a curious anticlimax.

John F. Kennedy: My own old fashioned belief is that every Presidential message should be a model of grace, lucidity and taste in expression. At the very least, each message should be (a) in English, (b) clear and trenchant in its style, (c) logical in its structure and (d) devoid of gobbledygook.

Walter Kerr: Creative writing is a harrowing business, a terrifying commitment to an absolute. This is *it,* the writer must say to himself, and I must stand or fall upon what I have put down. The degree of self-exposure is crucifying. And doubt is a constant companion. What if I am not as good as I thought? is a question that always nags, and can cripple.

Charles Lamb: I had thought of "Lycidas" as a full-grown beauty—as springing up with all its parts absolute—till, in an evil hour, I was shown the original copy of it . . . in the library of Trinity, kept like treasure to be proud of. I wish they had thrown them into the Cam, or sent them . . . into the Irish Channel. How it staggered me to see the fine things in their ore! interlined, corrected! as if their words were mortal, alterable, displaceable at pleasure! as if they might have been otherwise and just as good! as if inspiration were made up of parts, and these fluctuating, successive, indifferent! I will never go into the workshop of any great artist again.

Stephen Leacock: To write well it is first necessary to have something to say.

C. Day Lewis: I do not sit down at my desk to put into verse something that is already clear in my mind. If it were clear in my mind, I should have no incentive or need to write about it, for I am an explorer . . .

We do not write in order to be understood, we write in order to understand.

• • •

[The poet] has two conscious motives: to create an object in words, and to explore reality and make sense of his own experience.

He wishes this object to be both self-contained and elegant—elegant in the sense that a mathematician will call an equation "elegant." The poem must stand up after the poet has got out from underneath it; it must apply beyond the individual experience out of which it arose and carry meaning beyond the poet's own time and social environment . . .

Though the poet differs from the scientist in the method and field of his work, both start from one basic assumption—that there is pattern, or law, in the cosmos. . . .

Sinclair Lewis: Writers kid themselves—about themselves and other people. Take the talk about writing methods. Writing is just work—there's no secret. If you dictate or use a pen or type or write with your toes—it is still just work.

Archibald MacLeish: What distinguishes Homer and Shakespeare is not only their extravagant gifts as masters of words and makers of images, but what we call, inadequately enough, their "universality," meaning their inexplicable ability to hold together in a single form the contradictions and perversities of the familiar world.

Thomas Mann: At bottom [talent] is a compulsion; a critical knowledge of the ideal, a permanent dissatisfaction.

Katherine Mansfield: It's a very queer thing how *craft* comes into writing. I mean down to details. *Par Example.* In *Miss Brill* I chose not only the length of each sentence, but even the sound of every sentence. I chose the rise and fall of every paragraph to fit her, and to fit her on that day of that very moment. After I'd written it I read it aloud—numbers of times—just as one would *play over* a musical composition—trying to get it nearer and nearer to the expression of Miss Brill—until it fitted her.

Don't think I'm vain about the little sketch. It's only the method I wanted to explain. I often wonder whether other writers do the same—if a thing has really come off it seems to me there mustn't be one single word out of place, or one word that could be taken out.

Martial: He does not write at all whose poems no man reads.

W. Somerset Maugham: To write simply is as difficult as to be good.

Guy de Maupassant: For [the writer] no simple feeling exists. All that he sees, his joys, his pleasures, his suffering, his despair, all instantaneously become objects of observation . . .

He has not a spark of enthusiasm, not a cry, not a kiss that is spontaneous, not one instantaneous action done merely because it must be done, unconsciously, without reflection, without understanding, without noting it down afterwards. . . .

. . . he says to himself as he leaves the cemetery where he has left the being he has loved most in the world: "It is curious what I felt . . ."

He has seen all, noticed all, remembered all, in spite of himself, because he is first of all a literary man, and his intellect is constructed in such a manner that the reverberation in him is much more vivid, more natural, so to speak, than the first shock, the echo more sonorous than the original sound.

He seems to have two souls, one that notes, explains, comments upon each sensation of the other—the other being the natural soul common to all men. He lives condemned to be the mere reflection of himself and others; condemned to look on and watch himself feel, act, love, think, suffer, and never be free like the rest of man; simply, genially, frankly without analyzing his own soul after every joy and every agony.

Francois Mauriac: A writer is essentially a man who will not be resigned to solitude. Each of us is like a desert, and a literary work is like a cry from the desert, or like a pigeon let loose with a message in its claws, or like a bottle thrown into the sea. The point is: to be heard—even if by one single person.

William Maxwell: [The writer] may dream—he may dream that he had a dream in which the whole meaning of what he is trying to say is brilliantly revealed to him. Just so the dog asleep on the hearth-rug dreams; you can see, by the faint jerking movement of his four legs, that he is after a rabbit. The writer's rabbit is the truth—about life, about human character, about himself and therefore by extension, it is to be hoped, about other people. He is convinced that all this is knowable, can be described, can be recorded, by a person sufficiently dedicated to describing and recording; can be caught in a net of narration.

Phyllis McGinley: There is such a thing as inspiration (lower case), but it is no miracle. It is the reward handed to a writer for hard work and good conduct. It is the felicitous words sliding, after hours of evasion, obediently into place. It is a sudden comprehension of how to manufacture and effect, finish off a line or a stanza. At the triumphant moment this gift may seem like magic, but actually it is the result of effort, practice, and the slight temperature a sulky brain is apt to run when it is pushed beyond its usual exertions.

Vincent McHugh: Always the specific in a novel: the scene seen, the word heard, the deed done.

H. L. Mencken: His overpowering impulse is to gyrate before his fellow man, flapping his wings and emitting defiant yells. This being forbidden by the police of all civilized countries, he takes it out by putting his yells on paper. Such is the thing called self-expression.

James A. Michener: I have never thought of myself as a good writer. Anyone who wants reassurance of that should read one of my first drafts. But I'm one of the world's great rewriters.

I find that three or four readings are required to comb out the clichés, line up pronouns with their antecedents, and insure agreement in number between subjects and verbs. It is, however, this hard work that produces a style.

You write the first draft really to see how it's going to come out.

My connectives, my clauses, my subsidiary phrases don't come naturally to me and I'm very prone to repetition of words; so I never even write an important letter in the first draft. I can never recall anything of mine that's ever been printed in less than three drafts.

Alberto Moravia: In writing a novel, there is in the beginning what I would call a theme. It's not an idea but a feeling. Then this feeling goes on developing and unraveling itself, like a rope. This is why I say a novel writes itself. One writes a novel in order to know why one writes it. It is the same with life—you live not for some end, but in order to know why you live.

Edmund S. Morgan [Of Samuel Eliot Morison]: Every historian has to simplify, but usually the more he knows, the more he emphasizes the complexities of a situation. To simplify when you know little is easy. To simplify when you know a great deal requires gifts of a different order: unusual penetration of mind and, above all, sheer nerve.

Theodore Morrison: A writer is a man walking down the street thinking how he would describe himself as a man walking down the street.

A novelist is someone who wonders why people act as they do, and he doesn't know, so he imagines an explanation, and that's his novel.

Robert Motherwell: The more anonymous a work, the less universal, because in some paradoxical way we understand the universal through the personal.

Vladimir Nabokov: There is the first satisfaction of arranging it on a bit of paper; after many, many false tries, false moves, finally you have the sentence you recognize as the one you are looking for. . . .

Cardinal Newman: It is simply the fact that I have been obliged to take great pains with everything I have written, and I often write chapters over and over again besides innumerable corrections and interlinear additions . . . I think I have never written for writing's sake; but my one and single desire and aim has been to do what is so difficult—viz—to express clearly and exactly my meaning; this has been the motive principle of all my corrections and rewritings. When I have read over a passage which I had written a few days before, I have found it so obscure to myself that I have either put it altogether aside or fiercely corrected it; but I don't get any better for practice. I am as much obliged to correct and rewrite as I was thirty years ago.

Friedrich Nietzsche: The author must keep his mouth shut when his work starts to speak.

Frank O'Connor: "Get black on white" used to be de Maupassant's advice—that's what I always do . . . it's the design of the story which to me is most important.

Sean O'Faolain: I suggest it is a true image of both scientists and writers to see them all as a scattered processing of explorers, small as ants as compared to the world, each climbing his grass-blade to view the universe, uttering triumphant cries now called a poem, now a scientific fact, one here, one there, until the world we know gets mapped and remapped, over and over; that is to say, gets invented again and again in every generation: made up. . . .

• • •

Form! I kept on saying the word to myself, striking the table as I worked; this chaos of life must be reduced, somehow, to form!

George Orwell:

(i) Never use a metaphor, simile or other figure of speech which you are used to seeing in print.

(ii) Never use a long word where a short one will do.

(iii) If it is possible to cut a word out, always cut it out.

(iv) Never use the passive where you can use the active.

(v) Never use a foreign phrase, a scientific word or a jargon word if you can think of an everyday English equivalent.

(vi) Break any of these rules sooner than say anything barbarous.

Pascal: When we encounter a natural style we are always surprised and delighted, for we thought to see an author and found a man.

Walter Pater: Perfection is achieved by a series of disgusts.

Pablo Picasso: A picture is not thought out and settled beforehand. While it is being done it changes as one's thoughts change. And when it is finished, it still goes on changing, according to the state of mind of whoever is looking at it.

Ezra Pound: Good writers are those who keep the language efficient. That is to say, keep it accurate, keep it clear.

J. B. Priestley: Perhaps it would be better not to be a writer, but if you must, then write. If all feels hopeless, if that famous "inspiration" will not come, write. If you are a genius, you'll make your own rules, but if not —and the odds are against it—go to your desk, no matter what your mood, face the icy challenge of the paper—write.

Max Raphael: Originality is not the urge to be different from others, to produce the brand-new; it is to grasp (in the etymological sense) the origin, the roots of both ourselves and things.

Jules Renard: Talent is a question of quantity. Talent does not write one page: it writes 300.

Edwin Arlington Robinson: This morning I took the hyphen out of Hell-hound and this afternoon I put it back.

Ben Shahn: . . . I think it can be said with certainty that the form which does emerge cannot be greater than the content which went into it. For form is only the manifestation, the shape of content.

William Shakespeare: The truest poetry is the most feigning.

Percy Bysshe Shelley: Poetry is not principles, but processes. The poet is a doer, not a thinker.

George Simenon: I am an artisan; I need to work with my hands. I would like to carve my novel in a piece of wood.

Sydney Smith: In composing, as a general rule, run your pen through every other word you have written; you have no idea what vigor it will give your style.

Stephen Spender: One line is given to the poet by God or by nature, the rest he has to discover for himself.

Stendhal: I see but one rule: to be clear.

Wallace Stevens: The purpose of poetry is to make life complete in itself.

Jonathan Swift: Proper words in proper places make the true definition of a style.

Henry David Thoreau: How vain it is to sit down to write when you have not stood up to live.

• • •

Nothing goes by luck in composition. It allows of no tricks. The best you can write will be the best you are. Every sentence is the result of a long probation. The author's character is read from the title-page to end. Of this he never corrects the proofs.

Leo Tolstoy: I can't understand how anyone can write without rewriting everything over and over again. I scarcely ever reread my published writings, but if by chance I come across a page, it always strikes me: all this must be rewritten; this is how I should have written it. . . .

G. M. Trevelyan: The idea that histories which are delightful to read must be the work of superficial temperaments, and that a crabbed style betokens a deep thinker or conscientious worker, is the reverse of the truth. What is easy to read has been difficult to write. The labor or writing and rewriting, correcting and recorrecting, is the due exacted by every good book from its author . . . the easily flowing connection of sentence with sentence and paragraph with paragraph has always been won by the sweat of the brow.

Turgenev: I have never started from ideas but always from character.

John Updike: Writing and rewriting are a constant search for what one is saying.

Edward Lewis Wallant: We speak of art and we speak of illumination; in order to illuminate for others, one must obviously first be able to see for himself. Seeing is my key word, seeing with the heart, with the brain, with the eye . . . Normally we see others only as they relate to our own immediate needs, and for that, normal vision is often sufficient. Yet there are times when we have a need we cannot recognize, a sudden hunger to know what lies in the heart of others. It is then that we turn to the artist, because only he can reveal even the little corners of the things beyond bread alone.

You read the great books and your vision of the world is sharpened, heightened, colors become more true, voices more poignant and meaninful, faces unique. The actions and reactions, the pains and joys of humans, assume a clarity that makes them memorable and recordable. You see with the power of a thousand ancestral eyes.

Robert Penn Warren: The image that fiction presents is purged of the distractions, confusions and accidents of ordinary life. We can now gaze at the inner logic of things—of a personality, of the consequences of an act or a thought, of a social or historical situation, of a lived life. One of our deepest cravings is to find logic in experience . . . By showing a logical structure, it relieves us, for the moment at least, of what we sometimes feel is the greatest and most mysterious threat of life—the threat of the imminent but "unknowable," of the urgent but "unsayable."

Eudora Welty: . . . it [is] the business of writing, and the responsibility of the writer, to disentangle the significant—in character, incident, setting, mood, everything—from the random and meaningless and irrelevant that in real life surround and beset it.

E. B. White: The main thing I try to do is write as clearly as I can. Because I have the greatest respect for the reader, and if he's going to the trouble of reading what I've written—I'm a slow reader myself and I guess most people are—why, the least I can do is make it as easy as possible for him to find out what I'm trying to say, trying to get at. I rewrite a good deal to make it clear.

Virginia Woolf: . . . if there is one gift more essential to a novelist than another it is the power of combination—the single vision. The success of the masterpieces seems to be not so much in their freedom from faults—indeed we tolerate the grossest errors in them all—but in the immense persuasiveness of a mind which has completely mastered its perspective.

Jerrold Zacharias (physicist): If you can't put it into English it means you don't understand it yourself.

The Writing Teacher's Library

The teacher of writing should develop his own library of materials which illuminate the process of writing and the process of teaching writing. The library will be a resource for the teacher to which he should return when he faces a problem in his teaching. It should also include examples of good writing which will refresh him. Above all, it provides the teacher with an inventory which makes flexibility possible. With a good library he is able to adjust his teaching for the particular class and the individual student.

I have made an effort to compile a fairly complete bibliography, but the selection of the books is inevitably personal.

Desk Books and Texts

The writing teacher should have books on his desk which will help him and his student identify writing problems and their solution.

Altick, Richard D. *Preface to Critical Reading,* 4th ed. New York: Holt, 1960.

Baker, Sheridan. *The Complete Stylist.* New York: Thomas Y. Crowell, 1966.

Barzun, Jacques, and Henry F. Graff. *The Modern Researcher.* New York: Harcourt, 1957. (cloth and paper)
The best book on the problems of research and their solution. It also includes some fine advice on writing.

Bernstein, Theodore M. *The Careful Writer: A Modern Guide to English Usage.* New York: Atheneum, 1965.

Cain, Thomas H. *Common Sense About Writing.* Englewood Cliffs, N.J.: Prentice-Hall, 1967. (cloth and paper)

Corbett, Edward P. J. *Classical Rhetoric for the Modern Student.* New York: Oxford, 1965.
The best book of its kind.

Cosbey, Robert C. *The Writer's Job.* Glenview, Ill.: Scott, Foresman, 1966. (paper)

Cowing, Amy. *Writing Words That Work.* Washington, D.C.: Dept. of Agriculture—PA No. 466, 1961. (paper)

Dorsch, T. S., trans. *Classical Literary Criticism.* New York: Penguin, n.d. (paper)
Includes Aristotle, "On the art of poetry"; Horace, "On the art of poetry"; Longinus, "On the sublime."

Engle, Paul, ed. *On Creative Writing.* New York: Dutton, 1964. (cloth and paper)

Ferguson, Charles W. *Say It With Words.* New York: Knopf, 1959.
Mr. Ferguson is a biographer and a *Reader's Digest* writer-editor whose lively book states and demonstrates the professional writer's approach to his job.

Flesch, Rudolf. *The Art of Plain Talk.* New York: Harper, 1946. (paper: Collier Books)

———. *The Art of Readable Writing.* Evanston, Ill.: Harper, 1949. (paper: Collier Books)
Mr. Flesch may have made too much of a good thing, but his early book still speaks strongly for brevity and clarity.

Follett, Wilson, *Modern American Usage,* ed. Jacques Barzun. New York: Hill & Wang, 1966.

Gilman, William. *The Language of Science: A Guide to Effective Writing.* New York: Harcourt, 1961.
An excellent book for science writers which is a valuable aid for all writers and teachers of writing.

Gowers, Sir Ernest. *Plain Words, Their ABC.* New York: Knopf, 1954. (paper: Penguin)

Graves, Robert, and Allen Hodge. *The Reader Over Your Shoulder.* New York: Macmillan, 1961.

Gunning, Robert. *How to Take the Fog Out of Writing.* Chicago: Dartnell, 1964. (paper)
A fascinating pamphlet which attacks wordy phrases effectively.

Hall, Milton. *Getting Your Ideas Across Through Writing.* Washington, D.C.: U.S. Dept. of Health, Education, and Welfare, 1950. (paper)

Hunter, Laura Grace. *The Language of Audit Reports.* Washington, D.C.: U.S. General Accounting Office, 1957. (paper)

Jones, W. Paul, and Quentin Johnson. *Essays on Thinking and Writing in Science, Engineering and Business.* Dubuque, Iowa: W. C. Brown, 1963. (paper)

Lambuth, David. *The Golden Book on Writing.* New York: Viking, 1965. (cloth and paper)
This is a good change of pace if you've been using Strunk and White.

Lucas, F. L. *Style.* New York: P. F. Collier, 1962. (paper)

McCrimmon, James M. *Writing with a Purpose,* 4th ed. Boston: Houghton Mifflin, 1967.

Nicholson, Margaret. *A Practical Style Guide for Authors and Editors.* New York: Holt, 1967.

O'Hayre, John. *Gobbledygook Has Gotta Go.* Washington, D.C. U.S. Govt. Printing Office, 1960. (paper)

Payne, Lucile Vaughan. *The Lively Art of Writing.* Chicago: Follett, 1965. (cloth and paper)
An excellent text for the secondary school student.

Perlmutter, Jerome H. *A Practical Guide to Effective Writing.* New York: Random House, 1965. (paper: Dell)
The author, Chief of Publishing for the State Department, fulfills the promise of the title. Particularly helpful for students interested in business.

Rathbone, Robert R. *Communicating Technical Information.* Reading, Mass.: Addison-Wesley, 1966. (paper)

Read, Herbert. *English Prose Style.* Boston: Beacon, 1955. (paper)

Shapiro, Karl, and Robert Beum. *A Prosody Handbook.* Evanston, Ill.: Harper, 1965.
By far the most effective handbook on poetry.

Shidle, Norman. *Clear Writing for Easy Reading.* New York: McGraw-Hill, 1951. (paper)

Struck, Herman R., and Robert J. Geist. *Concise Writing.* East Lansing, Mich.: Michigan State, 1959. (paper)

Strunk, William J., and E. B. White. *The Elements of Style.* New York: Macmillan, 1959. (cloth and paper)
Deserves its reputation as the best book of it kind.

Tichy, H. J. *Effective Writing for Engineers - Managers - Scientists.* New York: John Wiley & Sons, 1966.

The most complete book of its kind. Excellent.

U.S. Dept. of Health, Education, and Welfare. *Getting Your Ideas Across Through Writing.* Washington, D.C.: U.S. Govt. Printing Office, 1960. (paper)

Vrooman, Alan H. *Good Writing: An Informal Manual of Style.* Exeter, N.H.: The Phillips Exeter Academy Press, 1966. (paper: Atheneum)

Writers on Writing

The teacher of writing should listen to what the writer has to say about his craft and his art.

Allen, Walter E., ed. *Writers on Writing.* Boston: The Writer, 1959. (paper: Dutton)

Allott, Miriam, ed. *Novelists on the Novel.* New York: Columbia, 1959. (cloth and paper)

Bowen, Elizabeth. *Seven Winters and Afterthoughts.* New York: Knopf, 1962.

Brean, Herbert, ed. *The Mystery Writer's Handbook.* New York: Harper, 1956.

Conner, Jack E., and Marcelline Krafchick. *Speaking of Rhetoric.* Boston: Houghton Mifflin, 1966. (paper)
A worthwhile collection of essays about writing by writers.

Cowley, Malcolm. *The Literary Situation.* New York: Viking, 1954. (cloth and paper)
His chapters on "A Natural History of the American Writer" are particularly interesting.

———, ed. *Writers at Work* ("The Paris Review Interviews"). Series 1-3. New York: Viking, 1958. (cloth and paper)

Day, A. Grove. "How to be a Writer," *James A. Michener.* New Haven, Conn.: College & University Press, 1964. (paper)
Interesting chapter on a writer by a writer and collaborator.

Ellmann, Richard, and Charles Feidelson, Jr., eds. *The Modern Tradition: Backgrounds of Modern Literature.* New York: Oxford, 1965.
A good resource in spite of some questionable cutting of a few of the anthologized articles.

Frost, Robert. "The Figure a Poem Makes," *Selected Poems of Robert Frost.* New York: Holt, 1963. (paper)

Gehman, Richard. *How to Write and Sell Magazine Articles.* New York: Harper, 1959.

Gwynn, Frederick L., and Joseph L. Blotner, eds. *Faulkner in the University.* New York: Random House, 1965. (cloth and paper)
Stimulating tape-recorded classroom discussions by Faulkner.

Hall, Donald. "A Clear and Simple Style," *The New York Times Book Review,* CXVI (May 7, 1967), 2, 30.

———, ed. *The Modern Stylists.* New York: The Free Press, 1968. (paper)

Hull, Helen, ed. *The Writer's Book.* New York: Barnes & Noble, 1956. (paper)
Dated, but still helpful.

Kilpatrick, James J. "Be Clear," *Boston Herald,* May 8, 1967.

Maugham, W. Somerset. *The Summing Up.* New York: New American Library, 1951. (paper)

Michener, James. "I Would Not Minimize That Apprenticeship . . ." An interview in *Northwest Review,* IV (Spring 1961), 5-27.

Moore, Thomas H., ed. *Henry Miller on Writing.* New York: New Directions, 1964. (paper)

Morison, Samuel Eliot. *History as a Literary Art.* (Old South Leaflet, Series II, No. 1.) Boston: The Old South Association, n.d. (paper)

Nell, Edward and Onora. "War Words," *College English,* XXVIII (May 1967), 603-6.

Orr, Peter, ed. *The Poet Speaks.* London: Routledge & Kegan Paul, 1966.

Orwell, George. "Politics and the English Language," *Shooting an Elephant.* New York: Harcourt, 1950.
This superb essay is included in many anthologies.

Roberts, Kenneth. *I Wanted to Write.* New York: Doubleday, 1949.

Thurber, James. *The Years With Ross.* Boston: Atlantic Monthly, 1959.

Watkins, Floyd C., and Karl F. Knight, eds. *Writer To Writer: Readings on the Craft of Writing.* Boston: Hougton Mifflin, 1966. (paper)

West, William W., ed. *On Writing, By Writers.* Boston: Ginn, 1966.
Written for the high school student, it includes a particularly interesting article, "The Light Side of the Moon," by Phyllis McGinley, some interesting pieces by John Ciardi, and a fascinating piece by John Updike on how his short story, "A Sense of Shelter," developed.

Wright, Walter F., ed. *Joseph Conrad on Fiction.* Lincoln, Neb.: University of Nebraska, 1964. (paper)

Yates, Elizabeth. *Someday You'll Write.* New York: Dutton, 1962.
A book written for the very young fiction writer.

Manuscript Studies

The teacher of writing and his students should both have the opportunity to see and examine the manuscript evidence of the writer ruthlessly attacking his own words.

Bartlett, Phyllis. *Poems in Process.* New York: Oxford, 1951.

Force, Gerald, ed. *The Jefferson Drafts of the Declaration of Independence.* Washington, D.C.: Acropolis Books, 1963. (paper)

Ginsberg, Robert, ed. *A Casebook on the Declaration of Independence.* New York: Thomas Y. Crowell, 1967. (paper)

Haber, Tom Burns. *The Making of a Shropshire Lad.* Seattle: University of Washington, 1966.
A definitive work which shows various versions of poems which are particularly enjoyed by young men and women.

Hildick, Wallace. *Word for Word.* London: Faber and Faber, 1965.
Norton has published an abridged American version of this interesting study in paper covers.

———. *Writing with Care.* New York: David White, 1967 (paper)

Kuehl, John, ed. *Creative Writing and Rewriting: Contemporary American Novelists at Work.* New York: Appleton-Century-Crofts 1967. (paper)
A valuable addition to the writing teacher's library.

Mearns, David C., and Lloyd A. Dunlap. "Notes and Comments on the Preparation of the Address," *Long Remembered: Facsimiles of the Five Versions of the Gettysburg Address*... Washington, D.C.: The Library of Congress, 1963. (paper)

Scott, A. F. *The Poet's Craft.* New York: Dutton, 1966. (paper: Dover)

The Story of the Bill of Rights: An Exhibit. Washington, D.C.: The

National Archives, 1966 (paper)

Taylor, Robert H., *Authors at Work*. New York: Grolier, 1957.

Master Writers

The student should be able to see a variety of writers at work. Since the usual English course includes the great writers of the past, with emphasis on fiction, drama, and poetry, this list will focus on contemporary non-fiction writers, with some exceptions.

Agee, James, and Walker Evans. *Let Us Now Praise Famous Men*. Boston: Houghton Mifflin, 1960. (paper: Ballantine)

Beston, Henry. *The Outermost House*. New York: Viking, 1961. (cloth and paper)

Breslin, Jimmy. *The World of Jimmy Breslin,* eds. James G. Bellows and Richard C. Wald. New York: Viking, 1967.

Brogan, Denis William. *The American Character*. New York: Knopf, 1944. (paper: Random House)

Capote, Truman. *In Cold Blood*. New York, 1966. (paper: New American Library)
Capote has consciously used most of the techniques of contemporary non-fiction writing, so that the book is filled with examples of technical virtuosity.

Carson, Rachel. *Silent Spring*. Boston: Houghton Mifflin, 1962. (paper: Fawcett)

Clark, Eleanor. *The Oysters of Locmariaquer*. New York: Random House, 1966. (cloth and paper)

Connell, Evans S., Jr., *Mrs. Bridge*. New York: Viking, 1959. (cloth and paper)
This novel, composed of 117 short incidents, should be read by every teacher of writing, and it could be read with great benefit by the high school writing student. It is an ideal book to use for demonstrations of brevity and description, the incident and the paragraph. Some of the most useful sections are: No. 3, Preliminary Training; No. 10, Table Manners; No. 13, Guest Towels; No. 17, Good-bye Alice; No. 26, Tower; No. 35, One Summer Morning; No. 45, The Clock; No. 47, Tea Leaves; No. 77, Beautiful Luggage; No. 99, Gloves; No. 109, Winter; No. 117, Hello?

Davis, Robert Gorham, ed. *Ten Masters of the Modern Essay*. New York: Harcourt, 1966.

Defoe, Daniel. *A Journal of the Plague Year*. London: Falcon, 1950 (paper: Penguin)

Fadiman, Clifton, ed. *Profiles from the New Yorker*. New York: Knopf, 1938.

Forster, E. M. *Two Cheers For Democracy*. New York: Harcourt, 1962. (cloth and paper)

Hall, Donald. *String Too Short to be Saved*. New York: Viking, 1961.

Harrington, Michael. *The Other America*. New York: Macmillan, 1962. (paper: Penguin)
This might be used in a unit with Agee's *Let Us Now Praise Famous Men* and Orwell's *Down and Out in Paris and London*.

Harrison, James, ed. *Scientists as Writers*. Cambridge, Mass.: M.I.T. Press, 1965. (cloth and paper)
A fine anthology.

Hart, Moss. *Act One*. New York: Random House, 1959. (paper: New American Library)

Hartog, Jan de. *The Hospital*. New York: Atheneum, 1964.

Hersey, John. *Here to Stay*. New York: 1963. (paper: Bantam)
Includes "Hiroshima."

Lang, Daniel. *An Inquiry Into Enoughness: Of Bombs and Men and Staying Alive*. New York: McGraw-Hill, 1955.

Leighton, Isabel, ed. *The Aspirin Age*. New York: Simon and Echuster, 1963. (cloth and paper)

Lewis, Anthony. *Gideon's Trumpet*. New York: Random House, 1964. (cloth and paper)
A fine piece of reporting, and a book that will provoke discussion.

Love, Edmund G. *Subways are for Sleeping*. New York: New American Library, 1959. (cloth and paper)

MacDonald, Dwight. *Against the American Grain*. New York: Random House, 1962. (cloth and paper)

McPhee, John. *A Sense of Where You Are: A Profile of William Warren Bradley*. New York: Farrar, Straus & Giroux, 1965. (paper: Bantam)
A profile of Bill Bradley, the basketball star, which should help the class athlete appreciate well-organized, specific writing.

Masters, Edgar Lee. *Spoon River Anthology*. New York: Macmillan, 1941. (paper: Collier)

Mitchell, Joseph. *The Bottom of the Harbor*. Boston: Little, Brown, 1960.
One of the best non-fiction stylists writing today.

Moynihan, William T., Donald W. Lee, and Herbert J. Weil, eds. *Reading, Writing and Rewriting: A Rhetoric Reader*. Philadelphia: Lippincott, 1964.
This has some interesting material on rewriting.

Orwell, George. *A Collection of Essays by George Orwell*. New York: Doubleday, 1954. (cloth and paper)
Superb.

———. *Down and Out in Paris and London*. New York: Harcourt, 1933. (paper: Berkley)

———. *Homage to Catalonia*. New York: Harcourt, 1952. (paper: Beacon)

———. *The Orwell Reader,* ed. Richard Rovere. New York: Harcourt, 1956. (paper)

———. *The Road to Wigan Pier*. New York: Harcourt, 1958. (paper: Berkley)

Reston, James. *Sketches in the Sand*. New York: Knopf, 1967.

Ross, Lillian. *Reporting*. New York: Simon and Schuster, 1964.
Fine pieces of work by a perceptive, incisive reporter.

Roueché, Berton, *Eleven Blue Men, and Other Narratives of Medical Detection*. Boston: Little, Brown, 1965. (paper: Berkley)

———. *A Man Named Hoffman, and Other Narratives of Medical Detection*. Boston: Little, Brown, 1965. (paper: Berkley)

Updike, John. *Assorted Prose*. New York: Knopf, 1965. (paper: Fawcett)

Watt, William W., and Robert W. Bradford, eds. *An E. B. White Reader*. New York: Harper, 1966. (paper)
A fine anthology arranged by rhetorical types for convenient classroom use.

White, E. B. *Here Is New York*. New York: Harper, 1949.

———. *One Man's Meat*. New York: Harper, 1944. (cloth and paper)

———. *Points of My Compass*. New York: Harper, 1962.

———. *The Second Tree From the Corner*. New York: Harper, 1954. (cloth and paper)

Every student of writing should be familiar with E. B. White's style.

Wolfe, Tom. *The Kandy-Kolored Tangerine-Flake Streamline Baby.* New York: Farrar, Straus & Giroux, 1965. (paper: Farrar, Straus & Giroux and Pocket Books)
An antidote to the emphasis on tight, taut, telegraphic writing.

The Teaching of Writing

The writing teacher should have some books on his shelf which allow him to share his problems with other professionals. The National Council of Teachers of English does a fine job of distributing books on the teaching of writing, and the writing teacher should, of course, belong to that organization and subscribe to its journals.

Archambault, Reginald D. *Tolstoy on Education.* Chicago: University of Chicago, 1967.
"Are the Peasant Children to Learn to Write From Us?" is especially interesting.

Arnstein, Flora J. *Children Write Poetry: A Creative Approach.* New York: Dover, 1967. (paper)
Revised version of *Adventures Into Poetry,* published in 1951.

Booth, Miriam B., ed. *Writing: A Portfolio.* Champaign, Ill.: National Council of Teachers of English, 1958. (paper)

Braddock, Richard, Richard Lloyd-Jones, and Lowell Schoer. *Research in Written Composition.* Champaign, Ill.: National Council of Teachers of English, 1963. (paper)
Note pp. 56-64.

Brown, Rollo Walter. *How the French Boy Learns to Write.* Champaign, Ill.: The National Council of Teachers of English, 1965. (paper)
Note pp. 56-58.

Ciardi, John. "On Writing and Bad Writing," *Saturday Review* (Dec. 15, 1962), pp. 10-12.

Clegg, A. B. *The Excitement of Writing.* London: Chatto & Windus, 1965.
This is available through NCTE.

Coles, W. E., Jr. "The Teaching of Writing as Writing," *College English,* XXIX (November 1967), 111-16.

Commission on English. *Freedom and Discipline in English.* Princeton: College Entrance Examination Board, 1965. (paper)

———. *Kinescripts.* New York: College Entrance Examination Board, 1965. (paper)
Of special interest is "Teaching Biography in the Secondary School" by Henry Darcy Curwen and "The 'Speaking Voice' and the Teaching of Composition" by Walker Gibson.

Conant, James Bryant. *The Comprehensive High School: A Second Report to Interested Citizens.* New York: McGraw-Hill, 1967. (cloth and paper)

Corbin, Richard. *The Teaching of Writing in Our Schools.* New York: Macmillan, 1966. (paper)

Dixon, John. *Growth Through English.* London: National Association for the Teaching of English, 1967. (paper)

Fader, Daniel N., and Morton H. Shaevitz. *Hooked on Books.* New York: Berkley, 1966. (paper)
A book on reading which has some important ideas on getting the most disadvantaged students to write.

Fischer, John. "Why Nobody Can't Write Good," *The Stupidity Problem and Other Harassments.* New York: Harper, 1964.

Gerberr, John C., ed.. *The College Teaching of English.* New York: Appleton-Century-Crofts, 1965.

Ghiselin, Brewster, ed. *The Creative Process.* Berkeley, Calif.: University of California, 1952. (paper: New American Library)

Gordon, Edward J. *Writing and Literature in the Secondary School.* New York: Holt, 1965. (paper)
Reports of the Yale Conference on the Teaching of English.

———, and Edward S. Noyes. *Essays on the Teaching of English.* New York: Appleton-Century-Crofts, 1960.
More excellent essays from the Yale Conference. The article by Richard B. Sewall, "The Content of Student Writing," describes the Yale Theme-A-Day Program in detail.

Gregg, Alan. *For Future Doctors: Language and the Practice of Medicine.* Chicago: University of Chicago, 1957. (cloth and paper)

Hamilton, Mary Glenn. *A Creative Approach to Writing.* Pleasantville, N.Y.: Educational Division, Reader's Digest Services, Inc., n.d. (paper)

———. *Expository Writing: A Motivated Approach.* Pleasantville, N.Y.; Educational Division, Reader's Digest Services, Inc., n.d. (paper)

Holbrook, David. *Children's Writing: A Sampler For Student Teachers.* London: Cambridge University, 1967. (paper)

———. *English For Maturity.* London: Cambridge University, 1962. (paper)

———. *English For the Rejected.* London: Cambridge University, 1964. (paper)

———. *The Exploring Word; Creative Disciplines in the Education of Teachers of English.* London: Cambridge University, 1967. (paper)
Stimulating books by a controversial British composition teacher.

Holt, John. *How Children Fail.* New York: Pitman, 1964. (paper: Dell)

———. *How Children Learn.* New York: Pitman, 1967.
Mr. Holt makes a significant contribution by showing the writing teacher how to observe what he is doing — and not doing — in his classroom.

Incorporated Association of Assistant Masters in the Secondary Schools of England. *The Teaching of English.* London: Cambridge University. 1966.

Jewett, Arno, and Charles E. Bish. *Improving English Composition.* Washington: The National Education Association, 1965. (paper)
Interesting reports on the NEA–Dean Langmuir Project on Improving English Composition.

Jones, W. Paul, and Quentin Johnson, eds. "Why Study English," *Essays on Thinking and Writing in Science, Engineering and Business.* Dubuque, Iowa: William C. Brown, 1963.

Judine, Sister M. *A Guide for Evaluating Student Compositions.* Champaign, Ill.: National Council of Teachers of English, 1965. (paper)
Note especially pp. 56-84.

Kitzhaber, Albert F. *Themes, Theory and Therapy: The Teaching of Writing in College.* New York: McGraw-Hill, 1963.

Kohl, Herbert R. *36 Children.* New York: New American Library, 1967.
A superb book which includes examples of student writing and takes you inside a classroom to

show what can be done by an excellent teacher under the worst conditions.

———. *Teaching the "Unteachables."* New York: New York Review, 1967. (paper)

Leavitt, Hart Day. "To Write or Not to Write: and How?" *Writing and Literature in the Secondary School,* by Edward J. Gordon. New York: Holt, 1965.

London Association for the Teaching of English. *Assessing Compositions.* Glasgow: Blackie and Son, 1965. (Available through NCTE.)

MacLeish, Archibald. "The Teaching of Writing," *Harpers Magazine* (October 1959), pp. 158-72.

Macrorie, Ken. *Writing to be Read.* New York: Hayden, 1968. (paper)
A stimulating method of teaching writing.

Moffett, James. "Learning to Write by Writing," *Report of the 13th Yale Conference on the Teaching of English.* Unpublished [1967].

———. *A Student-Centered Language Arts Curriculum, K–13: A Handbook for Teachers.* Boston: Houghton Mifflin, in press.

Muller, Herbert J. *The Uses of English.* New York: Holt, 1967. (paper)

Payne, Lucile Vaughan. "Teaching Students to Write," *NEA Journal* (November 1966), pp. 28-30.

Rubinstein, S. Leonard. "From Need to Desire," *College English,* XXIX (November 1967), 126-8.

Sauer, Edwin H. *English in the Secondary School.* New York: Holt, 1961.
The best of the texts for English Education students.

Schulberg, Budd. *From the Ashes: Voices of Watts.* New York: New American Library, 1967.
His introduction shows how long it can take to reach the unmotivated student, and the anthology proves how important it is we make the effort.

Stoehr, Taylor. "Some Practical Advice for the Student Writer," *College English,* XXIX (November 1967), 116-21.

Tate, Gary, and Edward P. J. Corbett. *Teaching Freshman Composition.* New York: Oxford, 1967. (paper)

West, William W. *Developing Writing Skills.* Englewood Cliffs, N.J.: Prentice-Hall, 1966.

Woodford, F. Peter. "Sounder Thinking Through Clearer Writing," *Science* (May 12, 1967), pp. 743-5.

Writing: A Portfolio Produced by a Subcommittee of the Secondary Section Committee. Champaign, Ill.: National Council of Teachers of English, 1958.

Helping the Student See

Each teacher of composition will have its own materials in this area but some of the following books may indicate what can be used effectively.

Carson Rachael, *The Sense of Wonder.* New York: Harper, 1965. (cloth and paper)

Churchill, Winston S. *Painting as a Pastime.* New York: Cornerstone Library, 1961. (paper)

Duncan, David Douglas. *The Private World of Pablo Picasso.* New York: Harper, 1958.

Henri, Robert. *The Art Spirit.* Philadelphia: Lippincott, 1960 (cloth and paper)

Kellogg, Rhoda, with Scott O'Dell. *The Psychology of Children's Art.* San Diego, Calif.: CRM, Inc.–Random House, n.d.

Kirstein, Lincoln, and Beaumont Newhall. *Photographs by Cartier-Bresson.* New York: Grossman, 1963.

Leavitt, Hart Day, and David A. Sohn. *Stop, Look and Write!* New York: Bantam, 1964. (paper)
Every composition teacher should be familiar with this book.

Levitt, Helen, and James Agee. *A Way of Seeing.* New York: Viking, 1965.

Newhall, Nancy, ed. *Edward Weston, Photographer.* New York: Grossman, 1965.

Rieger, Robert. *The Pros: A Documentary of Professional Football in America.* New York: Simon and Schuster, 1960.

Schwartz, Tony. "New York 19." Folkways Records, No. 5558.

———. 'Sound of My City." Folkways Records, No. 7341.

Steichen, Edward. *The Family of Man.* New York: Maco, 1955. (paper: New American Library)

Biographies of Writers

The better writers' biographies give a flavor of the writer's struggle.

Ellmann, Richard. *James Joyce.* New York: Oxford, 1959. (cloth and paper)

Fitzgibbon, Constantine. *The Life of Dylan Thomas.* Boston: Little, Brown, 1965. (cloth and paper)

Gelb, Arthur and Barbara. *O'Neill: A Biography.* New York: Harper, 1962. (paper: Dell)

Kaplan, Justin. *Mr. Clemens and Mark Twain.* New York: Simon and Schuster, 1966.

Schorer, Mark, *Sinclair Lewis: An American Life.* New York: McGraw-Hill, 1961. (paper: Dell)

Simmons, Ernest J. *Leo Tolstoy.* 2 vols. New York: Random House, 1956 (cloth and paper)

Steegmuller, Francis. *Flaubert and Madame Bovary,* rev. ed. New York: Farrar Straus & Giroux, 1950.
A magnificent double study of a man and his work.

Thompson, Lawrence. *Robert Frost: The Early Years.* New York: Holt, 1966.

Trollope, Anthony. *An Autobiography.* New York: Doubleday, 1883.

Troyat, Henri. *Tolstoy.* New York: Doubleday, 1961.

Letters of Writers

Writers' correspondence reveals their concern with money, fame, and sometimes craft.

[Fitzgerald.] Turnbull, Andrew, ed. *The Letters of F. Scott Fitzgerald.* New York: Scribner's, 1963. (paper: Dell)

[Flaubert.] Steegmuller, Francis, ed. *Selected Letters of Gustave Flaubert.* New York: Farrar, Straus & Giroux, 1954.

[Frost.] Thompson, Lawrence, ed. *Selected Letters of Robert Frost.* New York: Holt, 1964.

[Perkins.] Wheelock, John Hall, ed. *Editor to Author: The Letters of Maxwell E. Perkins.* New York: Scribner's, 1950. (cloth and paper)
A revealing look at a most influential teacher of writing.

[Thomas.] Fitzgibbon, Constantine, ed. *Selected Letters of Dylan Thomas.* New York: New Directions, 1967.

Writers' Journals

Even though self-conscious and pretentious, writers' notebooks still take the reader into the writer's workshop.

Camus, Albert. *Notebooks 1934-1942*, trans. Philip Thody. New York: Knopf, 1963.

———. *Notebooks 1934-1951*, trans. Justin O'Brien. New York: Knopf, 1965.

Fitzgerald, F. Scott. *The Crack-Up*, ed. Edmund Wilson. New York: New Directions, 1945. (paper)

Flaubert, Gustave. *Intimate Notebook 1840-1841*, trans. Francis Steegmuller. New York: Doubleday, 1967.
The journal of a teen-age writer.

Gide, André. *The Journals of André Gide*. 4 vols. New York: Knopf, 1947-1951. (paper: Random House)

James, Henry. *The Notebooks of Henry James*, eds. F. O. Matthiesen and Kenneth B. Murdock. New York: Oxford, 1961. (paper)

The Novelist

The following books will help the teacher of writing to understand the problems of the novelist and his solutions to those problems.

Bowen, Elizabeth. "Notes on Writing a Novel," *Writers on Writing*," ed. Walter E. Allen. Boston: The Writer, 1959.
The best introduction to the problems of fiction as seen by the writer.

Buckler, William E. *Novels in the Making*. Boston: Houghton Mifflin Co., 1961. (paper)

Butt, John, and Kathleen Tillotson. *Dickens At Work*. New York: Oxford, 1957.

Dostoevsky, Fyodor. *The Notebooks for Crime and Punishment*, ed. Edward Wasiolek. Chicago: University of Chicago, 1967.

———. *The Notebooks for The Idiot*, ed. Edward Wasiolek. Chicago: University of Chicago. 1967.
Other Dostoevsky notebooks will be published by the University of Chicago Press.

Forster, E. M. *Aspects of the Novel*. New York: Harcourt, 1947. (cloth and paper)
The best book of its kind.

Frankau, Pamela. *Pen to Paper: A Novelist's Notebook*. New York: Doubleday, 1962.

Gordon, Caroline. *How to Read a Novel*. New York: Viking, 1964. (cloth and paper)

Hale, Nancy. *The Realities of Fiction*. Boston: Little, Brown, 1962.
An exceptional job.

James, Henry. *The Art of the Novel*. New York: Scribner's, 1934. (cloth and paper)

Lubbock, Percy. *The Craft of Fiction*. New York: Viking, 1957. (cloth and paper)

Macauley, Robie, and George Lanning. *Technique in Fiction*. New York: Harper, 1964.

Mann, Thomas. *The Story of a Novel*. New York: Knopf, 1961.

Miller, James E., Jr., ed. *Myth and Method: Modern Theories of Fiction*. Lincoln, Neb.: University of Nebraska, 1960. (paper)
A collection of articles about the novel.

O'Hara, Mary. *Novel in the Making*. New York: David McKay, 1954.

Robbe-Grillet, Alain. *For a New Novel: Essays on Fiction*, trans. R. Howard. New York: Grove Press, 1966. (cloth and paper)

Scholes, Robert. *Approaches to the Novel*. San Francisco: Chandler, 1961. (paper)
A collection of essays on the novel.

Wolfe, Thomas. *The Story of a Novel*. New York: Scribner's, 1936.

The Poet

The poet's attempt to use the language with precision makes some of the studies of the poet at work exceptionally revealing.

Cane, Melville. *Making a Poem: An Inquiry into the Creative Process*. New York: Harcourt, 1962. (cloth and paper)

Engle, Paul, and Joseph Langland, eds. *Poet's Choice*. New York: Dial, 1962 (paper)
A fascinating anthology with revealing comments by the poets about their own poems.

Fussell, Paul, Jr. *Poetic Meter and Poetic Form*. New York: Random House, 1965. (cloth and paper)
Excellent.

Gibson, Walker. *Poems in the Making*. Boston: Houghton Mifflin, 1963. (paper)

Gross, Ronald. *Pop Poems*. New York: Simon and Schuster, 1967. (paper)

Lewis, C. Day. "The Making of a Poem," *The Saturday Evening Post* (January 21, 1961), pp. 18-9, 67-8.

Nemerov, Howard, ed. *Poets on Poetry*. New York: Basic Books, 1965.

Norman, Charles, ed. *Poets on Poetry*. New York: Macmillan, 1965. (paper: Free Press)

Scully, James, ed. *Modern Poetics*. New York: McGraw-Hill, 1965. (paper)

Shapiro, Karl, ed. *Prose Keys to Modern Poetry*. New York: Harper, 1962. (paper)

Spender, Stephen. *The Making of a Poem*. New York: Norton, 1962. (paper)

Valéry, Paul. *The Art of Poetry*. New York: Random House. (paper)

The Short Story Writer

O'Connor, Frank. *The Lonely Voice: A Study of the Short Story*. Cleveland, Ohio: World, 1963. (cloth and paper)

———. *Stories by Frank O'Connor*. New York: Random House, 1956. (cloth and paper)
A fine collection of short stories.

Trask, Georgianne, and Charles Burkhart, eds. *Storytellers and Their Art*. New York: Doubleday, 1963. (paper)
A collection of interesting quotations by writers.

Updike, John. *Olinger Stories*. New York: Random House, 1964. (paper)
A fine collection, particularly appropriate to the high school.

The Biographer

Altick, Richard D. *Lives and Letters: A History of Literary Biography in England and America*. New York: Knopf, 1965.

Bowen, Catherine Drinker. *The Writing of Biography*. Boston: The Writer, 1952.

———. *Adventures of a Biographer*. Boston: Little, Brown, 1959.

Clifford, James L., ed. *Biography as an Art: Selected Criticism 1560-1960*. New York: Oxford, 1962. (paper)

Davenport, William H., and Ben Siegel, eds. *Biography Past and Present*. New York: Scribner's, 1965. (paper)

Edel, Leon. *Literary Biography*. New York: Doubleday, 1959.

Garis, Robert, ed. *Writing About Oneself: Selected Writing*. Boston: D. C. Heath, 1965. (paper)
A very valuable reader for use in a unit on autobiography.

Garraty, John A. *The Nature of Biography*. New York: Knopf, 1957. (cloth and paper)
Especially valuable.

Kendall, Paul Murray. *The Art of Biography*. New York: Norton, 1965. (cloth and paper)

The Journalist

Adler, Ruth, ed. *The Working Press: Special to the New York Times.* New York: Putnam's, 1966.

Berger, Meyer *The Story of the New York Times, 1851–1951.* New York: Simon and Schuster, 1951.

Bernstein, Theodore M. *More Language That Needs Watching.* New York: Atheneum, 1964.

———. *Watch Your Language.* New York: Atheneum, 1965 (paper: Pocket Books)

Cater, Douglass. *The Fourth Branch of Government.* Boston: Houghton Mifflin, 1959. (paper: Random House)

The Danger of Libel. New York: The Associated Press, 1964. (paper)

Garst, Robert E., and Theodore M. Bernstein. *Headlines and Deadlines,* 3rd ed. New York: Columbia, 1961. (paper)

Hohenberg, John. *The Professional Journalist.* New York: Holt, 1960.

Indiana Committee on Journalism. *Teacher's Guide to High School Journalism.* The Indiana State Department of Public Instruction in cooperation with The Newspaper Fund of The Wall Street Journal, 1965. (paper)

Jordan, Lewis, ed. *New York Times Style Book.* New York: The New York Times, 1962. (paper)

Miller, Carl G. *Modern Journalism,* rev. ed. New York: Holt, 1962.
Aimed at the high school journalist.

Snyder, Louis L., and Richard Morris, eds. *A Treasury of Great Reporting.* New York: Simon and Schuster, 1949. (cloth and paper)
A magnificent anthology.

Woodward, Stanley, with Frank Graham, Jr. *Sportswriter.* New York: Doubleday, 1967.

Writing for the AP. New York: The Associated Press, 1959. (paper)

ndex

"Abundance, write from," 6, 9, 51
Action, 177, 178, 179, 189
Alsop, Stewart, 82–3
Analysis, 41, 176
Andler, Kenneth, 176–84
Art as writer's resource, 30, 31
Artist, endeavor of, 235
Assignments: directions for, 111; effective, 133–5; sources of, 162, 165–70; types of, 166
Audience: and communication, 3–5; and the writer, 33, 42, 129, 161, 203, 209, 228
Author revealed in his work, 188, 244. *See also* Personal involvement

Bowen, Elizabeth, 28, 62
Bronowski, [J.], 186
Burke, Kenneth, 166

Characterization, 189, 198, 200, 206, 208, 214
Churchill, Winston S., 70–1
Clarity of expression, 185, 186, 202, 233, 245
Class environment, 103
Classroom as writing laboratory, 109–10
Cliché, 12, 88–9, 182
Coach, teacher as, 18, 151, 170
Coherence, 11, 12, 53, 81, 82
Commonplace, use of, 227–8, 234
Communication: skills, 16, 42, 215; as writer's purpose, 3–5, 170
Comparison, 185, 186
Composition: in college, 103, 215; in high school, 103, 105, 215; myths in teaching of, 105–7, 219–22. *See also* Writing; Writing program
Conant, James Bryant, 105, 108
Conference, techniques of, 132, 133, 150–1
Conflict, 190, 191
Connell, Evan S., Jr., 198–202
Connotation, teaching of, 22
Content and form, 2, 8, 12, 192, 243
Content of writing course, 152
Continuity, 181
Contrast, 208, 212
Control. *See* Subject
Coordinating writing course with other courses, 162, 169, 218
Correction of papers: by student, 138; by teacher, 135–7, 139–46. *See also* Editing
Craftsmanship, 183
Creativity and discipline, 22–3
Criticism: by audience, 129; by classmates, 131, 132; purpose of, 21; by self, 10–11, 237, 239; by teacher, 221–2

Curiosity, 34

Deadline, 72, 169
Definitions in context, 177
Denotation, teaching of, 22
Description, 37, 47–9; 225. *See also* Specifics
Design, 6–8, 51, 55–8, 63, 183, 187, 242. *See also* Form; Structure
Detachment, 34
Details. *See* Description; Specifics
Development of idea, 186, 205
Diagnosing, 19–20, 129,–31; by student, 166; by teacher, 129–30
Discipline: 134, 161, 167, 238; and creativity, 22–3
Documentation, 175, 177, 178. *See also* Specifics
Doherty, Matthew F., 222–5
Draft, first or rough, 8–10, 71–2, 230. *See also* Facsimile drafts

Editing, 100, 101, 131; of students' papers, 137, 138–50. *See also* Self-editing
Editor's role, defined, 187
Education as writer's resource, 30–1
Emotional involvement. *See* Personal involvement
Emphasis: 11, 12, 53, 81, 82, 178, 182, 183, 190, 198, 199; examples of, 54
Endings, emphatic, 229
English teacher: extra duties of, 104–5, 107–8; as reading teacher, 104; as writing teacher, 104, 105
Essay as guide for writing, 217–8, 220–1
Ethics of relationship between teacher and students, 111
Experience as writer's resource, 27–8, 30–1, 37, 177, 191–2
Experimental course as teaching device, 167
Exposition, 180, 189
Expression, clarity of, 185, 186, 202, 233, 245

Facsimile drafts, 14, 26, 85–7, 95–100, 102, 128, 172, 193–7
Faraday, Michael, 36–7
Farrockhrooz, Louise, 35–6
Faulkner, William, 6, 30
Figures of speech, 186
Flexibility: of lesson plan, 112; of teacher, 20–1, 173
Foreshadowing, 180, 204
Form: 8, 27, 34, 192, 231, 233, 234, 236–7, 243; and audience, 3, 4–5, 69; and content, 2, 12, 243; and poetry, 234; in rewriting, 11; universal need for, 170. *See also* Design; Structure
Found Poetry, 167–8
Frost, Robert, 172, 236–7

Generalization, 3, 32, 37, 164, 177, 188, 191
Gerdy, Robert S., biography of, 187–8
Grading papers, 137–8, 149
Grammar, 100, 215, 216, 221, 233
Greene, Mike, 146–9
Gross, Ronald, 167–8

Hawthorne Effect, 167
Hearing, 31–2. *See also* Listening
Hemingway, Ernest, 6, 222
History, 31, 33, 40–1
Honesty in writing, 153
Humor: 35, 200; teacher's sense of, 24

Idealist, writer as, 34
Identifying with subject, 228–9
Implication, 33
Independence of student, 131
Inspiration, 73–4, 233, 241, 243
Interpretation, 41
Introduction, 7
Irony, 34, 182

Judgment, 173

Kennan, George F., 40–1
Kennedy, John F., 89–91
Knowledge as writer's resource, 37

Language: 34, 42, 187, 188; limitations of, 23
Leads: 7, 59–63, 178, 180, 183, 187; examples of, 60–3
Leech, Margaret, 44–6
Lesson plans: 103, 113–24; necessary elements of, 111–12
Lewis, Sinclair, 128, 240
Listening: as teaching skill, 15–8, 151, 152, 153, 157–8; as writer's resource, 31
Literature, study of as guide to writing, 216, 219–20

McCarthy, Mary, 175
MacLeish, Archibald, 17
Maintaining position as teacher, 23–5
Mann, Thomas, 8
Masters, Edgar Lee, 158–9
Melville, Herman, 26
Metaphor, 185, 192, 215
Mitchell, Joseph, 62, 173
Models, aid to teacher and writer, 175
Mood, 180, 190, 199
Motivating students, 111, 151–3

Myths in teaching of writing. *See* Composition

New England School Development Council, xi–xii
Newspaper writers, rules for, 101
Novel: defined, 242; source of, 238

Observation. *See* Seeing
O'Dea, Paul, 219–22
Organization, 176, 227
Originality, defined, 243
Orwell, George, 54–5, 60, 173
Outline, 7, 53

Pace, 190, 199
Padding, harm of, 230
Paragraphs, 11–12, 53, 54–5, 175
Payne, Lucile Vaughan, 215–8
People, sense of, 32
Personal involvement, 33, 41, 152–3, 226, 228, 234, 242
Personality collage, 169
Personality revealed in writing, 225
Plagiarism, 111
Poetry: 233, 236, 243; and form, 234; uses of, 167, 234, 240, 244
Point of view, 41, 57, 187, 212, 245
Preface, rough drafts of, 94–100
Pre-writing, 8–10
Problems as writer's resource, 33
Psychiatry, classroom no place for practice of, 24, 150, 154
Publication of students' papers, 161–2

Questions from students as teaching device, 169
Quintilian, 15
Quotation, 165

Reader's Digest, xii, 63
Reading: as basis for writing, 216; as writer's resource, 30
Reading aloud, 161, 230, 240
Realist, writer as, 34
Reality, examples of, 188, 210
Repetition, examples of, 179, 181, 206, 214
Resources for writer. *See* Art; Education; Experience; History; Knowledge; Listening; Questions; Reading; Seeing; Self; Skepticism; Smell; Solutions; Talking; Taste; Touch
Rewriting: 11–12, 72, 165, 176, 192, 230, 235–6, 241–2, 244, 245; how to teach, 224–5. *See* Doherty, Matthew F.
Rhetorical tools of student, 73
Rhythm, examples of, 200
Roosevelt, Franklin Delano, 83–7
Ross, Lillian, 202–14
Rosten, Leo, 162–5

Schlesinger, Arthur, 88–91
Seeing, 12, 31, 37, 48–9, 225, 227–8, 234, 239, 240–1, 244–5
Self as writer's resource, 6
Self-diagnosing by student, 130–1
Self-editing, 229–30, 244
Senses, use in writing, 31–6, 226, 229
Sentences, in rewriting, 12
Setting the scene, 198, 201, 208
Shahn, Ben, 30–1
Shaw, George Bernard, 102
Shelley, Percy Bysshe, 14, 243
Sherwood, Robert E., 83–4
Short story as assignment, 167
Show, not tell, 35, 176, 177, 183, 187, 190, 209, 226, 228. *See also* Description; Personal involvement; Specifics
Simile, 174
Skepticism as writer's resource, 32–3
Skills: of water, summary, 12–13; of writing teacher, 15–25
Small group teaching, 131–3
Smell as writer's resource, 32
Solutions as writer's resource, 33
Specifics, 5–6, 32, 35, 43–51, 55, 56, 75, 77–81, 169, 174, 175–8, 180, 182, 184, 187, 188, 198, 203, 207, 211, 226, 239, 241
Spelling, 16, 215
Structure, 51, 53, 217–8, 245. *See also* Design; Form
Student: as critical craftsman, 176; as individual, 16–7, 18, 20,112, 170, 173, 176; as reporter, 201
Style, 185, 189, 232, 233, 234, 243, 244
Subject: change of, 68–9; choosing, 2–3, 27, 28–30, 48, 66–7, 220; control of 7, 59, 153; elements of, 27, 39; limiting, 39–41, 67–8, 227; researching, 68; testing, 68
Success, measurement of writer's, 1, 161
Superlatives, 182
Suspense, 189, 201
Sweet, John, 225–30
Syntax, problems, 19

Talking as writer's resource, 31
Taste as writer's resource, 32
Taubman, Howard, 37–9
Teacher: influence of, 160; personal experiences of, 215; role of, 1, 133, 149, 152, 187; skills of, 15–25; source material for, 162; writes with students, 137
Teaching devices, 72, 166–70
Techniques for writing, 226–30, 243
Tenses, use of, 100
Thesis, 54
Time essential for teaching writing, 222, 223
Tone, 27, 35, 177, 179, 182, 184, 185, 187, 192, 199, 202
Touch as writer's resource, 32
Transition, 54, 55, 181, 189
Tuchman, Barbara, 46, 63–4

Understatement, 190
Unity: 11, 12, 53, 79, 81, 82, 175, 211; examples of, 54, 55

Verbs, 176, 177, 182, 190
Voice, active and passive, 100–1

West, Rebecca, 173–5
White, E. B., 23, 63, 173, 184–5
Williams, Thomas A., 188–92; rough draft of article, 193–7
Wordiness, 12
Words, choice of, 12, 22, 82, 83, 199, 232, 233, 236, 238
Workbook as teacher's aid, 221
Writer: as authority, 177; basic skills of, 2–13; decisions made by, 65; motivation of, 4; successful, defined, 1, 161
Writing: barriers to teaching, 103–8; defined, 1, 51, 225; for children, 237; models for teacher, 173; reason for, 238; reason for teaching, 154; rewards of, 239; steps in, 58–9, 66–70, 126–7; by teacher, 21–2
Writing course: coordination with other courses, 111, 125–6; scope of, 112
Writing process, elements of, 123
Writing program: elements for teaching of, 217, 219; high school, 215. *See also* Composition